Social System and Legal Process

Theory, Comparative Perspectives,
and Special Studies

Harry M. Johnson

Editor

Social System and Legal Process

Jossey-Bass Publishers
San Francisco • Washington • London • 1978

SOCIAL SYSTEM AND LEGAL PROCESS
Theory, Comparative Perspectives, and Special Studies
by Harry M. Johnson, Editor

Social System and Legal Process, edited by Harry M. Johnson, is a
special double issue of *Sociological Inquiry* (Volume 47, Nos. 3-4,
1977), journal of the National Sociology Honor Society, a quarterly
publication of the United Chapters of Alpha Kappa Delta.

Library of Congress Catalogue Card Number LC 77-93676

International Standard Book Number ISBN 0-87589-364-3

Manufactured in the United States of America

JACKET DESIGN BY WILLI BAUM

FIRST EDITION

Code 7804

The Jossey-Bass
Social and
Behavioral Science Series

Preface

As we hope to make clear in *Social System and Legal Process,* a special double issue of *Sociological Inquiry,* the sociology of law, although a well-recognized field, is still not cultivated as much as it deserves to be. Some theorists emphasize the idea that "law" is connected, above all, with the "public interest"— the interest in social order with justice and the interest in the effective pursuit of societal goals. Other theorists stress the idea of "law" as an instrument for pursuing private individual interests or the interests of subcollectivities of society, rather than those of the whole society. Both types of theorists are "obviously" correct, yet the exact relationship between the two requires careful theoretical analysis before, as well as after, empirical investigation. In any case, "law" is deeply involved whether we attempt to define the public interest substantively or whether we content ourselves with a conception based on procedural criteria—a conception that would focus on the institutionalized processes of decision making in relation to policies and goals at every level and in every kind of collective activity.

The public interest is notoriously difficult to define substantively. For example, although we "all" benefit from high economic production, we do not benefit equally. As another, more extreme example, the citizens or subjects of a country might not benefit equally even from military protection against a potentially exploitative foreign power. Thus, the public interest can seldom guarantee the absence of differential advantages to particular interests; there are cases where advantage to one individual or group is clearly at the expense of others. The long-run "public interest," however, requires protecting legitimate differential gains for "private" individuals and groups.

As my quotation marks have indicated, one problem that theory must address is the very definition of "law." Among other questions considered in this book are the following: What are the general connections between the legal system and other aspects of society? What are the functions of law and the sources of legal effectiveness? What are the basic types of law? How can we explain the relative neglect of law in sociology? What are the focal points in the comparison of legal systems? What are the criteria (if any) of legal evolution? What are the relative merits of different existing legal systems? All of these questions are at least touched on; none, of course, can be given definitive treatment in one volume.

The classification of the eleven chapters is somewhat arbitrary. Almost all of the chapters have theoretical concerns; those of Lon L. Fuller and Talcott Parsons in Part One are specifically classified as "theoretical" because of their wide range and far-reaching implications. Similarly, and almost of necessity, all of the chapters are comparative. In the chapters grouped under Part Two, "Comparative Perspectives," comparison is relatively explicit, although Robert Sharlet's chapter on Soviet law assumes that readers will be able to make their own comparisons with Western democratic law. The four chapters in Part Three, "Special Studies," deal mainly with American experience, yet all would also be relevant to theoretical and comparative concerns.

Urbana, Illinois   Harry M. Johnson
November 1977

Contents

Contributors

Harry M. Johnson is professor of sociology at the University of Illinois, Urbana-Champaign, and editor of *Sociological Inquiry*. He has taught at Simmons College (1942-1963) and the Massachusetts College of Art (1945-1955). In addition, he has been a visiting professor during summers at the Salzburg Seminar for American Studies (1961); the Heimvolkshochschule, Falkenstein (1962); Columbia University (1964); and the University of Munich (1970).

At Harvard University, Johnson earned his bachelor's degree (1939) in English literature, master's degree (1942) in sociology, and doctor's degree (1949) in sociology; his doctoral dissertation examined the social structure of France between the two world wars.

Johnson served as associate editor of the *American Sociological Review* (1964-1965); has written articles on ethnic relations, religion, and the mass media; and is the author of *Sociology: A Systematic Introduction* (1960). He is planning a special double issue on the sociology of religion for *Sociological Inquiry* and is working on a book about intrasocietal ethnic relations.

Lon L. Fuller, Carter Professor of General Jurisprudence emeritus, Harvard Law School, is the author of many articles and several books, including *The Law in Quest of Itself, The Morality of Law, Legal Fictions,* and *Anatomy of the Law.*

John Hagan, associate professor of sociology at the University of Toronto, has written many articles on juvenile delinquency and criminal justice; his most recent book is *The Disreputable Pleasures.*

Travis Hirschi, professor in the School of Criminal Justice, State University of New York, Albany, is the author of *Causes of Delinquency,* as well as many articles.

Robert L. Kidder, professor of sociology at Temple University, is the author of papers on law in India.

Charles W. Lidz, assistant professor of psychiatry and sociology at the University of Pittsburgh, is doing research on the legal control of psychiatry. He is coauthor, with Andrew L. Walker, of *Connections: Notes from the Heroin World* and *The Moral Core.*

Jeffrey Leon, lecturer, Center of Criminology, University of Toronto, is completing work for his LL.B. He is involved in research concerning children's legal representation and legal issues connected with drug abuse.

Talcott Parsons, professor emeritus of sociology at Harvard University, has been the central figure in the developing "theory of action" for many years. Since leaving Harvard, he has taught at the University of Chicago, the University of Pennsylvania, and Rutgers. His most recent collection of articles and essays is *Social Systems and the Evolution of Action Theory.*

Dietrich Rueschemeyer, professor and chairperson of sociology at Brown University, is the author of *Lawyers and Their*

Society: A Comparative Analysis of the Legal Profession in Germany and the United States and the editor and translator into German of collected theoretical essays by Talcott Parsons.

Robert Sharlet, professor of political science at Union College, is the coauthor (with Z. L. Zile and J. C. Love) of *Legal Aspects of Verification in the Soviet Union* and *The Soviet Legal System and Arms Inspection: A Case Study in Policy Implementation.*

Susan Bowker Schwarz, assistant professor of sociology at Syracuse University, is currently working on a book about regression and an income-prediction study based on the National Longitude Study.

Rita James Simon, professor of sociology and director of the Law and Society Program at the University of Illinois, Urbana-Champaign, is the current editor of the *American Sociological Review* and the author of *The American Jury: The Plea of Insanity, Payment for Pain and Suffering* (with J. O'Connell), *Public Opinion in America, 1930-1970,* and *Women and Crime.*

Andrew L. Walker, assistant professor in the division of social science at Stephens College, is interested in the study of deviance and social control. With Charles W. Lidz, he is coauthor of *Connections: Notes from the Heroin World* and *The Moral Core.*

Barbara Yngvesson, associate professor of anthropology at Hampshire College, has carried out research on dispute management in Scandinavia and the United States and is concluding a study of a community forum that processes criminal cases in an Eastern-seaboard district court.

Social System and Legal Process

*Theory, Comparative Perspectives,
and Special Studies*

Part 1

Theoretical Perspectives

~~~~~~

Many terms are available for the normative aspect of "social structure." Some writers prefer a definition of "law" broad enough to apply to at least some of the normative structure in any society. Other writers prefer a more restrictive definition, such that we might be able to say that some societies do not have "law" or that they have it only in embryonic form. Although all definitions of technical terms in social science are somewhat arbitrary, we stray from "common" usage with misgiving even if we have reasons for doing it. Common usage of the term law, *however, is of little help anyway.*

On the whole, Lon Fuller perhaps leans toward a rather "inclusive" definition, while Talcott Parsons, like Max Weber, is more restrictive. What is most striking, however, is the broad agreement between our two theorists concerning the nature and functions of law. Perhaps we could recognize the existence of social evolution and of transitional phenomena by adopting what is sometimes called a "cluster" definition, according to which norms are most appropriately called "law" if, at the "center" so to speak, they clearly have all the defining characteristics, while the term law *would become less appropriate at*

1

the periphery, where one or another of the cluster of character-istics is lacking, uncertain, or inchoate. Accordingly, a code of law is, first, a more or less coherent set of norms defining rights and obligations. Second, interpretation of the code for particu-lar situations is specialized; that is, at need or as required, dis-putes concerning the precise application of the code can be authoritatively settled in "courts" set up for that purpose. Third, the law, and consequently the decisions of courts, can at need be backed up ("enforced") by negative situational sanc-tions; that is, the law is in principle binding; compliance, al-though it may well be voluntary, can be coerced. Fourth, enforcement is in the hands of one or more specialized agents or agencies. Fifth, in the ideal-typical case, law is itself "legiti-mated" through its agreement with widespread morality; or—to put it more technically—full-fledged "law," as applied in prac-tice, can be reasonably regarded as a specification and imple-mentation of generalized value commitments. Parsons (1969b) uses the term "generalized value commitments" to refer to a kind of symbolic medium that can be institutionalized; can grow or decline in "value," like money; can be "spent" in the form of specific decisions and messages in processes of "inter-change"; and can, like money, be exhausted or replenished in processes of "circular flow." Ultimately, the cultural value system that is maintained through the spending of generalized value commitments of individuals and collectivities, has some kind of "religious" basis. In highly evolved cases, however, codes of law are "secularized," in the sense of being differen-tiated from religion, even though religion may and typically does provide indirect support for secularized legal systems. We are still speaking of an "ideal type." Sixth, the moral legitimacy and normativeness of law for interaction are "shared" to a con-siderable extent; that is, they are cultural and institutionalized. Especially important, as Fuller stresses, is the extent to which law is equally binding on governments (and therefore law en-forcers) and on citizens or subjects and "private" collectivities.

On this rather elaborate cluster definition of law, several comments are appropriate. First, as Fuller remarks in passing, we do not have law only or mainly because morality is lacking or weak. Although generalized value commitments can certainly guide very specific decisions, as when Christians decide, after perhaps long consideration, how the commandment to love all "neighbors" applies in highly specific situations, yet by definition generalized *value commitments by themselves are not specific enough and not necessarily interpreted with enough consensus in specific situations to facilitate adequate mutual adjustment of expectations for purposes of planning and detailed interaction. In highly differentiated and complex systems of interaction, therefore, "smooth" functioning may "require" the specification and sanctioned bindingness of law. Secondly, the existence of negative sanctions does not necessarily mean that law is not widely accepted or regarded as moral. As Parsons has emphasized in a basic paper (1969a), negative sanctions may and often do* symbolize *the serious and binding character of power-bearing "decisions," including law; the negative sanctions symbolize the fact that* collective *interests are presumptively involved. This remains true and important even though, as Fuller remarks, law is often so fully settled, so widely institutionalized, that enforcement may be virtually unnecessary in practice. Indeed, this point leads into my third comment: that "law" need not even be fully explicit for all those whose interaction is partly guided by it. I am reminded of the emphasis of the great Polish-Russian theorist Leo Petrażycki, who thought of "law" as consisting of "impulsions" to carry out felt obligations towards others (see Petrażycki, 1955; Gorecki, 1975); such "impulsions" may or may not be consciously verbalized.*

For discussion of the functions of law (about which I think our two theorists largely agree), it is at least convenient but also, I think, theoretically important, to have in mind Parsons's famous classification of the functional problems of action systems (1971), a classification, therefore, also of problematical functions.

Very briefly, functional problems and functions may be distinguished, first, according to whether they have to do, primarily, with relations internal to the system (say, a society) or whether they primarily have to do with the relations between the system and one of its "environments." In a technical sense,

the "units" of a social system are "roles" and "collectivities,"
both of which are defined in abstraction from the "concrete"
biological organisms and "concrete" personalities of the role
occupants (and participants in collectivities). Given this techni-
cal, abstract conception of social system, its internal relations
are relations among its subcollectivities and roles. The (external)
environments of the social system, with which it has continuous
relations on which it depends for its very existence and continu-
ity, include, then, not only the physical environment of land,
sea, sky and their nonhuman inhabitants but also the organisms
of the participating human actors themselves, their personali-
ties, social systems other than the system of reference, and
systems of cultural symbols.

The fundamental distinction between internal and exter-
nal problems is referred to as the "horizontal" axis of differen-
tiation because it can be conceived graphically and metaphori-
cally as a line dividing the internal subsystems "above" from the
external subsystems "below." The internal and external sub-
systems are themselves conceptual abstractions that make sense
because of the fact that there is a strong empirical tendency for
the units of social systems to be structurally differentiated
according to their relative emphasis on internal or external func-
tional problems.

There is also a "vertical" axis of differentiation. In more
"advanced" social systems, both the internal and the external
functional specializations tend to be further divided between
"instrumental" and "consummatory" emphases. Let us briefly
consider, first, the instrumental systems thus differentiated and
then the consummatory.

For the "units" of social systems (roles, or persons-in-
roles, and collectivities, or more or less goal-directed organiza-
tions of persons-in-roles), there "must" be commitments to
common values, that is, conceptions of the ideal social system.
Such conceptions are the highest-level cultural and normative
guides in the complex processes of detailed decision making in
interaction. They do not all by themselves determine action
and decisions; but, the more firmly and widely they are institu-
tionalized, the more they do tend to guide or "control" lower-

level normative elements (such as "law") and, ultimately, specific decisions in concrete action. If we view the matter statistically, we could say that generalized value commitments more or less strongly bias *"concrete" action and decisions in a certain direction, well beyond what would result on a purely random basis. Referring, then, to the vertical axis of differentiation, the internal-instrumental subsystem "works" by inculcating and maintaining and, in the longer run, changing these very high-level generalized value commitments. For example, units we call* families *and* churches *perform (more or less effectively) in this way. Technically, such units are said to be primarily "pattern maintenance" units; for the* social system, *they are also said to be "fiduciary."*

Turning to the external-instrumental subsystem, called "adaptive," it provides generalized resources in the form of economic "utility," consisting of "goods" and "services."

Pattern maintenance or fiduciary units and adaptive or economic units are "instrumental," in that generalized value commitments and generalized utility are means or resources for the social system, resources that, in "proper" combination with other elements, "pay off," as Parsons puts it, in the form of solidarity and collective goal attainment.

Solidarity and collective goal attainment are the functional "products" of the two "payoff" or consummatory subsystems. The internal consummatory subsystem, called "integrative," provides various levels and degrees of consensus, mutual concern of system units, and loyalty to the society, which together make up solidarity. The external consummatory subsystem, called "political," builds on pattern integrity and solidarity and produces collective goal attainment.

As Parsons makes clear (1966, 1971), one aspect of evolutionary *change in social systems is the tendency toward more pronounced structural-functional differentiation of the four functional subsystems: the pattern-maintenance system, producing the pattern integrity of fiduciary generalized value commitments; the integrative system, producing solidarity; the goal attainment or political system, producing collective effectiveness vis-à-vis environments; and the adaptive or economic sys-*

*tem, producing generalized utility. This evolutionary tendency
toward differentiation has often been recognized in the historical development of the theory of action; the Parsonian version
is an improvement over its predecessors in clarity, precision, empirical adequacy, and integrative power in the scientific sense.
The brief account just given is misleading in at least one respect.
The distinction between "internal" and "external" is in fact a
relative one. The "internal" subsystems, unlike the "external,"
deal with relations between units of the system or with the state
of units, but in addition the internal subsystems have somewhat
specialized relations with particular "environments" of the social system as a whole. For example, the fiduciary system depends on developments in cultural systems. Furthermore, all the
functional subsystems of the social system are interdependent;
thus, the "internal" subsystems cannot perform their functions
without the cooperation, so to speak, of the "external" subsystems.*

*The "four-function paradigm" is important in the theory
section of* Social System and Legal Process *in two ways. First,
"process" is functionally significant (functional or dysfunctional) action (communication of message decisions), and
"process" is therefore not random action but tends to be controlled by structure, which is normative. (I like to distinguish
between the* structure *of a social system and its* composition:
*Class "structure," for example, should suggest a normative
order of values, law, and less formal norms, which helps to organize both the consensual and conflict aspects of the class
composition; the class composition, in turn, could be represented in the statistics classifying units according to wealth,
power, and so on.) The four-function scheme is used in Parsons' essay, then, to "locate" the legal system in the social
system as a whole, both structurally and processually, "structure" and "process" being defined relative to "function." I shall
return to the functions of law in a moment. Secondly, Parsons
uses the four-function scheme to help explain the relative neglect of "law" in the social sciences. Briefly, because "law" is a
complex combination of structures and processes involved in all
four of the functional subsystems, it is easy to focus too nar-*

*rowly on one or two elements and in a sense "miss" or under-
estimate the phenomenon as a whole. Parsons illustrates this
general fact systematically by showing that ideological reduc-
tions of this kind tend to be classifiable in terms of the four-
function scheme. I hope that my brief discussion will help
readers who are not familiar with this scheme or are familiar
only with hostile and frequently distorted accounts of it. Above
all, I have sought to bring out the fact that it is an analytical
tool, not a simple description of concrete reality. For example,
Parsons has never had the "utopian" ideas that social system
units all have or should have the same values, that conflicts of
orientation and interests are altogether undesirable or elim-
inable (let alone nonexistent), or that systemic functional problems all by themselves somehow automatically determine the
content of human interaction. On the contrary, functional
problems, being problematic, may or may not be solved, are
never more than to some extent solved, and require organized
human effort for the partial "solutions" we see in the empirical
world.*

*Before attempting to classify the functions of law, we
might enumerate its actual functions as they are presented
above all in the chapters by Fuller and Parsons but also, at least
implicitly, in several other chapters.*

1. *Even if interacting parties cannot agree and are in conflict,
   law is a complex code for communication.*
2. *Law is a basis for having more or less realistic mutual expectations. As a preexisting code, it is less specific than agreements tailored to unique situations, but a good deal more
   specific than moral principles.*
3. *Closely related to the functioning of law as a code for
   smooth interaction is the function of authoritative settlement
   of disputes. Adjudication contributes to the code and helps
   to keep it up to date, and the code provides the main basis
   for further adjudication.*
4. *The settlement of disputes through enforced judgments requiring restitution, compensation, or punishment has a social
   control function in a special, relatively narrow sense: It serves*

to check or counteract possible tendencies to deviant behavior, which would (and does) disrupt the processes of orderly, predictable, dependable interaction. Because court judgments are more or less predictable, two things happen: First, many interacting parties settle their disputes out of court (although possibly with the help of lawyers), and, second, many people no doubt are able to imagine negative results to themselves if they yield to the temptation of violating the rights of others. It would be ridiculous to assume that negative sanctions, including the sheer opprobrium of negative court judgments, have no deterrent effect, even though they do not deter all crimes or all irresponsibility. One function of lawyers is to help their clients to avoid litigation and negative court judgments.

All these functions can be classified as "integrative." Even if people cannot agree on the terms of their interaction, they are at least able to contain their conflict, thus to enjoy some integration or mutual adjustment, through being able to communicate in terms of a common code and to define the points in dispute. Conflict is always a matter of degree, and if there were no actual or potential conflict there would be no "need" for integrative processes. Thus, the settlement of actual disputes is an integrative process, as is the forestalling of disputes. In thinking about these functions of law, we should remember Merton's distinction between function and purpose ([1949] 1968, p. 78). People do not go to court in order to integrate society, but their doing so is objectively integrative. This integrative function is not necessarily undermined by the use of legal processes to pursue differential advantage. Both private and public collectivities are often competing for scarce resources to be used for working toward goals all of which are "good." Law defines acceptable means to be used in this competition. It also inevitably protects vested interests (this is virtually a circular statement, since "vested" interests are for the most part interests legally defined and protected). Further, as we shall see in Parsons's chapter, "individualism," which is frequently treated, without reflection, as "selfish," may ac-

tually contribute to the public welfare. Thus conflicts of interest do not necessarily involve conflicts at the level of values and law.

All the functions we have just noted are integrative. However, there are laws more or less specialized for almost every kind of activity we can think of, economic, political, and fiduciary, as well as integrative. Furthermore, these laws not only restrict units in their goal attainment activities; as lawyers are likely to emphasize, the law in advanced societies may also actually facilitate all kinds of valued goal attainment by making resources flexibly reallocatable and by providing "prefabricated" forms of organization for all sorts of "free enterprise"— not only business (see Chayes, 1966). Thus we may say that law has functions of all four of the categories distinguished earlier. It is primarily "integrative" in two related senses: First, it facilitates the mutual adjustment of units in the social system; secondly, it facilitates the mutual adjustment of all four functional subsystems.

Little need be said here about the different types of law distinguished by Lon Fuller. His discussion is remarkably lucid and self-explanatory. I should like to emphasize only one point, namely, that the intergradations of the four types he distinguishes reveal the continuity of "law" from nonliterate and less differentiated to the more "advanced" societies, or from the "periphery" of our cluster definition of law to the "center." Fuller explicitly remarks that we can easily find in modern advanced societies the counterpart of phenomena that are more characteristic of "primitive" societies.

The part of Fuller's chapter that deals with the different kinds of appropriateness of the four types of law will be found to provide a good framework for integrating many points made in subsequent chapters, notably those by Yngvesson and Kidder.

References

Chayes, A. "The Modern Corporation and the Rule of Law." In E. S. Mason (Ed.), *The Corporation in Modern Society.* Cambridge, Mass.: Harvard University Press, 1966.

Gorecki, J. (Ed.). *Sociology and Jurisprudence of Leon Petrażycki.* Urbana: University of Illinois Press, 1975.

Merton, R. K. "Manifest and Latent Functions." In R. K. Merton, *Social Theory and Social Structure.* (rev. ed.) New York:
Free Press, 1968. (Originally published 1949.)

Parsons, T. *Societies: Evolutionary and Comparative Perspectives.* Englewood Cliffs, N.J.: Prentice-Hall, 1966.

Parsons, T. "On the Concept of Political Power." In T. Parsons,
Politics and Social Structure. New York: Free Press, 1969a.

Parsons, T. "On the Concept of Value Commitments." In T.
Parsons, *Politics and Social Structure.* New York: Free Press,
1969b.

Parsons, T. *The System of Modern Societies.* Englewood Cliffs,
N.J.: Prentice-Hall, 1971.

Parsons, T. "Some Problems of General Theory in Sociology."
In T. Parsons, *Social Systems and the Evolution of Action
Theory.* New York: Free Press, 1977.

Petrażycki, L. *Law and Morality.* (H. W. Babb, Trans.) Cambridge, Mass.: Harvard University Press, 1955.

1

Talcott Parsons

Law as an Intellectual Stepchild

After the brilliant start by Durkheim and Max Weber about the turn of the century, it is something of a mystery why the social sciences and particularly, perhaps, sociology have shown so little interest in the study of law and legal systems. That Johnson, for his first venture as editor of *Sociological Inquiry,* has chosen this field is to me a very welcome sign of a change.

This chapter is to a slight extent an essay in the sociology of knowledge and will move a little, I hope, toward explaining this relative neglect of law. My thesis will be that this neglect has resulted from a constellation of factors in the intellectual situation of modern society and especially the United States. I shall discuss four tendencies that, although at first sight they seem unrelated, all converge on two broad themes. First, they all stress that individualism is a basic characteristic of contemporary society, and, secondly, they all regard this characteristic as deplorable because it allegedly undermines community. This negative evaluation of individualism grows out of the sociological stress on what I sometimes call *Gemeinschaft* romanticism.

The emphasis on individualism and its negative effect on community appears in a variety of formulas, but they all have to do with the prominence of economic concerns, often of the "capitalistic" order, and with the "utilitarian" pursuit of self-interest. The general tone is pronounced pessimism about the prospects of the kind of society in which these characteristics are prominent.

This is where law comes in. From a sociological point of view, law is significant, above all, as an institutional instrumentality of "social control." In the quarters I have in mind, however, the tendency is to presume that the "play of interests" is in fact not being effectively controlled and therefore that the instrumentality that by long tradition has had a central place in this functional context cannot be very important after all. Put a little differently, the implication is that Durkheim must have been wrong about the importance, the *effectiveness*, of the mechanisms he summed up under the heading of "organic solidarity." There is a tendency to identify "community" with "mechanical" solidarity in Durkheim's sense and to presume that any diminution in the relative prominence of this set of components must mean a diminution of solidarity generally.

Before outlining the movements of thought I have in mind, I should like briefly to cite one counterexample, which seems to me to be a highly important harbinger of what I hope will become a major sociological trend. This is a study by John Akula (1973) of the effect of legal action in the United States on the status of black people over a full century, broadly since just after the Civil War.[1] He takes account of both legislation and court decisions and somewhat less account of administrative action, and, very importantly, he investigates both the state and the federal level. His broad conclusion is quite clear: In the light of the historical evidence, the action of governmental agencies through legal measures has, over the period, had a *major* effect in the clear direction of strengthening civil rights.

Furthermore, and particularly important for the present argument, Akula demonstrates—to my mind, conclusively—that the predominant social science views of this record have been heavily biased against attributing much effectiveness to legal action. They divide, according to Akula's analysis, into two principal groups: those who lay the principal emphasis on economic factors (for example, the need for black labor in northern industry) and those who emphasize political factors. Political factors, of course, intertwine in complex ways with the legal, but they are analytically distinguishable. For example, political decision making has legal consequences, through legislation, but the factors that operate in bringing about a Congressional decision such as the Civil Rights Acts of 1964 and 1965, are not to be simply identified with the legal consequences of these decisions for the many different parties to the conflicts and controversies involved.

In the analytical sense, law is a phenomenon of the social system. The four trends of thought I shall discuss here have been concerned with four different primary aspects of the society as a whole. These aspects are, first, economic problems and structure; second, political; third, integrative aspects, which have to do with what I call the "societal community"; and, fourth, the problems of the fiduciary system, which focus to a certain extent on morality. I shall deal with the economic emphasis in terms of a few points about the defenders and critics of the market system in modern society; here I shall focus on the "orthodox" economists and the Marxian movement. For the political emphasis, I shall consider the structure of government and other power systems and focus on certain themes in Max Weber's work. The third emphasis, on the integrative, it will be convenient to treat with reference to the work of a legal scholar, Roberto M. Unger, who has recently emerged into prominence; I shall view Unger's work against the background of the sociological conception of community, especially in the work of Durkheim. Finally, it has seemed best to focus the discussion of the moral problem on the work of Robert Bellah, especially his recent book, *The Broken Covenant* (1975), which has received a good deal of attention.

The four tendencies—they are not definitely enough "structured" to be called *movements*—diverse as they are, have at least three "ideological" features in common, although all four are bound up with serious and highly competent work in social science. Of these "ideological" aspects, the most important is a tendency toward what I have come to call "absolutism." This operates at a variety of levels, but has to do especially with functional subvalues of the societal value system. These functional subvalues cluster about the four system aspects or categories I have just outlined: the economic, the political, the integrative, and the fiduciary. The general pattern common to all four of the tendencies I shall examine is anxiety concerning the value component that the writer or thinker has come to regard as central and with respect to which his* intellectual interests and his "practical" convictions converge, anxiety either that this value component is losing out in the process of development of the society or of those sectors for which he has a special concern or that the value component is not being given its due attention in the work of certain practitioners of his intellectual art.

A second characteristic of the four tendencies I distinguish can be referred to as "dedifferentiation" in a broad sense, including inhibitions against carrying through certain steps of intellectual differentiation. Like absolutism, this characteristic dedifferentiation is itself only a tendency of thought and analysis. An illustration we shall return to later is the Marxist labor theory of value, a single-factor theory dogmatically adhered to in the face of the classical economists' theory of three factors (labor plus land and capital), which, with the addition of Alfred Marshall's "organization," eventually became a widely accepted four-factor theory. Dedifferentiation is linked to absolutism by the fact that concentration on the one salient factor or value encourages a constriction of emphasis at other levels to a minimum of elements that have maximally salient connections with the focus of attention, and causes other, less obvious elements to be ignored. The single-factor theory of production is an example.

*Editor's Note: The traditional use of the pronoun *he* has not yet been superseded by a convenient, generally accepted pronoun that means *he* or *she*. Therefore, the author will continue to use *he*, while acknowledging the inherent inequality of the traditional preference of the masculine pronoun.

A third common characteristic is that each of the four forms of absolutism I shall deal with finds itself opposed to a "counterabsolutism"; that is, its position is polemically oriented against something it regards as its special enemy, a special danger to the society. Needless to say, the antagonism between the original absolutism and its "counter" is generally mutual.

My thesis is that all four tendencies have converged on modern individualism as the focus of their anxiety. Law tends to be the loser by implicit derogation and, often, neglect.[2]

The Economic Complex

It is most convenient by far to start with the economic complex, including the market system and "utilitarian" individualism. Deep ambivalence toward things economic is very ancient indeed. In Western society, it goes back at least to the Greeks; witness Aristotle's discussion, in the *Politics,* of "natural" and "unnatural" acquisition and his hostility to what he called "chrematistics." His discussion can be linked to the problem of usury in Hebrew tradition and in medieval Christian ethics (Nelson, 1969). There is a sense in which modern culture has inherited these ancient suspicions and ambivalences.

A major new phase, however, came with the industrial revolution, I think, because it was this primary social change that "mobilized" the factors of production by drawing them into the market "orbit" and thereby established, for the first time, a high level of *differentiation* of the economy from the societal community. One major reaction to this, in the intellectual community, was the first modern development of economic theory as a scientific discipline, especially with Adam Smith and the classical economists, notably David Ricardo. This development was on the background of the utilitarian movement in the more general field of thought about "man and society."

Almost concurrently, but crystallizing somewhat later, came an intellectual countermovement, namely socialism. After various antecedents, this came to a culmination in Marxism, of which the first prominent public expression was the *Communist*

Manifesto of 1848. Marxism soon captured the leadership of the anticapitalist movement and has maintained its lead ever since. It is highly significant that it articulated, theoretically, *very directly* with the classical economists, notably Ricardo.

As a conceptual scheme, the classical economics was oriented to specifically economic problems. Marxist theory, on the contrary, was diffusely oriented to problems of the status of the *total* society. Thus, for Ricardo, labor was essentially a factor of production in the technical sense of economic theory. His view of it as the primary determinant of "value" in the strict economic sense was arrived at in the context of dealing with a specifically economic theoretical problem. For Marx, on the other hand, labor was only incidentally a factor of production. Much more centrally, Marx treated labor as the primary *symbol* of the meaning of the human condition under "capitalism." This was essentially a religious frame of reference of symbolization, quite directly derived from Christian antecedents. To be "forced to labor" was the latter-day version of the "curse of Adam" in the book of Genesis, from which the individual would, by an act of God (read "revolution"), be freed for the "eternal life" of Communism.

The counterabsolutism to the Marxist absolutism is one major branch of orthodox economic theory, most prominently represented in the United States today by Milton Friedman. Its characteristic is to hypostatize the free and competitive market to the highest degree, not only as an effective institutional mechanism of facilitating economic productivity but as so important that any "tampering" with its operations is, to say the least, deplorable.[3]

In spite of the prominence of corporate actors in the modern industrial type of economy, the Friedman type of ideology puts the stress on the market freedom of "the individual," be he or she consumer or producer. By contrast, the Marxist contention is that under "capitalism" there is a maximal restriction of freedom, most obviously for "labor," but the Marxist analysis extends this to "capitalists" themselves, in that they too are allegedly "forced" by market competition and the discipline of the "profit system" to act as they do.

In this case, the version of individualism that is the primary focus of contention among the adversaries is clearly that which stresses the economically rational pursuit of self-interest, with its background in utilitarian thought. Its ideal institutional form is the competitive market. It is notable that the classical economists all talked in terms of individuals and their economic decisions, thus "the" worker, "the" landlord, and "the" capitalist, meaning the holder of capital funds in a position to invest them. They, especially Adam Smith, were highly suspicious of "combinations" and "monopolies."

By and large, Marx followed the classical model in this as in other respects. He paid virtually no attention to the structure of the firm as a social organization, simply stating that it involved two "classes," laborers and "capitalists," who were in the first instance owners but who of course also were "managers." Even the involvement with kinship, as in the case of family firms, was never explicitly analyzed but was implicit in the conception of a capitalist "class." Even at the level of the dichotomy between the ideal-typical owner-manager and the worker roles, the firm was surely more of a social organization than either the classical economists or Marx made clear.

The issue is important because on theoretical grounds we postulate that the structure and determinants of interests are very different according to whether they are attributed to individuals as actors or to collectivities; even a collectivity of two members, such as a married couple, is only by legal fiction *an* individual or person. In an analytical sense, the problem of individual interest comes to focus in economic terms, whereas that of collective interest is primarily political.

The historic formula "the rational pursuit of self-interest" is clearly primarily individual in reference and has linked up with economic rather than political analysis. The philosophy called *utilitarianism* served well as an underpinning for the development of economics, precisely because it tended to absolutize both the individualism and the rationalism underlying that formula. We should, however, be very careful about transposing this pattern and its implications to the analysis of political phenomena.

Both the two primary categories of reference in this discussion, human "individuals" and "collectivities," are such that there are some sectors of their action systems in which the "rational pursuit of interests" in the social system context can claim primacy and there are others in which it cannot. For example, the worker, whether he seeks employment in a "profit-making enterprise" or another type of organization, certainly is under pressure to consider economic interests, particularly level of money pay relative to that in other employment opportunities. A "housewife" shopping for family food supplies is under similar pressure. These individuals, however, have large sectors of their role involvements, such as concern for their children, in which such considerations are not primary. The absolutism common to utilitarianism and to much of economic theory consists of overextending the sphere governed by self-interest in this sense relative to other spheres. It should follow that no human individual, even one of Marx's classical capitalists, can be oriented *only* in terms of self-interest in all connections. And what about a small child? The question is one of balance among several modes of orientation.

Parallel considerations apply to the case of collective interest. For the collectivities we call *firms,* economic interest is primary at the *collective* level. What that implies for individual participants, however, is highly problematical and may vary over a wide range. Other collectivities, such as universities, hospitals, churches, indeed agencies of government, surely are not mainly "profit-making" organizations. They, however, like and including family households, must carefully consider their economic problems in such contexts as level of income and "cost of living" or, for nonfamilial cases, cost of operations. For example, academic people have become painfully aware in recent years of the budgetary exigencies of colleges and universities.

The primary symbol of primacy of economic orientation on the part of individuals and of collectivities has been *profit.* This concept is susceptible of theoretically precise definition, along the line of the *economic advantage* derived, in the past or the future, from a set of transactions between one unit of

action and its social environment. In modern institutional settings, the overwhelmingly predominant relevant sector of the
economic environment is the market system, and advantage is
usually measured in money terms. The concept profit, however,
being an affect-laden symbol, has tended to be generalized along
lines of connotation that are theoretically at variance with its
technical theoretical meaning, which I insist should be economic.

Perhaps the most egregious example of this tendency is
the common usage of the phrase "the profit motive." The scien-
tifically correct use of the concept *motive* refers to the action
of the individual. The phrase is, however, frequently applied to
collectivities, such as business corporations. But these entities,
whatever else they are, are not human individuals and are not
actuated by "motives" in the sense that the latter are. I have no
objection to saying that business corporations have "interests"
and that among these interests that which can be called *economic* has primacy. But every other kind of social collectivity
also has interests. For many, other than firms, economic interests are secondary to others; thus we suppose that for universities the "advancement of knowledge and its transmission to
others" takes precedence over financial profit. At the same
time, the economic interests of a university are of formidable
importance. But to recognize this is *not* to assert that these interests "govern" the whole policy of the organization, subordi-
nating all else.

The allegation of a profit "motive," extended from the
individual to the collectivity, is often carried still further in
ideological discussion. It may, thus, in certain radical circles, be
alleged that the universities in a society are subservient to the
economic interests of large business corporations; for example,
through training both competent and "compliant" manpower
for employment by such corporations. Such allegations have
been with us, in my personal experience, since the 1920s, and
surely much longer. But cannot social science come up with
more sophisticated accounts of these (admittedly complex) relationships?

The adversary relationship—to borrow a legal term—

between the procapitalistic economic absolutists and their anti-capitalistic, broadly socialist counterparts tends to squeeze out other concerns. It is striking that, in the period of more than a century in which this conflict of interpretive formulas about the "real" processes in modern society has been prominent, it has steadily focused on the salience of the society's predominantly economic organization. Thus, government has, on the one hand, been minimized through the idealization of the "night watch-man state," where the minimal functions of enforcement of contracts and external defense have been stressed; on the other hand, the state has been alleged to be the "executive committee of the bourgeoisie," which has simply operated as a "tool" of the capitalistic interests. Virtually nothing has been said about other important structures in the same society. One of these, with which I have been especially concerned, is the educational system, especially that of higher education (Parsons and Platt, 1973; Parsons, in press).

The case of special interest here, however, is the legal system. The economists, leading up in the absolutist direction, have grudgingly conceded that a legal order is needed notably in the areas of the law of property and contract, but it is striking how little stress has been placed on these themes in the theoretical literature of economics, especially since the days of such figures as John R. Commons. Indeed, the importance of such contributions as Willard Hurst's *Law and the Conditions of Freedom* (1956), especially where he dealt with the development of the legal legitimation of corporate organization and the legal devices for its implementation in the second half of the nineteenth century, has not figured prominently in economic literature.

On the other side, notably in Marxist literature, the tendency has been to play down the independent significance of the legal order and of legal action. This has taken two principal forms. On the one hand, it is alleged that what has determined the actual state of affairs in modern society has been the "pressure" of economic interests—predominantly capitalistic interests, of course—and that the legal framework has had little to do with the development of the hated "capitalistic system," except as a dependent variable. On the other hand, in the socialist movement, remedial action has been seen overwhelmingly in the context of political, not legal, action. Where *political* decision making has had legal consequences, these have been seen overwhelmingly as simple consequences of the political, not as having any independent significance. Let me give two examples of this neglect. First, David Little (1969) in a study that I think would have been very congenial to Weber, had he lived to see it, and that I gather has been congenial to Bellah, included an impressive analysis of the relation between Puritanism and the development of the common law in early modern England—the sixteenth and seventeenth centuries. This, like Merton's work (1938) on the relations between Puritanism and science in the same period, is a complement to Weber's study of the relations between the Protestant ethic and the motivation of "capitalistic" economic activity—by individuals, I may note. I regard Little's work as an important contribution to understanding the background of more recent developments in modern societies, but one that has surely been neglected in economic discussions.

The second example is an unfinished, posthumously published work (1965) of Perry Miller, perhaps the most distinguished historian of Puritanism in New England. It concerns the aftermath of the religious crises of the eighteenth century, especially the "Great Awakening" in the early nineteenth century in America. The important point is that, along with revivalism, Miller emphasizes the emergence of concerns with the law and the prominence of the legal profession. After Independence and the acceptance of the Constitution, law, especially in the common law tradition, acquired a new level of importance. This involved the emergence into salience of the U.S. Supreme Court, especially under Chief Justice Marshall, with his assertion of the doctrine of judicial review, but also the role of two other major figures, Justice Story and Chancellor Kent. This is a development that most economics-oriented historians of this period would find too unimportant to receive their attention. This impression of the importance of the adoption of the common law is confirmed by the work of Roscoe Pound (1921).

To conclude this introductory and tone-setting section, I

should like to make more than footnote reference to what I regard as a very important recent book: Louis Dumont, *From Mandeville to Marx: The Genesis and Triumph of Economic Ideology* (1977). This is a comprehensive review, in the best tradition of French intellectual history, as typified in the work of Elie Halévy ([1901-1904] 1952), of the background and essential themes of the rise of the "economic" complex of primary symbols in the culture of Western society from the eighteenth century to the present. Dumont has brought to this work the contrasting perspective derived from his studies of Indian culture (*Homo Hierarchicus: The Caste System and Its Implications*, 1970). In my opinion, he has done a masterly piece of work in comprehensively analyzing what we may call the "economic primacy complex" in the development of Western cultural symbolism. Above all he has systematically related the strand in the tradition that comes from utilitarianism and the classical economics, to the Marxist strand, with its background in German idealistic philosophy. Particularly impressive is his contention, which seems to me valid, that Marx did not transcend the utilitarian version of individualism but that his "collectivism" was mainly pragmatic-political, rather than, in the philosophical sense, "principled."

In my opinion, for the theoretically serious student of these matters, careful study of Dumont's book is a *must*. He does more than any other recent author to clear away many of the confusions and misunderstandings that have plagued so many discussions of these subjects.

There are, however, two problems that I do not think Dumont adequately handles and about which I will briefly raise questions at the end of this chapter. The first is, given the correctness of Dumont's thesis of the "triumph" of the economic, how the economic complex is to be related theoretically to the other aspects of the social system and, beyond that, of the general system of action. The second question is, given the unsatisfactoriness of the economic-utilitarian conception of individualism, including its Marxist version, must the idea of individualism be dropped or is there a way to correct and supplement these received ideas?[4]

The Political Context

Let us now turn to the second context in which "absolutisms" produce conflicts leading to downplaying law as a social phenomenon. This is the political context. Much of the all-too-voluminous literature, reaching back for centuries, is relevant here; I have, however, chosen to deal with the problem only in terms of the work of Max Weber. I am not an historian of political theory, but over the years I have devoted a great deal of time to the study of Weber, and, rightly or wrongly, feel that I know his work rather well. Moreover, Weber was, in terms of his "intellectual psychology," if that term is admissible, an exceedingly complex personality, and I think all the essential tensions and conflicts are, for the sensitive student, visible in his work.

Let me start by reporting a difference of interpretation. Reinhard Bendix, certainly one of the leading interpreters of Weber's work, has strongly asserted that Weber was in the first instance a political sociologist whose primary concern was the understanding of political phenomena (Bendix and Roth, 1971). At about the same time I stoutly asserted that the center of Weber's sociological concern lay in his sociology of law, which was "flanked" on one side by his interests in economic and political phenomena, on the other by those in the sociology of religion (Parsons, 1967, chap. 3; original in German, 1964). After having had several years to mull it over, I am prepared to stand by that statement of 1964, which was made on a rather special occasion, namely the Heidelberg meeting commemorating the hundredth anniversary of Weber's birth.

It is, of course, a matter of record that Weber was initially trained in jurisprudence and had a promising beginning of a career in academic law before turning away from it for economics and then sociology. More important is the fact that references to the importance of law ran all through his works from his dissertation on medieval commercial law to the "Author's Introduction" to his series of studies in the sociology of religion, which was one of the last things he wrote ([1920] 1930). The major monograph on the sociology of law was one of the centerpieces of *Economy and Society* (1968), the final arrangement for which was not his, but was the choice of his posthumous editors.

More important still, however, is the theoretical logic of his position. I think that Weber's focal point of reference for the analysis of societies lay in the concept of *legitimate order*. He grounded the concept of legitimacy itself in the beliefs or conceptions (*Vorstellungen*) of actors. It should be noted that he placed the concept of legitimate order at a higher level than that of *Herrschaft* (translated by Bendix and Roth as "domination" and by myself, when it is qualified by the adjective *legitimate,* as "authority"). A legitimate order, then, is called "convention" if the mechanisms of its enforcement are informal—for example, diffuse disapproval of infraction—and is *law* when its enforcement is in the hands of a specially authorized organization.

It seems to me symptomatic that, at this very critical point in his classification of ideal types, Weber singled out the agency of enforcement as the criterion to distinguish law from convention. This is consistent with the fact, which emerges from reading his sociology of law, that he tended to be impressed by the relative "irrationality" of English common law and, indeed, rather tended to play down its importance. Of course, he had in mind the contrast with the Roman law traditions of continental Europe, especially those of his native Germany. It is also highly important that Weber did not define law as a sociological concept in terms of government or the state. *Any* collectivity may have law so long as there is a body of rules and the function of enforcement is entrusted to a specialized agency within it.

Important as it is, I should say that enforcement is only one of the primary functions performed in a legal action system. It is itself part of a larger set of functions that may be called "administration." Thus, when a legislature enacts a tax law, the collection of money from individuals and collectivities liable under it must be carried out by an organization that not only has to deal with resistances to payment but also has to make rulings about the detailed definition of liability, since a "law," as an act of a legislature, is seldom precise enough. Legislation itself is another function, but presumably it would be too specific for Weber's criterial purposes.

Another particularly important legal function is *interpretation*. The regulation-making function of administrative agencies involves this, but in some legal systems it is, at higher levels, entrusted to special courts, especially the "appellate" courts. By the decisions they make, such courts say which, among the possible meanings of a set of norms, are to have legally binding effect. The function of interpretation in this sense is to be distinguished from legislation on one side. A court decision is not a legislative enactment, although concretely, as in so many cases, there are often indistinct boundaries. At the same time, such courts typically do not perform enforcement functions, which are the province of administration or executive agencies.

The prominence of the interpretive function or of "adjudication" is an especially important feature of the Anglo-American legal systems, which Weber—not radically, but perceptibly—tended to deprecate. This is the feature of the legal system that in the American case is focused on the background of the written Constitution, the federal structure of government, and the separation of powers, which it is most important, sociologically, to stress as clearly legal, not political.

The function of enforcement is built on the assumption that *what* the legitimate normative order requires of persons and collectivities acting in relation to it is not in question. What is in question is their compliance, and the primary function of agencies of enforcement is to ensure that compliance, by dealing with situations where noncompliance occurs or is suspected or threatened. The function of interpretive courts, on the other hand, is quite different. Their function is to "define the situation" for those who act in relation to a normative order, so that they know better what their rights and obligations are and what the consequences of alternative courses of action will be for themselves and for others with whom they are concerned.

Courts of law are made responsible for rendering adjudicative decisions, but this articulates with one of the most important of the functions of members of the legal profession. Of course, most courts are manned by professional lawyers. Also, it is mainly lawyers, through "arguments" or briefs, to whom the judges listen in trying to decide their cases. Furthermore, lawyers have a highly important role in advising clients, not only those who are or may be involved in a court case but also, short of that, clients who want to know what actions it would be in their interest to take in the light of the structure of the legal system and its trends of change, including change by future judicial decisions.

I have selected Weber's work to illustrate the possibilities of drifting toward a political absolutism, as distinguished from the kind of economic absolutism discussed earlier. It is clear from the discussion thus far that Weber did not neglect the importance of legal systems as such economists as Milton Friedman and the economically focused Marxists have done. What I do suggest is that Weber's orientation to the legal system was selective and that his stress on enforcement rather than on interpretation is symptomatic of what, in this sense, is a "bias."

This, I think, connects with his emphases among possibly important political phenomena. But before going into these, I should like to say a little about Weber's treatment of economic problems. No more than law, surely, did Weber neglect this sphere in any general sense. After all, he was the author of *The Protestant Ethic and the Spirit of Capitalism,* and he wrote many other things about what are empirically economic problem areas. Furthermore, unlike Marx and most Marxists, Weber, with the advantage of coming a generation later, was thoroughly conversant with the main structure of *modern,* as distinguished from *classical,* economic theory.

It seems to me that there is a clue to Weber's selectivity of emphases in his special treatment of the "spirit" of capitalism. As a German, brought up in Berlin and trained there in academic law, Weber may well have been struck, I suggest, by the similarity of the concept of *duty* as it permeated both the Prussian army and the civil service, the latter of which in the higher reaches was made up overwhelmingly of people trained in the law faculties of the universities (Rueschemeyer, 1973), and the concept of the *calling* as this was developed by the

English Puritan divines of the seventeenth century, and applied to economic enterprise but more generally to work in *any* secular occupation.

Weber developed this association just when large-scale organization was coming to be characteristic of the "capitalistic" economy, as it was then in Germany and at about the same time in the United States. It should not be altogether surprising then, that Weber saw as the most characteristic *structural* feature of what he called modern "rational bourgeois capitalism" the linking of *bureaucratic organization*—note, not the interests of individuals, in utilitarian fashion—to orientation to profit through the market. It was this bureaucratized capitalism that, given certain other concerns of his, came to constitute the "iron cage" of his famous statement at the end of the essay on the Protestant ethic.[5]

Whatever the merits of Weber's case for the "orientational"—I avoid the expression "motivational"—equivalences of the Puritans' "ascetic Protestant man" and the latter-day "bureaucratic man," the "iron cage" from which Weber felt alienated was not the "rational pursuit of self-interest" of the utilitarians and the classical economists, if only because bureaucracy is not a phenomenon of *individual* self-interest coming to be free of "moral" discipline. If anything, the discipline was very stringent but, for Weber, of the *wrong kind,* in the wrong cause.

Of Weber's many contributions to thinking about modern society, I think it is significant that, along with the iron cage and charisma, about which a few things will be said presently, his ideal type of "bureaucracy" has had a vast resonance in modern thought. The first point to be clear about is that it is in the first instance a *political* category. It is not a mode of individual action, whatever the participants' motives may be, but a mode of the *organization* of the coordinated actions of many individuals. It has in common with economic rationality that it is oriented to increasing efficiency and effectiveness—in short, to rationality. Since this is true, there is a special significance in the linking of the two, which in the present context I regard as the principal significance of Weber's "genial" combination of

them. Indeed, Weber very strongly stressed that bureaucratic organization was overwhelmingly the most efficient that had been
arrived at in human societies anywhere. Moreover, it was applicable in a wide variety of fields, by no means only that of governmental administration.

Another indication of Weber's political "slant" in these
matters is that he treated bureaucracy within the context of
types of *authority,* not of legitimate order more generally nor
anything like John Locke's conception of liberties and interests,
either in terms of the pursuit of individual self-interest or of the
natural rights underlying a social contract.

A centrally important fact is that, among Weber's three
types of legitimate authority—traditional, charismatic, and rational-legal—the last, under which the bureaucratic type falls, is
the only one that by definition includes any direct reference to
law. In his more general chapter ([1922] 1947, chap. 3) on
types of *Herrschaft,* there is some discussion of constitutional
democracies, parties, separation of powers, and the like, but
clearly his primary attention was focused on the three types.
Moreover, he started his discussion with the rational-legal type,
clearly making it the centerpiece. Then traditional authority,
certainly in relation to the modern world with which he was so
deeply preoccupied, essentially serves as a kind of background
scenery. The important alternative to the rational-legal type was
the charismatic.

Weber's characterization of the bureaucratic type was
very much in the ideal-type format of an accentuation of certain salient features. It stressed what we have come to call "line
authority," proceeding strictly from the top down. It stressed
specificity of function on the part of participants, contrasted
with more diffuse "whole person" involvements. It stressed
"leadership" in the sense of centralization of top authority.
Thus, one of Weber's key concepts was that of the *Verband*—
which I somewhat awkwardly translate as "corporate group."
The prime characteristics of the *Verband* are a "leader" or
chief, and a staff, and below that those whose prime function is
to follow direction from above. The bureaucratic organization is
essentially the accentuation of these more general characteristics.

Bureaucracy is one major type of primarily political organization, but only one, standing at a relative extreme in a range of variation. One might suggest that the opposite end of the range should be the "participatory democracy" of recent idealization. As in the case of law, here also Weber has selected one rather extreme type to stand as representative for the whole —but with one outstanding exception.

The exception is that of charismatic authority. It is, first, significant that Weber deals with charisma, as he does with bureaucracy, in the context of his theory of authority, with its strong hierarchical emphases. This is also related to the extent of his association of the concept *charisma* with a type of *personal* influence. Thus his definition runs: "resting on devotion to the specific and exceptional sanctity, heroism or exemplary character of an individual person, and of the normative patterns or order revealed or ordained by him" ([1922] 1947, p. 328). I think it probable that a main reason for this stress on the individual person was not a "psychological" concern, but an emphasis on the *role* of leadership. This word is indeed very frequently linked with charisma. Just as a rational-legal *Verband* will have a leader or chief, so will a charismatic movement. This interpretation is consistent with Weber's introducing the concept of charisma in the context of the analysis of authority.

In addition, I think that the concept charisma has two other primary features. The first is that it is in part a residual category, but in one direction, whereas the category traditional is residual in another. Both are in the first instance contrasted with the rational-legal, and their prime characteristic is that they are *not* rational-legal. The characteristic of traditionalism for Weber is its "closedness," as expressed in his phrase "belief in the sanctity of immemorial traditions." By contrast, the prime characteristic of charismatic authority is its openness to change, its role of introducing innovations. The charismatic leader stands in conscious opposition to "established" norms. An example is Weber's frequent reference to the Gospel statement by Jesus, "It is written, but I say unto you [something in conflict with what is written]."

The other feature of the concept to which I wish to call attention is the religious reference of charisma. Weber, of course, borrowed the term from early Christian usage. In the definition just quoted, the normative patterns or order is said to be "revealed or ordained by him," which is surely religious terminology. In terms of recent analyses, charisma is a reference to what we have been calling telic sources of legitimation, but of change, not of a status quo (Parsons, in press).

To go back to the terminology of "alienation," Weber was certainly a deeply alienated man, relative not only to "capitalism" but also to rational-legal authority more generally, not least in governmental organization. His deepest hopes were for a charismatic release from the bureaucratic iron cage. The one element of prognostication of which he felt rather sure was that the agency of such release had to be political, in the present *analytical* sense.[6] It had to come through a movement that could achieve a high level of collective organization under leadership.

It seems to be quite clear that what preoccupied Weber was not the socially disintegrative effects of "the rational pursuit of self-interest," which, as we shall see, preoccupy Robert Bellah and, if Dumont is right, preoccupied Marx. He was not worried about the breakdown of the moral discipline of the individual in the direction of the pursuit of individual interests at the expense of a common interest. This is basically a problem of what Dumont has called the triumphant "economic ideology."

Weber was, of course, worried about the impact of rational-legal organization on the individual, who, as he put it, was fated to live in an iron cage. But the problem of interests was shifted to another level, that of the organized collectivity. Here, however, there is another curious and interesting feature of Weber's position. He did not stress the conflict between private *collective* organizations and the common or public interest, but tended to treat especially big business and government as coordinated branches of what can probably most appropriately be termed a *rational-legal society*. This has become a prominent theme of much of neo-Marxism, and the contemporary political Left more generally.[7]

But even this was not Weber's primary problem. His primary concern, with reference to the formula of the rational pursuit of self-interest, even if "self" be interpreted to include a corporate reference, was not with that but with the word *rational*. As much of the literature on Weber has pointed out, his focal concern, both theoretical and existential, was, especially toward the end of his life, with the "process of rationalization," about which he was deeply ambivalent. On the one hand, more than almost anyone else he knew what a profound influence the developments of philosophy and science, of rational law and economic and political organization, had on Western civilization and specifically on the preeminence of the West ("Author's Introduction," [1920] 1930). But on the other hand he was extremely sensitive to the negative side, a sensitivity that came to focus in his preoccupations with religions, but also with art and a variety of other concerns.

Thus there is a sense in which bureaucratization, or at the more general level rational-legal authority, for Weber as it were "gobbled up" the field of law, as well as other fields. The consequence was to compromise if not destroy its independence as a structural sphere in the constitution of modern societies. The association of law and the state is in the nature of the case extremely close, but in my opinion it should not be asserted to constitute a virtual identity. However, Weber "tended" not only to identify them but also, aided by his analytical concept of things political, to extend the identity to the business enterprise and hence to arrive at a curiously monolithic conception of a bureaucratically rationalized society. This could be considered to be a case of the politicization of the law and much else, although very different, for instance, from recent leftist-promoted politicization of the university world. Perhaps bureaucratization, then, takes a place second only to profit orientation in the catalogue of evils of modern society.

With reference to my difference of opinion with Bendix (Bendix and Roth, 1971), mentioned at the beginning of this section, there is a sense in which we were both right. Among the functional emphases open to the theoretical analysis of modern societies, Weber stressed the political in the analytical sense, in marked contrast, for example, to the "triumph of the economic" of which Dumont speaks. On the deeper level of the main structure of analytical social theory, with which I am concerned, however, I think that the position still holds that law is more central than politics, not exclusively, but definitely, for Weber. The conflicts that have been outlined in this discussion, however, tended to constrict his treatment of legal phenomena in a way parallel to but different from the construction on the part of many whose preoccupation has been with the economic area of social life.[8]

The Societal Community

Going on around the functional "clock" (counterclockwise) for the analysis of a society as a system, one comes to focus attention on the integrative system, which in recent years I have been calling the *societal community* (Parsons, 1969). This subsystem of the society is of special importance for purposes of the present paper because, as part of the structure of a society, it is in this subsystem that I would place the legal system, in a sense of paramount functional significance, although of course concretely it involves other functional components, notably political.

For the limited purposes of the present discussion I have chosen to treat one book, *Law in Modern Society* (1976), by Roberto Mangabiera Unger. I should like to make it clear immediately that my relation to Unger's work is very different from that to Max Weber's. Whereas I have been intensively concerned with Weber for half a century, I have only read this one book of Unger's and that very recently—and, I confess it, in the first instance, because I agreed to write a review of it—and, of course, its subject interested me. I have not even read his preceding book, *Knowledge and Politics* (1975), although clearly, from its table of contents, it is in many respects pertinent to this discussion; the reason for that omission is simply pressure of time. Hence the scope of this discussion of Unger must be strictly limited.

As a lawyer and a law school teacher, Unger would not be expected to play down the importance of law. If anything, the contrary is true, and thus his book is an important corrective, conceived in a very broad perspective, to the tendencies with which the rest of this article has been and will be concerned. The book, however, raises complex problems about the articulation of the legal system in the rest of the society. Indeed, in the course of studying the book, I came to the conclusion that, in the sense in which I have been using the term *absolutist* in this article, it would be correct to call Unger a "legal absolutist." The interesting problems concern the features of his position that justify that label and some of their implications for social system theory.

Before entering into that, however, something needs to be said about my own conception of the place of law in the social system. First, I would follow Weber in treating it as a form of legitimate order, meaning order in the normative sense, as a set of prescriptions, permissions, and prohibitions bearing on social action and more or less systematically organized. I would also follow Weber in not confining the concept to government or the state, but extending it to private organizations.

This last point is exceedingly important to my own conception of the place of the legal order in the structure of a society, a placing that is not empirically evident except for highly differentiated societies. Its focus is the societal community, not the polity, and therefore its primary societal functions are integrative. Among these, the function of interpretation, as discussed earlier, is particularly salient. It, in turn, has become especially prominent in American society because, first, we have a written constitution, which can be amended, but only by a politically difficult procedure; second, it is a federal system; and, third, it institutionalizes the separation of powers in three "branches."

It is so common simply to identify the legal system with government that the implications of an analytical scheme must be considered with particular care at this point. If we think of the polity as concerned with the attainment of societal goals, this function can extend even to making a constitution, because only a government could take that order of responsibility on behalf of the society as a whole. The same is true of the legislative function, in that solution of a problem arising in the society may sometimes call for enacting a "law." As far as adjudication is concerned, then, there are two problems that could hardly be solved without governmental involvement. The first is enforcement, which Weber stressed so strongly, and the second is the manning of courts, because no agency not representing the society as a whole could be permitted to make appointments, for example, to the U.S. Supreme Court.

The focal point is that the law of the state is *binding* in the sense that not only is compliance defined as "obligatory" but coercive sanctions are also threatened or applied in case of noncompliance. For private associations, the "ultimate" negative sanction is generally exclusion from the rights and privileges of membership or other status components within the control of the association. In well-ordered modern societies, only government can legitimately use physical sanctions to coerce or compel compliance.

These considerations, however, do not imply that once a constitution has been ratified, or once an act of Congress has been enacted, the normative structure remains only part of government. The U.S. Constitution is the constitution of the United States *as a society,* not of the federal government. Thus, as amended and interpreted, it defines the powers of the branches of the federal government and their limits, vis-à-vis each other, vis-à-vis the state governments, and vis-à-vis the various parts of the "private sector." Hence there is a critically important sense in which, in societies with written or informal constitutions, there is a continuing dynamic relation between the governmental system and the societal community (see Evan, 1962). At certain points in their evolution as issues, some become governmentalized, but if something approaching a solution is attained, the normative structure is in a sense degovernmentalized and becomes part of the normative structure of the societal community or its relevant subsectors. It seems to me that this interpretation is consistent with Weber's centrally important point, that the concept of law should not be confined to government. The criterion of the private sector is that organizations within it can establish laws without resort to government. An important zone of interpenetration, then, is the field of regulation of private by governmental organizations and action. The obverse of this is the penetration of government by "interest" representation.

Weber's subsuming of law under the concept of *legitimate* order indicates the connections of a legal system with other sectors of the society in another direction—in our terminology, the *fiduciary* subsystem of a society. A close relative of Weber's term *legitimation* is *moral,* which was preferred by Durkheim. If a legal system is legitimate, in some degree compliance with its normative rules is binding not only legally but also morally. There are always problems of the justification of compliance with what are felt to be unjust laws, whether public or private. But it is very important to be clear that only at one extreme of a range is a whole legal system felt to be illegitimate. This can almost serve as the definition of a "revolutionary situation."

Social systems are, after all, complex in intricately ramified ways. Their normative requirements impinge on interests in a wide variety of ways, which are a function not only of the normative structure and content but also of the interests and the concrete situations in which they take shape. I think that the crux of the integrative problems of a social system can be said to lie in the ways in which normative components—among which the legal have a particularly important place—are related to each other and to the many kinds of interests on which they impinge. The criterion of legitimacy of course applies both to the norms and the interests involved and is *one* of the main ways of connecting them, but not the only one.

There is one further context of the present problem, with respect to which I think that Durkheim had an even surer insight than Weber had. This concerns the functions of law in relation to the economic sphere, particularly to the division of labor. It should be clear from the preceding sketch that the legal system, if its functions are in the *first* instance integrative, cannot have just the same kind of articulation with the economy and the structure of economic interests that it has with the polity on the one hand, the fiduciary system on the other. One way to put this difference is to point out that the "play" of economic interests, as such, does not involve either of the two kinds of "bindingness" just referred to. Indeed, as we have seen, the economy is the focus of the modern conceptualization of "naked interests"; this is why it is so often used as a generalized symbol of evil. The fact that the legal system, then, can mobilize sets of binding obligations from *two* analytically distinct sources makes it particularly important as a regulating mechanism in this field of the "pure type" of the "play of interests." It is the *combination* of the two components of normative regulation that is particularly important here.

On the one hand, idealists are continually averring how fine it would be if such regulation could be effected *only* through the moral authority of the necessary restraints. On the other hand, certain "realists" tend to say that the fact that the rules are *legally* binding, that is, that compliance is enforced by coercive sanctions, is the "real" basis of order. There seems to be ample evidence that neither alone will be sufficient, but there is something to be said for the view that the combination has certain advantages over a "policy" that virtually suppresses either one in favor of the other.

We may now return to Unger. I would first like to emphasize that his book is valuable because of his broad perspective, as I have already noted. This is, in a very good sense, both comparative and historical. For example, his discussion of the Chinese system of about 5 to 200 B.C., is a notable contribution to both aspects of perspective. The same is true of his treatment of the German record in two phases, the development there, especially in Prussia, of bureaucratic law and the erosion of it in the Weimar period.

More specifically these two merits come to focus in Unger's insight that the development of what he calls a "legal system" has been special to the "modern" West in the phase that he designates as "liberal society." My earlier discussion of Weber should make it clear that I am very much in agreement with this trend of thought and diagnosis.

In the shift to more technically analytical considerations, however, I have found myself forced (intellectually) to raise certain questions. In his characterization of this relatively unique historical phenomenon he calls a "legal system," Unger gives us four criteria, as follows.

First, law is "positive," by which I think he means that it is explicit in the definition of rights and obligations.

Second, it is "public"; I find Unger's discussion of this ambiguous, but my interpretation runs to the effect that by "public" he means "governmental" or pertaining to "the state," as he frequently says. If this interpretation is correct, it means that he does not accept the view that I have adopted from Weber, that the concept of law should be defined as crossing the line between the polity and the societal community, as a zone of interpenetration between them. Indeed, Unger speaks of the differentiation between the state and "society," not attempting to differentiate the various components of the latter that I have reviewed. Furthermore, in speaking of the state, he does not differentiate between the aspects of the governmental structure that are in the analytical sense political and those which are not. This is a serious difference of theoretical view (my first disagreement).

Unger's third criterion of a fully developed legal system he calls "generality," which he spells out as involving "generality in legislation and uniformity in adjudication" (1976, p. 53). This conception comes very close to what, in relation to Weber's work especially, I have been calling "universalism." It is surely one of the most important pattern types of modern society, not only in law, but in many other aspects of the modern world, perhaps especially science. It very much links with Weber's conceptualization of rationality, which was touched on earlier.

The fourth criterion is "autonomy," which is exceedingly important. He speaks of the autonomy of the legal system "within the state," which again raises my central problem. There can be different contexts of legal autonomy, but Unger—rightly, I think—stresses that of the process of adjudication and the social organization involved in it, namely the courts and their judicial personnel.

The most striking historical locus of this development, of course, was England, its main symbol being the struggle of Justice Coke against James I, well before the achievement of parliamentary ascendancy over the Crown. And then there was the especially important American development after the adoption of the constitution, which was cited in the previous section.

In a somewhat different context, which I interpret to be more a functional approach than Unger's four-fold classification, which seems to be one of criterial properties, he speaks of three aspects of a legal system, which he calls the *formal,* the *procedural,* and the *substantive.* It seems to me at least that for Unger, although he does not use the concept, these three categories can be interpreted to stand in a cybernetic hierarchy.

Thus it seems clear that for Unger the primary criterion of the "integrity" of a legal system is its adherence to formal considerations. Thus he says (1976, p. 194), "An ideal of justice is formal when it makes the uniform application of general rules the keystone of justice or when it establishes principles whose validity is supposedly independent of choices among conflicting values." There seems to be only one major difficulty here, namely that Unger seems, to me at least, to equivocate as to how far "formality" is to be construed in rational or logical terms; I gather he would not stress that feature as far as Weber did. Indeed, I find it rather strange, since Unger uses a contrast between formal and substantive, that there is in his book no reference to Weber's rather extended discussion of the contrast between "formal and substantive rationality," stated precisely in Weber's monograph (1968, chap. 8) on the sociology of law.

However that may be, it is clear that for Unger the essential contrast is between the formal and the substantive elements, while the intermediate category of the procedural does not figure at all prominently in his analysis. This emphasis is my second serious theoretical disagreement with Unger's position. In order to clarify this, however, it is necessary to outline a little more of his empirical position.

We have already noted that Unger suggests that a fully developed "legal system" in his sense has developed only once, in a special set of circumstances, namely, in the "liberal society" of the early modern Western world. But if it took almost unique circumstances to produce the conditions of such a legal system, there is no obvious set of reasons to believe that these conditions will remain stable over a long period. It is Unger's thesis that in what he calls "postliberal" society the situation has changed and the viability of the legal system in his sense is quite endangered, if it has not already seriously deteriorated.

The circumstances that made the development of this legal system possible, according to Unger, are two, namely what he calls "group pluralism" and "natural law." What he has in mind in speaking of group pluralism in this connection is the plurality of "estates" in early modern Europe, namely the monarchical—which, especially through the development of its bureaucracy, was the fountainhead of "the state"—the aristocratic, and the bourgeois, which was above all the seat of economic interests, although Unger includes the professions. He does not speak of the clergy, except indirectly, to say that a legal system was dependent on the secularization of law. He puts it, however, in terms of absorption of law into the state, leaving "religion" outside. Also, in that period the "working class" did not count as a power group.

Turning then to the pressures that Unger feels threaten the integrity of the legal system in postliberal society, he concentrates his attention on two categories, both of which in his opinion operate to shift the balance from the supremacy of formal considerations to that of substantive or, as he often says, "policy" considerations, using the latter phrase in pretty much the current political sense. These constitute the complex he calls the "welfare state" and a plural set of "interest groups"—this time not the estates of the earlier period, but a new set, in which he would of course include the standard "business" pressure groups, as well as others without primarily economic goals, such as "minority" groups. What is common among the different groups and those who are demanding "welfare"—not simply in the sense of "relief"—is that they demand "substantive justice," the granting of which cuts across the imperatives of "generality" and formality that are to him the main characteristics of a legal system. But the demand for substantive justice also tends to compromise the autonomy of the legal system, in that it tends to subordinate legal to political considerations. There is, of course, an important sense in which, under pressure, political considerations must take precedence over legal.

In the light of the preceding discussion, contrasting the special concern of the theorists of the economic complex with the play of individual interests, especially through market competition, with Weber's concern with the importance of collective interests, it is interesting to note that Unger does not strongly stress this issue. If anything, he is more interested in the impact of collective interests, a fact that is indicative of his position.

There are obviously important empirical problems in this area, concerning the magnitude of the pressures toward substantive primacy, the nature of the resistances to them, and the degree to which the formal integrity of the legal system has in fact been eroded by them. Both for reasons of space and of personal competence, I cannot undertake to review the relevant empirical evidence. It does, however, seem to me that the combination of the two theoretical considerations I have cited creates a presumption that Unger has been predisposed to exaggerate the extent to which the balance of forces has operated against the integrity of the legal system, at least to the extent that Unger claims it has.

First, the fact that Unger restricts his conception of law to the law of the state, seems to me to erect an "artificial" barrier between what are now commonly called the *public* and the *private* sectors of the society, with the effect of distorting the interchange between them; the state through its law and policies influences the private sector only by imposing rules, but private interests operate to "bend" the law away from these norms. If, for example, law is a feature of private collectivities, then treating private law as part of an extended legal system involves a presumption that in the course of the two-way interaction between the legal system of the state and the "interest groups" of the private sector, the commitment to law should tend to operate on both sides. However, Unger's way of posing the problem tends to suggest that the interchange is between "legally controlled" agencies on the one side and agencies or collectivities with no relation to law on the other.

In the case of the welfare state complex, as Unger puts it, the incidence of law on the "demand" side is somewhat different. Few of the claimants to what he thinks of as substantive decisions are collectivities with highly formalized substantive law in their own organization. In pressing their claims, however, they very definitely relate themselves to the great legal traditions of the society, which are at least partially publicly formulated in legal documents, such as the American Bill of Rights. In this sense, they are largely appealing to "the state" in its political capacity, but they are doing so in terms of *their own* legal tradition and conception of their legal and moral rights. Again, it is the fact that, according to my and Weber's conception, there is a "legal" component that is both public and private that makes probable a more highly integrative outcome of such interactions than Unger suggests is possible and likely.

There seems to be a genuine parallel to the situation that underlay the emergence of the legal system in Europe, according to Unger. The three group interest components he dealt with—the monarchies, the aristocracies, and the bourgeois groups—after all shared a common cultural heritage. In its secularized version, Unger deals with this under the heading of *natural law*. He suggests, but I am skeptical of his view, that any kind of belief in a basis of order transcending contemporary group interests has eroded.

Related considerations apply to my second main focus of disagreement with Unger, namely on the status of the category of procedure. Among the members of his triad, the formal component, dominated as it is by *generality* (his term) or *universalism* (mine), easily tends to transcend the interests or even concerns of the particular society or legal jurisdiction, for example, of private law systems. The category of substantive concern, on the other hand, tends to be tailored, as Unger says, to the situation and interests of the particular group the interests of which are being adjudicated or otherwise considered. Procedure is the great intermediate and mediating category, and one of my great disappointments with Unger's book was the scant attention he paid to it, and the low positive evaluation he gave it.

Procedural institutions are particularly prominent in a

major type of social structure that Unger also barely mentions, namely what I should call *associational structure,* specifically in contrast with both bureaucracy and market systems. One might characterize it by saying that it is not primarily hierarchical in the sense that bureaucracies are, nor is it primarily competitive in the sense that markets are, but in some sense it is "cooperative." It provides a framework within which "parties," whether they be individuals or groups, can be "brought together" to adjust their interests with each other under a normative order.

What courts of law do, in this sense, is to provide a forum within which opposed parties—sometimes one is not there voluntarily—can state their "cases" and be given a binding decision. The bindingness of court decisions involves an element of power, but arriving at a decision, the core of adjudication, involves a set of pertinent rules, the advocacy of positions and their defense, and some agency to render a decision—jury, judge, and so on.

Associational collectivities with prominent procedural institutions, however, extend far beyond courts of law. Within the Anglo-American type of government, of course, the other primary example is legislative bodies. These have to have elaborate procedural rules regulating debating time for speakers ("access to the floor"), the introduction and staging of bills, and many other things. The rules also have to be administered by a designated officer, such as the "speaker," but except for his procedural authority the members are all equal, and even the speaker either has only one vote or has none at all.

It is also evident that electoral rules are essentially procedural; they regulate who can vote in what elections and polling places, how ballots are made up, and how votes shall be counted, but they do not decide the outcome of elections. Outside of government, there are of course innumerable associational structures in which procedural institutions are highly prominent. The "committee" is a particularly prominent example, which regularly has members and a chairman, the latter being the procedural officer, typically with only one vote, like the chief judge in a multijudge court of law.

Not the least prominent field of the prevalence of procedural institutions is that of intellectual discourse. The prototype is perhaps the "conference," which has become so prominent in the modern intellectual world. But the conduct of classroom instruction is also closely regulated by procedural norms, and the instructor or teacher serves as a procedural officer as well as the purveyor of substantive information.

In all these nongovernmental settings, it seems to me that what I have tended to call *procedural institutions* involve a component of law, in Weber's and my sense, if not that of Unger. And this law is clearly continuous with that internal to government. Perhaps this is the most conspicuous field of which that continuity is definitive. It thus seems to me that this continuity in a way pins down my case that Unger, by confining the legal system to the state, introduces a serious bias into the argument, one major result of which is to exaggerate the erosive effects on the legal system of the features of what he calls the *postliberal society* that have just been outlined. In a slightly different context, however, he also asserts strongly the importance to him of the state's maintaining control of all "important" power. I do not think he means quite the same thing by *power* as I do, but our previous discussion of the political aspect of private collectivities should make it clear that the biasing effect of the "monopoly of power" doctrine about the state is of a piece with that of failing to mention procedural institutions outside of government and that of playing down the importance of procedure within the public legal system.

As between the other two core components of the legal system, once the procedural is downgraded, as it were, it is clearly the formal that is the core for Unger. It is the alleged erosion of this component that grounds his judgment that the legal system generally has a dim future in postliberal society. And it is above all his stress on the core significance of the formal component that is to me the principal basis of justification for my pinning the label of "legal absolutist" on Unger. I hope I have been able to convince the reader that this stress is not a function *only* of Unger's "free" empirical judgment of legal history and the present situation of the legal system, but that it also roots in *theoretical* factors, in the structure of the conceptual scheme Unger uses in analyzing the problems. It is this component in which I have been primarily interested. It will also not have escaped the reader that there is a certain intellectual kinship between Unger's selective emphases and those of Weber.[9]

Moral Absolutism

It is now possible to turn to the last of the four complexes of "structural absolutisms" with which I have planned to deal in this chapter. This I call "moral absolutism," which I conceive to be anchored in the fiduciary subsystem of the society. In the great sociological tradition of both Weber and Durkheim, with their different emphases, it stresses the importance of common values in the constitution of social systems, especially at the macrosocial level of analysis.

As a case study in this field, I have chosen the recent work of Robert Bellah, as documented in his book *The Broken Covenant* (1975), which deals with American society in a historical perspective. Bellah, however, is also a distinguished comparativist, with special reference to East Asia, and has specialized in the sociology of religion. In addition, he has worked within the framework of the "theory of action," a circumstance that in part derives from long personal association with me, which goes back to his undergraduate student days at Harvard.

At the level of empirical specificity, the primary relevant reference here is to the conception of the *covenant* with God, with which the Puritan settlers of Atlantic North America defined their mission into the wilderness. In a keynote reference, Bellah gives great prominence to the sermon delivered by John Winthrop to his flock on shipboard the evening before the landing in Massachusetts Bay in 1630. Winthrop there described the covenant that to him should define the normative pattern for the new community and that Bellah holds, "was broken almost from the beginning."

Of course, the major emphasis was religious; this aspect is particularly well analyzed in Perry Miller's *Errand into the Wilderness* (1956), both the title essay and the book as a whole.

The covenant was a covenant *with God,* a conception taken over by the Puritans from the ancient Hebrews, which also established a relation of solidarity among men, who assumed obligations in the first instance toward God but at the same time toward each other.

In Bellah's interpretation, the overwhelming emphasis is on the *collective* aspect of the covenant. It is on both religious and social obligation. For this reason, I think, Bellah is particularly sensitive to any assertion of unit interest that is in any way in conflict with the collective interest and, among unit interests, to those of particular individuals. I think it can correctly be said that the major antinomy for Bellah, under the ascetic Protestant conception, is that between the collective obligation under the covenant and the interests of the individual, potentially— indeed, presumptively—in conflict with those obligations.

In the background, as Bellah explicitly discusses, is the critical innovation of the Reformation, collapsing the duality of the Catholic system and enjoining human communities to work for the establishment of the "Kingdom of God on Earth." To be single-mindedly devoted to that task is, almost by definition, to subordinate one's self-interest to that of the covenanted "holy" community. Indeed, in Calvinism this note extends even to the sphere of salvation. As Bellah notes, the doctrine of predestination declared the individual's pursuit of his personal salvation to be essentially meaningless, since his action could have no effect on it, even by faith.

Another consequence of this collapse of the two spheres held apart in Catholic doctrine is to equate the religious and moral spheres. To be religiously "conscientious" is to be morally so, and vice versa. Indeed, with the powerful concern of this religious orientation with the things of *this world,* which was what Weber meant by "inner-worldly asceticism," the accent on the collective focus of moral obligations was strongly emphasized. This essentially, I think, was the covenant that in Bellah's view was broken almost from the beginning, as he put it. From this point of view, almost *any* concern for individuality, either religious or moral, or still more in spheres indifferent to morality, could be felt to be both religiously and morally suspect.

There is, however, another trend within what Weber called *ascetic* Protestantism, which historically became differentiated from the original Calvinism and which may be called *liberal* Protestantism. As Miller has shown, this movement was already well under way in the orientations of the early Puritan settlers in this country and, before independence, had already become dominant in the colonies (see Loubser, 1964). Otherwise, it would be incomprehensible that the First Amendment to the U.S. Constitution could have been adopted. This movement institutionalized the individual pursuit of salvation, religious freedom and toleration and, by 1790, the separation of church and state, and it made clear that the national community should be religiously pluralistic, in the course of time including non-Protestants, Catholics, Jews, and eventually adherents of non-Western religions.

The development of what I have called *liberal* Protestantism and its associated movements at a variety of levels, religious, moral, intellectual-cultural, political, and economic, certainly involved an increase of "individualism." These individualisms are of several distinguishable varieties, all of which, however, stand in some kind of contrast and often of conflict with the religiomoral collectivism of the seventeenth-century Puritan covenant. How far and in what more specific respects, these various currents of individualism can properly be construed as "breaking" of the covenant, seems to me far from being a simple question. The strands of what may be called individualistic thought in the history of Western culture since the seventeenth century are surely various.

From the vantage point of his devotion to—and I think personal commitment to—a religiomoral collective ideal, Bellah (1975) singles out *one* of these strands, and of course it is a very prominent one, namely "utilitarian individualism," for his excoriation, and the tone of his discussion surely makes use of that term appropriate. Referring back to the section on economics of this chapter, the reader should be familiar with it as the "rational pursuit of self-interest." This concept has been abstracted from a whole range of contextual associations, with the consequence that, in a *social* setting, it becomes mainly the pursuit of *economic* interest, by the unit specifically as contrasted with the collectivity. Thus for Bellah its immorality has a dual reference, with a third in the background. The first is that it is individual, not collective, and this is the main explicit point. The second is that it is an assertion of "interest," not of concerns transcending interests in any "worldly" sense. In the background are reservations about the acceptability of the conception of "rational."

Bellah's treatment of the background of utilitarian and therefore economic individualism is largely in terms of the classical utilitarian writers themselves. He, like myself, finds Locke a somewhat weak reed so far as protection against force and fraud is concerned, and he tends to stress that Hobbes stated the core problem of human behavior. There is a latent "war of all against all" in the rather near background, sometimes breaking through.

In the light of Bellah's close familiarity with Weber's work, I find it puzzling that he does not give more emphasis to the Puritan doctrine of the calling, which is surely an authentic child of the Puritan branch of Protestantism and which surely could, unless Weber was completely wrong, help to motivate economically oriented action at the level of the individual actor. Commitment to work in a calling from religious motives is surely not the same thing as domination by the "passions" of Hobbes or as the "rational pursuit of self-interest" of the economic utilitarians.

The themes of Weber's analysis are also relevant to another context of Bellah's position. It would be expected that he would extend his condemnation of utilitarian individualism to "capitalism" more generally. The collective, corporate aspect of the latter raises some questions to which I shall return presently. But there is a third target of his strong suspicion, from his moral point of view, namely science. I personally have long been convinced by Merton's case (1938) that concern with science, certainly in the seventeenth century, was, sociopsychologically, one might say a first cousin of concern in the economic sphere, indeed a case of devotion to a calling. Cultivation of science, however, has usually not been primarily associated

with economic individualism or the profit motive. I have, on
what I think to be a good Weberian background, tended to treat
it as very much part of the professional complex, which, in
modern societies, should not be identified with the market
economy.

I suspect that Bellah's attitude in this context has less to
do with the self-interest component or with utilitarianism than
it does with the rationality of science. If this is correct, there is
an overlap between the meaning of Weber's "iron cage" and
Bellah's equivalent one. Even if one could see adequate control
of the self-interest component, that would not be enough for
Bellah; there must also be emancipation from what to him is the
overrationalization of modern society.

The theme of the meaning of science leads over to that of
other parts of what I have called the *professional complex.* By
no means the least important of these is law, so at this point we
can make contact with our earlier discussions of Weber and
Unger. At one level, Bellah has a good deal to say about American law, namely, the level of its constitutional framework. Even
here, however, there are moral problems for him. He is inclined
to give rather strong approval—in his case, always mainly moral
—to the Bill of Rights, even beyond the first ten amendments.
Thus he refers to the "great" Fourteenth Amendment.

He gives even stronger approval, however, to the Declaration of Independence and broadly contrasts it with the Constitution itself (see especially Bellah, 1976). The main theme of
the contrast is that the Constitution, with its well-known set of
checks and balances, gives much more scope to the play of
interests and the presumptive self-interested types of individualism that underlie it. We might put it that it opens the door to
the development of the nation as an aggregate of self-interested
units, individual and collective.

What is striking to me, however, about Bellah's treatment
(1975, 1976) of American law is his almost total ignoring of
what might be called the "subconstitutional" stratum of the
legal system. This reaches "up" to the constitutional level especially through the role of the Supreme Court, but as a relatively
integrated normative subsystem it reaches "down" to an elabo-

rately complex context of everyday life of the society. Above all, the phase of adjudication that I emphasized in the last section, as well as its relation to the less generalized features of the law, is not mentioned at all by Bellah.

There is also an important historical point to be noted. Particularly in the notable study by David Little (1969), it has been shown, to my satisfaction at least, that in the development of the common law in England in the sixteenth to seventeenth centuries, the Puritan influence was very important. My impression is that it was sufficiently important to justify putting the development of law together with that of the devotion to callings in economic enterprise and in science, and indeed in the development of parliamentary government, as all belonging to what may be called the "Puritan complex" of orientation to secular society. All four of the constituent parts of this complex have their individualistic aspect and make room for competitive and conflicting interests. They also have their integrative aspects.

In the case of the legal system, another feature not figuring at all in Bellah's discussion is the importance of a private legal profession, especially its intimate relation to the adjudicative system. One prominent keynote is the often discussed adversary system, in which court action is generally structured about two parties, a plaintiff and a defendant. Furthermore, in most court actions both parties are represented by attorneys, who belong to the legal profession but who are by no means necessarily government officials. This system surely recognizes, at one level, not only the inevitability but also the legitimacy of "conflict of interest," but it is also an institutionalized way of dealing with such conflicts with, it is hoped, on balance integrative consequences in the social system. In an assessment of the moral qualities of America, as of other modern societies, I think the legal system merits more attention than Bellah gives it.

Just a brief word may be said about the collective aspect of social structure in the range intermediate between the covenanted total society and the individual. To me, the striking thing about the Bellah discussion is the extent to which he

tends to squeeze out this vastly complicated range in his dichot-
omization of what may be called "covenanted collectivism" on
one side and individualism on the other, with the latter presumptively utilitarian and hence self-interested. It seems to me,
however, that telling evidence has been submitted earlier against
the presumption that *only* total-society commitments are not
self-interested, either in actual modern societies or in the Protestant ethic complex, which embraces several kinds of action in a
calling, including law. This dubious presumption makes it easy
to go from imputing self-interest alone to the individual to imputing self-interest alone to corporate groups as well, with
equally dubious legitimacy. As I emphasized earlier in this chapter, individual interests and collective interests at the level
below the total society should be treated somewhat differently;
putting both together under the heading of "capitalism" does
not help work out the nature and implications of their analytical separateness.

Indeed, in that earlier discussion I suggested that there is
another thread besides the problem of individualism, which was
evident for Weber's case, namely that of rationalization. We
have at least hints that this is an issue for Bellah as well, but it is
not featured in his main indictment, which is, of course, his
relative derogation of science. This seems to explain why Bellah
is sympathetic to some sorts of individualism that have been
recently prominent, namely those having to do with "self-
expression" in the context of what has been called the "coun-
terculture." On grounds such as these, I suspect that, for Bellah,
as for Weber, the deeper source of his alienation from recent
trends of Western society is not so much the problem of self-
interest or indeed of individualism in a totally general sense as it
is the problem of rationalization. In this sense, he is a Weberian,
but with reversed accent, as it were, stressing not the political,
but the moral. Both, however, seek a kind of charismatically
based socialism,[10] which will resolve all three of these sources of
tension.

It is on such grounds that I have ventured to call Bellah a
moral absolutist, and that I have maintained that he has tended,
like the others in different ways, to treat law as an intellectual
stepchild.[11]

Conclusion

In conclusion, I would like to make only a few brief points. First, with the exception of the section on the economic complex, as I have called it, I have discussed the problems that concern me in terms of the works of three particular authors. In each case, and also in the less personalized discussion of the economic case, I have maintained that, with respect to the position of law in modern social systems, they have manifested a bias, which in some way will have to be overcome or at least mitigated if, by my theoretical standards, the position of law is to be adequately dealt with.[12]

Admittedly, in discussing the relevant works, my emphasis on issues and the like has been selective. Had I been writing a review of their work for other sociological purposes, my emphases would have been different. But I hope that the reader will appreciate that the central concern of *this* discussion has been with the theoretical framework of the interpretation of the nature and significance of legal systems within the structure and the processes of functioning of modern societies. It is in *this* context and only in this that I have charged them with either downgrading the importance of legal systems or, as in the case of Weber and Unger, with presenting a "slanted" interpretation of their nature and significance. Again, in each case I have suggested that to this unsatisfactory treatment of legal systems corresponded an "absolutist" stress on the overwhelming centrality of one functional aspect of the societal system. Again, in each case I have no doubt about the very great importance of each of the foci, but surely they cannot *all* be right in the contention that the focus of *their* concern should take precedence over all others.

Therefore I come to the conclusion that if a more satisfactory—from the point of view of the use of sociological theory in the understanding of modern societies—account of the place of law is to be attained, it must be through some kind of synthesis that refuses to accept any one of these points of view as "proven" yet that also tries to incorporate all of the valid considerations presented by all of them.

My concern as a theoretical analyst of modern societies

transcends all four of these positions. It is specifically, at present, with the integrative problems of such societies, which are surely of sufficient complexity. They include assessment of the states of integration-malintegration of such societies. They include identification of the principal sources of malintegration and of the kinds of institutions and other mechanisms by which such tendencies are counteracted and/or controlled or fail to be. They include assessment of the principal modes of conflict such systems entail and the probable consequences of the existence of such conflicts.

It is my conviction that the legal system, in the sense in which that concept has been used in this article, broadly constitutes what is probably the single most important institutional key to understanding these problems of societal integration. Within this context, I believe that a more "catholic" understanding of the problems than any of those reviewed is necessary.

I think that the most promising approach from major currents of sociological theory comes from the tradition of Durkheim. Among the theorists reviewed in this article, Bellah clearly has paid the greatest attention to Durkheim's work. I have, however, the impression, without going back to his distinguished introduction to the selection from Durkheim's work that he edited ([1898] 1973), that Bellah has somewhat overstressed the salience in Durkheim's work of the moral component. Its centrality is quite clear, but it must also be balanced by consideration of Durkheim's treatment of more "internal" features of the society—notably, I think, the division of labor and organic solidarity.

This leads to a final word about individualism. It is to me as curious as Bellah's omission of reference to a number of Weber's concerns that in *The Broken Covenant* he concentrates so heavily on utilitarian individualism and does not give much if any attention (Bellah's book has no index, so this is difficult to check) to Durkheim's conception of individualism, which, in a loose way, I have been calling *institutionalized individualism*, specifically in contrast to *utilitarian individualism*. Durkheim himself associated this with what he called the "cult of the indi-

vidual" as a major part of the common culture of modern societies. The religious character of the word *cult* is clearly not for-
tuitous.

With reference to a central problem of this chapter, the
relation of the collectivity as a moral community to the status
of the individual, I happen to think that a conception such as
that of institutionalized individualism is much more fruitful to
work with than the dichotomy between collective interest and
individual self-interest. This emphasis surely has something to
do with the problems of this chapter, the status of law in the
analysis of social systems.[13]

Notes

1. Akula is one of the few who have combined full formal
training in sociology and in law. After completing his Ph.D., he
entered Harvard Law School and received his law degree in
1977.

2. For the first section, especially pertinent references are
Fuller (1968); Pollock and Maitland ([1895] 1952); Hurst
(1956); Pound (1921); Kelsen ([1934] 1970); and Akula
(1973).

3. Thus, recently, in his column in *Newsweek,* Friedman
(1977) stated that President Carter's energy program would be
"disastrous" to the economy and that the only way to improve
the energy situation is to free the energy producers from governmental regulation. This is a much more "absolutist" stance
than, for example, that taken by Friedman's rival, Paul Samuel-
son.

4. For the second section, especially pertinent references
are, for historical background, Halévy ([1901-1904] 1952), and
Dumont (1977); and, for the contemporary problem of corporate economic interests, Vernon (1977).

5. Perhaps it is well to remind the reader that I, not
Weber, was responsible for the expression "iron cage." As translator of Weber's essay into English, I found it awkward to render his phrase, *ein stahlhartes Gehäuse;* "iron cage" was the
nearest equivalent I could think of. It seems to have caught on.

6. It may be worth remarking that I feel I owe the insight
on which that theoretical view is based, namely that the "politi-

cal" should be an analytical category, more to Weber than to any other source. See my essay "On the Concept of Political Power" (1963).

7. Thus, in his political writings during World War I (see Weber, 1958), Weber stressed what he felt to be the irresponsible tendency of his own government, under Wilhelm II, to pursue a kind of national self-interest in a way that presumed there would be no effective opposition to such policies. Perhaps the primary example was the initiation of unrestricted submarine warfare, which Weber correctly predicted would bring the United States into the war against Germany.

8. For the third section, especially pertinent references are Weber, *Economy and Society* (in my translation, Weber, 1947, chap. 1, "The Fundamental Concepts of Sociology" and chap. 3, "The Types of Authority and Imperative Co-ordination" and his "The Sociology of Law," which may be conveniently found in Weber, 1968, Vol. 2).

9. Unger seems to be rather clearly more in the continental tradition of jurisprudence, of which I think of Hans Kelsen as a particularly important representative (not mentioned in Unger's index). My own inclination is palpably toward the common law tradition. It has been influenced by conducting for two years a joint seminar in law and sociology with Lon L. Fuller. The especially pertinent reference for the fourth section is, of course, Unger (1976).

10. For Bellah, this is explicit. For Weber, it is inferred, so the word "socialism" should be put in quotation marks. Weber was also highly skeptical of utopianism and, as noted, for him the problem of self-interest was not so central as it is for Bellah.

11. Especially pertinent references for the fifth section are Bellah (1973, 1975).

12. Another reason the authors discussed earlier, or their culture heroes, need not feel especially aggrieved by being called various kinds of "absolutists" is that they are part of a much larger company. I have singled out the four versions of value absolutism that seem to me to correspond to the main functional exigencies of modern society as a system. In the society as a concrete entity, however, there are quite a number of other strong currents of thought that would merit the label "absolutist." Not least are the various explicitly religious absolutisms

or fundamentalisms—to cite only one example, the Jehovah's Witnesses. Then there are absolutisms of health; and "scientism," which seems to be the preferred new label for positivism; and the absolutism of the ultimate value of "self-expression." This is by no means to exhaust the list. It did not seem feasible, however, to take up these and other absolutisms within the limits of the present article.

13. For the sixth section, see Durkheim ([1893] 1960, [1898] 1973).

References

Akula, J. "Law and the Development of Citizenship." Unpublished doctoral dissertation in sociology, Harvard University, 1973.

Bellah, R. N. "Introduction." In R. N. Bellah (Ed.), *Emile Durkheim: On Morality and Society; Selected Writings.* Chicago: University of Chicago Press, 1973. (Originally published 1898.)

Bellah, R. N. *The Broken Covenant: American Civil Religion in Time of Trial.* New York: The Seabury Press, 1975.

Bellah, R. N. Paper presented at the plenary session of the Society for the Scientific Study of Religion, Philadelphia, October 1976.

Bendix, R., and Roth, G. *Scholarship and Partisanship: Essays on Max Weber.* Berkeley: University of California Press, 1971.

Commons, J. R. *The Legal Foundations of Capitalism.* New York: Macmillan, 1924.

Dumont, L. *Homo Hierarchicus: An Essay on the Caste System.* (M. Saintsbury, Trans.) Chicago: University of Chicago Press, 1970.

Dumont, L. *From Mandeville to Marx: The Genesis and Triumph of the Economic Ideology.* Chicago: University of Chicago Press, 1977.

Durkheim, E. *The Division of Labor in Society.* (G. Simpson, Trans.) New York: Free Press, 1960. (Originally published 1893.)

Durkheim, E. "Individualism and the Intellectuals." In R. Bellah (Ed.), *Emile Durkheim on Morality and Society*. (M. Traugott, Trans.) Chicago: University of Chicago Press, 1973. (Originally published 1898.)

Evan, W. M. "Public and Private Legal Systems." In W. M. Evan (Ed.), *Law and Sociology: Exploratory Essays*. New York: Free Press, 1962.

Friedman, M. "A Monstrosity." *Newsweek,* 1977, *89,* 20-21.

Fuller, L. L. *Anatomy of the Law*. New York: Praeger, 1968.

Halévy, E. *The Growth of Philosophic Radicalism*. (M. Morris, Trans.) London: Faber and Faber, 1952. (Originally published 1901-1904; Beacon Press paperback, 1955.)

Hurst, J. W. *Law and the Conditions of Freedom in the Nineteenth-Century United States*. Madison: University of Wisconsin Press, 1956.

Kelsen, H. *The Pure Theory of Law*. (M. Knight, Trans.) Berkeley: University of California Press, 1970. (Originally published 1934.)

Little, D. *Religion, Order, and Law: A Study in Pre-Revolutionary England*. New York: Harper & Row, 1969.

Loubser, J. J. "Puritanism and Religious Liberty: A Study of Normative Change in Massachusetts, 1630-1850." Unpublished doctoral dissertation in sociology, Harvard University, 1964.

Marshall, A. *Principles of Economics: An Introductory Volume*. (8th ed.) New York: Macmillan, 1920.

Merton, R. K. "Science, Technology and Society in Seventeenth Century England." *Osiris,* 1938, *4* (part 2), 360-632.

Miller, P. *Errand into the Wilderness*. Cambridge, Mass.: Belknap Press of Harvard University Press, 1956.

Miller, P. *The Life of the Mind in America, from the Revolution to the Civil War*. New York: Harcourt Brace Jovanovich, 1965.

Nelson, B. *The Idea of Usury: From Tribal Brotherhood to Universal Otherhood*. (2nd ed.) Chicago: University of Chicago Press, 1969.

Parsons, T. "On the Concept of Political Power." *Proceedings of the American Philosophical Society,* 1963, *107*; reprinted in

T. Parsons, *Politics and Social Structure* (New York: Free Press, 1969).

Parsons, T. "Evaluation and Objectivity in Social Science: An Interpretation of Max Weber's Contribution." In T. Parsons, *Sociological Theory and Modern Society*. New York: Free Press, 1967.

Parsons, T. "Theoretical Orientations on Modern Societies." In T. Parsons, *Politics and Social Structure*. New York: Free Press, 1969.

Parsons, T., and Platt, G. M. *The American University*. Cambridge, Mass.: Harvard University Press, 1973.

Parsons, T. *Action Theory and the Human Condition*. New York: Free Press, in press.

Pollock, F., and Maitland, F. W. *The History of English Law Before the Time of Edward I*. 2 vols. (2nd ed.) Boston: Little, Brown, 1952. (Originally published 1895.)

Pound, R. *The Spirit of the Common Law*. Boston: Marshall Jones, 1921.

Rueschemeyer, D. *Lawyers and Their Society: A Comparative Analysis of the Legal Profession in Germany and the United States*. Cambridge, Mass.: Harvard University Press, 1973.

Unger, R. M. *Knowledge and Politics*. New York: Free Press, 1975.

Unger, R. M. *Law in Modern Society: Toward a Criticism of Social Theory*. New York: Free Press, 1976.

Vernon, R. *Storm over the Multinationals: The Real Issues*. Cambridge, Mass.: Harvard University Press, 1977.

Weber, M. *The Protestant Ethic and the Spirit of Capitalism*. (T. Parsons, Trans.) Boston: Scribner's, 1930. (Originally published 1904-1905; Scribner's paperback, 1958.)

Weber, M. "Author's Introduction" [to the whole series on the sociology of religion, not just to *The Protestant Ethic*]. In M. Weber, *The Protestant Ethic and the Spirit of Capitalism*. (T. Parsons, Trans.) Boston: Scribner's, 1930. ("Author's Introduction" originally published 1920; paperback, 1958.)

Weber, M. *The Theory of Social and Economic Organization*. Part 1: *Economy and Society*. (A. M. Henderson and T. Parsons, Trans.) New York: Oxford University Press, 1947. (Originally published 1922.)

Weber, M. *Collected Political Writings.* (2nd ed.) Tübingen, Germany: Mohr, 1958.

Weber, M. *Economy and Society: An Outline of Interpretive Sociology.* 3 vols. (G. Roth and C. Wittich, Eds.) New York: Bedminster Press, 1968.

2

Lon L. Fuller

Law and Human
Interaction

As it is used in my title, I mean the word *law* to be construed
very broadly. I intend it to include not only the legal systems of
states and nations, but also the smaller systems—at least "law-
like" in structure and function—to be found in labor unions,
professional associations, clubs, churches, and universities.
These miniature legal systems are, of course, concerned with the
member's duties and entitlements within the association itself.
They find their most dramatic expression when the erring member is called up to be tried for offenses that may lead to his
being disciplined or expelled.

When the concept of law is given this broad coverage, it
becomes apparent that many of the central issues of today are,

Note: This essay is substantially the same as Lon Fuller's address to
the thirteenth annual meeting of the Board of Editors of *The American
Journal of Jurisprudence*, September 26, 1969. With Lon Fuller's approval
and specific control, the present editor has omitted, at places indicated, a
few passages that deal with interesting but somewhat peripheral points.
The full text may be found in *The American Journal of Jurisprudence*
(1969, *14*), to whose editors and to Lon Fuller himself we are grateful for
permission to publish this version.

in this extended sense, "legal" in nature. The pressure of our present predicament pushes us—as we have not been pushed for a long time—toward an effort at comprehension. We must come to perceive and understand the moral and psychological forces that underlie law generally and give it efficacy in human affairs.

Nature and Significance of "Customary Law"

If in search of this understanding we turn to treatises on jurisprudence, we shall find that they commonly begin by distinguishing two kinds of law. On the one hand, there is enacted or authoritatively declared law—what may be called "made" law; on the other hand, there is what is known as *customary* law. Customary law is not the product of official enactment, but owes its force to the fact that it has found direct expression in the conduct of men toward one another.

Between these two kinds of law, the treatises commonly devote almost their entire attention to enacted or declared law, to the law that can be found in statutes, judicial decisions, by-laws, and administrative decrees. The discussion of customary law is largely confined to the question, Why should it be thought to be law at all? After some discussion along this line and some treatment of its function in primitive societies, customary law is generally dismissed as largely irrelevant to advanced civilizations. It tends to be regarded as a kind of museum piece offering an object for serious study only to anthropologists curious about the ways of tribal peoples.

This neglect of the phenomenon called customary law has, I think, done great damage to our thinking about law generally. Even if we accept the rather casual analysis of the subject offered by the treatises, it still remains true that a proper understanding of customary law is of capital importance in the world of today. In the first place, much of international law, and perhaps the most vital part of it, is essentially customary law. On the successful functioning of that body of law, world peace may depend. In the second place, much of the world today is still governed internally by customary law. The newly emerging nations (notably in India, Africa, and the Pacific) are now engaged in a hazardous transition from systems of customary law to systems of enacted law. The stakes in this transition—for them and for us—are very high indeed. So the mere fact that we do not see ourselves as regulating our conduct toward fellow countrymen by customary law does not mean that it is of no importance to us as world citizens.

The thesis I am going to advance here is, however, something more radical than a mere insistence that customary law is still of considerable importance in the world of today. I am going to argue that we cannot understand "ordinary" law (that is, officially declared or enacted law) unless we first obtain an understanding of what is called *customary law.*

In preparing my exposition, I have to confess that at this point I encountered a great frustration. This arises from the term *customary law* itself. This is the term found in the titles and the indices, and if you want to compare what I have to say with what others have said, this is the heading you will have to look under. At the same time, the expression "customary law" is a most unfortunate one that obscures, almost beyond redemption, the nature of the phenomenon it purports to designate. Instead of serving as a neutral pointer, it prejudges its subject; it asserts that the force and meaning of what we call "customary law" lie in mere habit or usage.

Against this view I shall argue that the phenomenon called *customary law* can best be described as *a language of interaction.* To interact meaningfully, men require a social setting in which the moves of the participating players will fall generally within some predictable pattern. To engage in effective social behavior, men need the support of intermeshing anticipations that will let them know what their opposite numbers will do, or that will at least enable them to gauge the general scope of the repertory from which responses to their actions will be drawn. We sometimes speak of customary law as offering an unwritten "code of conduct." The word *code* is appropriate here because what is involved is not simply a negation, a prohibition of certain disapproved actions, but also the obverse side of this negation, the meaning it confers on foreseeable and approved actions, which then furnish a point of orientation for ongoing interactive responses. Parsons and Shils have spoken of the function, in social action, of "complementary expectations"; the term "complementary expectations" indicates accurately the function I am here ascribing to the law that develops out of human interaction, a form of law that we are forced—by the dictionaries and title headings—to call "customary law" (Parsons and Shils, 1951, p. 64).

I have already recorded my distress at having to employ the term "customary law" so frequently in this discussion. Both ingredients of the expression, the adjective and the noun, offer difficulties. I shall take up shortly the embarrassments created by the noun. Meanwhile, it would be well to explore more carefully than I have so far the problems involved in finding a satisfactory substitute for "customary." As I have already observed, the principal objection to this word lies in its suggestion that the mere repetition of some action by A will create in others a right that A shall repeat this action, with an added implication that the strength of this claim will vary directly with the duration in time of A's repetitive behavior. Of course, no theorist of customary law in fact embraces any such absurdity, however much the language employed may seem at times to suggest the contrary. My neighbor might for years have arisen every morning precisely at eight, yet no one would think that this settled practice could create any obligation toward me unless it entered into some coordination of our activities, as it might if I had come to depend on him to drive me to work in his car. Instead, therefore, of speaking vaguely of an obligation arising through mere "custom" or repetition, it would be better to say that a sense of obligation will arise when a stabilization of interactional expectancies has occurred so that the parties have come to guide their conduct toward one another by these expectancies.

The term "interactional expectancy" is itself, however, capable of producing difficulties. We shall be misled, for example, if we suppose that the relevant expectancy or anticipation must enter actively into consciousness. In fact, the anticipations that most unequivocally shape our behavior and attitudes toward others are often precisely those that are operative without our being aware of their presence. To take an example from a somewhat trivial context, experiments have shown that the distance at which people stand toward one another in carrying on ordinary conversations varies predictably among cultures and between individuals. At the same time, most people would not be able to state, without some preliminary testing, what they themselves regard as a normal conversational distance. My inability to define offhand a proper distance would not prevent me, however, from finding offensive the action of someone who projected his face uncomfortably close to mine, nor would it relieve my puzzlement and distress at the conduct of someone who kept retreating when I approached what seemed to me a normal speaking distance. Our conduct toward others, and our interpretations of their behavior toward us, are, in other words, constantly shaped by standards that do not enter consciously into our thought processes. The analogy of language is once again useful; often we only become aware of rules of grammar when they are broken, and it is sometimes their breach that leads us to articulate for the first time rules we had previously acted on without knowing it.

Any analysis in terms of "interactional expectancies" must also confront the problem of the man who is in some sense an outsider to the expectancies that organize the life of a particular group. He may be literally an outsider, a trader, for example, coming from a distance to sell his wares among a tribal people. Or, although born and raised within the group, he may be "alienated," too imperceptive to understand the system, or perhaps too perceptive to accept some of its built-in absurdities and anomalies. It would, of course, be impossible to undertake here any adequate analysis of the problems suggested. A guess may be hazarded, though, that it is to the intrusion of the true outsider—"the stranger" in Simmel's famous essay (Simmel, 1950)—that we owe, not only the invention of economic trade but also the more general discovery that it's possible for men to arrange their relations with one another by explicit contract.

Now for the difficulties produced by the noun in the expression "customary law." If we speak of "a system of stabilized interactional expectancies" as a more adequate way of describing what the treatises call "customary law," we encounter the embarrassment that many of these expectancies relate to matters that seem remote from anything like a legal context. For example, rules of etiquette fully meet the suggested definition, yet one would scarcely be inclined to call rules of this sort *rules of law.*

Interactional Foundations of Contract Law

The brief account of contract law that follows has been included here primarily for the light it may shed on customary law, which is often and properly said to contain a "consensual element." In this shared aspect, contract law and customary law are indeed near cousins, and a study of either will help to understand the other. In the course of the analysis that follows, I shall have occasion to revisit from a somewhat different perspective some of the questions already discussed, particularly that of knowing how to determine when patterns of interaction can properly be said to have created an obligation to persist in them.

In keeping with the general objective just outlined, we shall be concerned here with contract as a source of social order, as one means for establishing "stable interactional expectancies." As it is used in the heading for this section, the term "contract law," therefore, refers primarily, not to the law *of* or *about* contracts, but to the "law" a contract itself brings into existence. This employment of the word *law* represents, of course, a considerable departure from the conventions we ordinarily follow in using the term.

Our reluctance to apply the word *law* to the obligation created by a contract is, however, in many ways an anomaly. In enforcing contracts, courts purport to derive the legal rights and duties of the litigants from the terms of their agreement, much as if a statute were being applied. The Romans did not hesitate, at least in certain contexts, to apply the word *lex* to contractual provisions, and the Latin word seems indeed to have taken its origin in a contractual context. Today international lawyers list treaties as the prime source of their kind of law. Although the term "customary law" has been regarded by some legal theorists as an abuse of language, today most writers seem to have overcome any qualms about that expression; the acceptance of "customary law" and the rejection of "contractual law" are all the more remarkable, since, if what is associated with "law" is something like an explicit legislative process, the contract comes much closer to fitting that model than do the silent processes through which customary law comes into being. Finally, as proof that lawyers do not reject the expression "law of the contract" because it conflicts with any basic demand of legal logic, I cite their readiness to accept the thought contained in the expression, provided it comes decently clothed in paraphrase. Thus, I doubt if any lawyer would be deeply perplexed (although he might be slightly intrigued) by the statement contained in Article 1134 of the French Civil Code that a contract "serves as law" between the parties (*"Les conventiones légalement formées tiennent lieu de loi à ceux qui les ont faites"*).

If we permit ourselves to think of "contract law" as the "law" that the parties themselves bring into existence by their agreement, the transition from customary law to contract law becomes a very easy one indeed. The difficulty then becomes, not that of subsuming the two kinds of law under one rubric, but of knowing how to draw a clear line of division between them. We may say, of course (using the jargon I have inflicted on the reader here), that in the one case the relevant interactional expectancies are created by words; in the other, by actions.

But this is too simple a view of the matter. Where words are used, they have to be interpreted. When the contract falls within some general area of repetitive dealings, there will usually exist a body of "standard practice" in the light of which verbal ambiguities will be resolved. Here, in effect, interactional regularities in the world outside the contract are written into the contract in the process of interpretation. In commercial law generally, it is often difficult to know whether to say that by entering a particular field of practice the parties became subject to a governing body of customary law or to say that they have by tacit agreement incorporated standard practice into the terms of their contract.

The meaning of a contract may be determined not only by the area of practice within which the contract falls but also by the interactions of the parties themselves after entering their agreement. If the performance of a contract takes place over a period of time, the parties will often evidence by their conduct what courts sometimes call a "practical construction" of their agreement; this interpretation by deeds may have control over the meaning that would ordinarily be attributed to the words of the contract itself. If the discrepancy between the parties' acts and the words of their agreement becomes too great to permit the courts to speak of a "practical construction," they may hold that the contract has been tacitly modified or even rescinded by the manner in which the parties have conducted themselves toward one another since entering the agreement.

Generally, we may say that in the actual carrying out of a complex agreement between friendly parties, the written contract often furnishes a kind of framework for an ongoing relationship, rather than a precise definition of that relationship. For that definition, we may have to look to a kind of two-party customary law implicit in the parties' actions, rather than to the verbal formulations of the contract; if this is true of contracts that are eventually brought to court, it must be much more commonly so in situations where the parties make out without resort to litigation.

If the words of a contract have to be interpreted in their interactional context, or in the light of the actions taken under them by the parties, the actions that bring customary law into existence also have to be interpreted sometimes almost as if they were words. This problem of interpretation is at once the most crucial and most neglected problem of customary law; intrinsically difficult, it is made more so by inept theories about the nature of customary law, such as those explaining it as an expression of "the force of habit" that "prevails in the early history of the race."

The central problem of "interpretation" in customary law is that of knowing when to read into an act or a pattern of repetitive acts an obligatory sense such as that which may attach to a promise explicitly spelled out in words. All are agreed that a person, a tribe, or a nation does not incur an obligation—"legal" or "moral"—simply because a repetitive pattern can be discerned in his or its actions. All would probably also agree that the actions that create customary law must be such as enter into interactions, although a complication ensues when we recall that under some circumstances inaction can take on the qualities of action, as when it becomes appropriate to call it "acquiescence" or "forbearance." Beyond this, we encounter almost a vacuum of ideas.

Into this vacuum, there is projected at least one articulate attempt at formulating a test. This is found in the doctrine of *opinio necessitatis*. According to this principle (which still enjoys some esteem in international law) customary law arises out of repetitive actions when and only when such actions are motivated by a sense of obligation, in other words, when people behave as they do, not because they want to or because they act unreflectively, but because they believe they have to act as they do. This seems a curiously inept solution. In clear cases of established customary law, it becomes a tautology; in situations where customary law is in the process of being born, it defaults.

One might suggest that a better approach could be found in the principle contained in Section 90 of the American Law Institute's Restatement of Contracts. As formulated to fit the problem at hand, this principle would run along these (unfortunately somewhat complex) lines: Where by his actions toward B, A has (whatever his actual intentions may have been) given B reasonably to understand that he (A) will in the future in similar situations act in a similar manner, and B has, in some substantial way, prudently adjusted his affairs to the expectation that A will in the future act in accordance with this expectation, then A is bound to follow the pattern set by his past actions toward B. This creates an obligation by A to B. If the pattern of interaction followed by A and B then spreads through the relevant community, a rule of general customary law will have been created. This rule will normally become part of a larger system, which will involve a complex network of reciprocal expectations. Absorption of the new rule into the larger system will, of course, be facilitated by the fact that the inter-actions that gave rise to it took place within limits set by that system and derived a part of their meaning for the parties from the wider interactional context within which they occurred.

The familiar phenomenon of the spread of customary law from one social context to another suggests a further distinction between customary law and contract law that deserves critical examination here. It may be said that a contract binds only the parties to it, while customary law normally extends its rules over a large and at times somewhat unclearly defined commu-nity. The first observation is that while this spread of customary law is a common occurrence it is by no means inevitable. Some-thing that can be called *two-party* customary law can and does exist; it is, again, only linguistic prejudice that makes us hesitant about this employment of the word *law*.

Where customary law does in fact spread, we must not be misled as to the process by which this extension takes place. It has sometimes been thought of as if it involved a kind of in-articulate expression of group will; the members of Group B perceive that the rules governing Group A would furnish an apt law for them; they therefore take over those rules by an act of tacit collective adoption. This kind of explanation abstracts from the interactional processes underlying customary law and ignores their ever-present communicative aspect. Take, for example, a practice in the field of international relations, that of offering a twenty-one-gun salute to visiting heads of state. By a process of imitation, this practice seems now to have become fairly general among the nations. One may say loosely that its appeal lies in the appropriateness of a resounding boom of can-non as a way of signalizing the arrival of a distinguished visitor. But why twenty-one guns, instead of sixteen or twenty-five? It is apparent that once the pattern of twenty-one became familiar any departure from it could generate misapprehension; specta-tors would spend their time, not in enjoying the grandeur of cannon roar, but in counting booms, attributing all sorts of meanings—intended and unintended—to any departure from the last allocation. Generally we may say that where A and B have become familiar with a practice obtaining between C and D, A is likely to adopt this pattern in his actions toward B, not simply or necessarily because it has any special aptness for their situation, but because he knows B will understand the meaning of his behavior and will know how to react to it.

As for the proposition that a contract binds only those who made it, who actively and knowingly assented to its terms, a mere glance at modern contracting practice is sufficient to reveal how unreal and purely formal this proposition can become. Only a tiny fraction of the "contracts" signed today are actually negotiated or represent anything like an explicit accommodation of the parties' respective interests. Even contracts drafted by lawyers, and in theory specially fitted to the parties' situation, are apt to be full of traditional or "standard" clauses borrowed from other contracts and from general practice. These clauses are employed for a great variety of reasons—because the lawyer is in a hurry, or because he knows from the precedents how courts will construe them, or because the interests at stake are insufficient to justify the fee that would be appropriate to a more careful, specially tailored phrasing.

But the realities of contracting practice are much farther removed from the picture of a "meeting of minds" than is suggested by a mere reference to standard clauses. In fact, the overwhelming majority of contracts are embodied in printed forms, prepared by one party to serve his interests and imposed on the other on a take-it-or-leave-it basis. In recent years, American courts in dealing with such contracts have increasingly exercised the right to strike out clauses they regard as oppressive or grossly unfair. This practice stands in contrast with that of the homeland of the common law, where the courts are much more conservative in this matter, being inclined generally to enforce the contract "as written," that is, as printed from boiler plate. There is a certain irony in this, for from the time of Lord Coke the English courts have freely claimed the right to refuse enforcement to customary law deemed unreasonable and repugnant to the ordinary sense of fairness. If we were to search about in modern society for the nearest counterpart to the "repugnant" customary law of Coke's time, we might well find it in the standardized, printed contract, drafted by one party and signed unread by the other.

There remains for discussion one further distinction that can be made between contract law and customary law. This lies in the notion that a contract comes into effect at once, or when the parties stipulate it shall, while custom becomes law only through a usage observed to have persisted over a considerable period.

This is, again, too simple a view of the matter. The notion that customary law comes into effect gradually and only over a considerable period of time comes about, in part because of mistaken implications read into the word "customary," and in part because it is true that normally it takes some time for reciprocal interactional expectancies to "jell." But there are circumstances in which customary law (or a phenomenon for which we have no other name) can develop almost overnight. As an authority in international law has observed, "A new rule of customary international law based on the practice of States can emerge very quickly, and even almost suddenly, if new circumstances have arisen which imperatively call for regulation—though the time factor is never wholly irrelevant" (Fitzmaurice, quoted in Parry, 1965, p. 60). (The assertion sometimes encountered that to be accepted as law a custom must have existed "from time immemorial" is directed to a very special question, that is, When should custom be regarded as overriding provisions of the general law? This obviously can be something quite different from asking when custom should control an issue previously not regulated by law at all. The doctrine of *opinio necessitatis* probably originated in the same context, for it may make good sense to say that a man should not be held to have infringed at least some kinds of general law where he acted in the belief that a special or local customary law obligated him to conduct himself as he did.)

As for the notion that a contract binds at once and before any action has been taken under it, this is again a misleading simplification, especially when the matter is viewed historically. It is, of course, dangerous to attempt generalizations about the historical course of legal development in all societies.

Nevertheless, it is reasonably safe to say that the legal enforcement of contracts first emerges in two contexts. The first of these is that of the ritualistic promise, the promise accompanied by some traditional oath or the recital of a set verbal formula, for example. Here, indeed, the contract binds at once and without proof of any action under it. But the very formality of this process of "binding," or the distrust implied by an insistence on it, has no doubt always inhibited its use, as it does today in the case of its modern counterparts.

The second early legal manifestation of the contract principle involves the situation of the half-completed exchange. A delivers fish to B in return for B's promise of a basket of vegetables. B keeps the fish but refuses to deliver the vegetables. Plainly there is nothing mysterious about the fact that in this situation legal redress became available at an early period in history. It should be noted, however, that the obligation enforced rests not on mere words, but primarily on the action (and inaction) that followed the words.

It appears likely that in all legal systems the enforcement of the executory bilateral contract is a development that comes quite late. This is the situation where A and B agree on the exchange, let us say again, of fish for vegetables; when A comes to deliver the fish, B refuses his offering and repudiates the agreement. The recognition that A has a legal claim in this situation seems generally to have occurred contemporaneously with the development of something like a market economy. But in such an environment there is likely to be action, at least in the sense of forbearance, in the very act of entering the contract. A, in seeking for a chance to trade his fish for vegetables, forgoes, when he strikes his bargain with B, the chance to enter a similar trade with C, D, or E. So here once again the agreement becomes enforceable because its words have been underscored, as it were, by reliance on them—in this case, by an inferred neglect of other opportunities once the contract in question had been concluded.

Finally, it should be recalled that the promise of an outright gift retains to this day a somewhat uncertain legal status. There may exist cumbersome legal forms for making such prom-

ises enforceable, and the courts have sometimes shown remarkable ingenuity in finding tacit elements of exchange in what
appears on its face as an expression of sheer generosity. In the
United States, there has emerged a doctrine (now known generally as the Section Ninety Principle) whereby the promise may
become enforceable when the promisee has seriously and reasonably taken its anticipated performance into account in the
arrangement of his own affairs. As I have previously suggested,
this principle is not far removed from one that underlies customary law generally.

Interactional Foundations of Enacted Law

Early in this chapter, I stated my intention to advance a
thesis "more radical than a mere insistence that customary law
is still of considerable importance in the world of today. I am
going to argue that we cannot understand 'ordinary' law (that
is, officially declared or enacted law) unless we first obtain an
understanding of what is called 'customary law.' " The time has
come to attempt some fulfillment of the commitment implied
in this statement.

In the pages that have gone before, I have treated both
customary law and contract law as interactional phenomena. I
have viewed them as arising out of interaction and as serving to
order and facilitate interaction. Can anything like this be asserted of enacted law, as typified, for example, by the statute?
Can we regard enacted law itself as dependent on the development of "stable interactional expectancies" between lawgiver
and subject? Does enacted law also serve the purpose of ordering and facilitating the interactions of citizens with one another?

It cannot be said that there are no traces of ideas like
these in the literature. What can be said is that it requires some
diligence to find them. As for the general purpose of enacted
law, the standard formula—in both jurisprudence and sociology
—is to the effect that "law serves as an instrument of social control." Sometimes this conception is coupled with the notion
that the necessity for law arises entirely from man's defective

moral nature; if men could be counted on to act morally, law would be unnecessary. As for the way law is conceived to come into existence, it is by an exercise of authority and not from anything like an interplay of reciprocal expectancies. The law does not invite the citizen to interact with it; it acts on him.

Let us test the question whether enacted law serves to put in order and facilitate human interaction by inquiring how this conception applies to some actual branches of the law. First, consider the law embraced under the following headings: contract, agency, marriage and divorce, property (both private and public), and the rules of court procedure. All of these vital branches of the law serve primarily to set the terms of men's relations with one another; they facilitate human interaction as traffic is facilitated by the laying out of roads and the installation of direction signs. To say that these branches of law would be unnecessary if men were more disposed to act morally is like saying that language could be dispensed with if only men were intelligent enough to communicate without it. The fact that the branches of law just listed include restraints as well as enabling provisions detracts in no sense from their facilitative quality; there is no more paradox here than there is in the proposition that highway traffic can be expedited by signs that read, "NO LEFT TURN," "STOP, THEN ENTER."

An interactional theory of law can hardly claim acceptance, however, simply because it seems apt when applied to certain branches of the law, such as contracts, property, agency, and marital rights. The law of crimes, for example, presents a quite different test, for here an interactional view encounters an environment much less congenial to its premises. There would, for example, be something ludicrous about explaining the rule against murder as being intended to facilitate human interaction by removing from men's confrontations the fear that they may kill one another. Murder, we are likely to say, is prohibited because it is wrong, not because the threat of it can detract from the potential richness of man's relations with his fellows.

Viewed from a historical perspective, however, the matter assumes a very different aspect. Students of primitive society have seen the very inception of the concept of law itself in limitations on the blood feud. A member of Family A kills a member of Family B. In a primitive society, the natural response to this act is for the members of Family B to seek revenge against Family A. If no limits are set to this revenge, there may ensue a war to the death between the two families. There has, accordingly, grown up in many primitive societies a rule that blood revenge on the part of Family B must, in the case supposed, be limited to one killing, although the injured family is regarded as being entitled as of right to this degree of counterkill. A later development will normally prohibit blood revenge and require instead compensation in the form of "blood money" for the life of the man whose life was taken. Here, plainly, the law of murder serves to regulate interaction and, if you will, to facilitate interaction on a level more profitable for all concerned than killing and counterkilling.

Today the law against murder appears on the surface to have become entirely divorced from its interactional origins; it is seen as projecting its imperative, "Thou shalt not kill," over the members of society generally and without regard to their interrelations. But what has in fact happened is that interactional issues that were once central have, as the result of legal and moral progress, been pushed to the periphery, where they remain as lively as ever. The most obvious example is offered by the plea of self-defense; a man is still legally privileged to kill an aggressor if this is necessary to save his own life. But how shall we interpret *necessary* in this context? How far can we expect a man to run some risk to his own life in order to avoid taking the life of another? Again, there is the question of reducing the degree of the offense when a man kills in "hot blood," as when he comes on another making love to his wife. Finally, there are the disputed issues of killing to prevent a felony or to stop a fleeing felon. In all these much-debated cases, the rule against homicide may be modified, or punishment reduced, by a reference to the question, What can reasonably be expected of a man in these interactional situations?

I trust it is clear that I am not advancing here the thesis that law, in its actual formulation and administration, always serves exclusively the purpose of ordering and facilitating human interaction. There are, certainly, some manifestations of law that cannot readily be forced into this frame of thought. Perhaps the most significant of these lies in that portion of the criminal law relating to what have been called "crimes without victims." Included here are laws forbidding the sale of intoxicants and contraceptive devices, the use of marijuana, homosexual practices, prostitution, and gambling. Assuming that those involved are of sound mind and that there is no deception —the roulette wheel has not been rigged, for example—these laws, far from facilitating interaction, have as their purpose preventing forms of interaction desired by the participants and not directly designed, at least, to injure others.

It is no accident, I think, that it is in this area—the area precisely where legal restraint appears most unequivocally as an "instrument of social control"—that the grossest failures of law have everywhere occurred. It is an area characterized by corruption, selective and sporadic enforcement, blackmail, and the open tolerance of illegality. There is no need to argue here that this body of law requires critical reexamination. The problem is to know by what guiding principle to direct that reexamination.

We should begin by asking ourselves why the law fails so notably in this general area of "crimes without victims." The usual answer is that you cannot enforce morality by law. But this is not so. Keeping promises may be a moral obligation, yet the law can and does successfully force people to keep their promises. Not only that, but the legal enforcement of promises, far from weakening the moral sense of obligation, tends to strengthen it. Suppose, for example, a situation where men associated in some business enterprise are discussing whether they ought to perform a disadvantageous contract. Those who believe they are morally bound to do so are in a position to remind their less principled associates that if the contract is broken they will all be brought to court and will subject themselves, not only to the cost, but also to the opprobrium of an adverse judgment. There are areas of human concern, then, where the cliché that you cannot make men act morally by law does not hold. These are, I believe, precisely the areas where the law's sanctions reinforce interactional expectancies and facilitate a respect for them.

If we accept the view that the central purpose of law is to furnish base lines for human interaction, it then becomes apparent why the existence of enacted law as an effectively functioning system depends on the establishment of stable interactional expectancies between lawgiver and subject. On the one hand, the lawgiver must be able to anticipate that the citizenry as a whole will accept as law and generally observe the body of rules he has promulgated. On the other hand, the legal subject must be able to anticipate that government will itself abide by its own declared rules when it comes to judge his actions, as in deciding, for example, whether he has committed a crime or claims property under a valid deed. A gross failure in the realization of either of these anticipations—of government toward citizen and of citizen toward government—can have the result that the most carefully drafted code will fail to become a functioning system of law.

It is a curious fact of history that although the older books are full of discussions of the principle that law implies general rules, there is almost no explicit recognition that the enactment of general rules becomes meaningless if government considers itself free to disregard them whenever it suits its convenience. Perhaps there is here illustrated a phenomenon already discussed, that the anticipations that most firmly direct our actions toward others are often precisely those that do not rise to consciousness. Such anticipations are like the rules of grammar that we observe in practice without having occasion to articulate them until they have been conspicuously violated. Perhaps there is also operative here a confusion arising from the fact that we realize that normally a lawgiver can change any one of his laws simply by repealing it and providing a quite different law for the governance of events thereafter happening. It seems curious that the agency that can rewrite the whole book of laws should be held to respect the most insignificant of its enactments in judging events that occurred while it was still in effect. There is the paradox here, in Simmel's words, of "interaction within an apparently one-sided and passive submission" (1950, p. 186). Yet without that paradox the notion of enacted "law" would become empty and meaningless.

In the analysis now being concluded, three distinct kinds of law have been passed in review: customary law, contract law, and enacted law. This list omits a fourth expression of law, namely, adjudicative law as exemplified in the Anglo-American "common law." It is fashionable nowadays to consider the common law as being simply a form of enacted law, differing from statutory law only in its authorship, a statute being enacted by a legislature, a rule of common law being declared by a court. This view ignores the special qualities exemplified by the common law, qualities that once led men—with much justification— to speak of it as a form of customary law. For the common law, by virtue of its special way of making law case by case, projects its roots more deeply and intimately into human interaction than does statutory law—although, to be sure, in the country of its origin it seems to be losing the qualities that once distinguished it, perhaps because its judges have finally begun to conform their practice to the pattern legal theory has been ascribing to it for more than a century.

If we view law as serving the purpose of putting in order and facilitating human interaction, it is apparent that the making of law involves the risk that we may be unable to foresee in advance the variety of interactional situations that may fall within the ambit of a preformulated rule. A statute that reveals itself as a patent misfit for situations of fact that later come to court—situations plainly covered by the language of the statute, but obviously misunderstood or not foreseen by the draftsman —such a law certainly has no special claim to praise simply because it is clear in meaning and announced in advance. The virtue of the common law is that, proceeding case by case, it can fit and refit its prescriptions to the configurations of life as they reveal themselves in litigation. What the common law lacks in the way of clear advance formulation, it may more than make up for by its capacity to reshape and reword its rules in the light of the actual situations that offer themselves for decision.

The common law presents, then, a complex amalgam of lawmaking forms, intermixing explicit legislation with the tacit adjustments characteristic of customary law, sometimes expressing the best qualities of both systems, and, on rare occasions, displaying the worst qualities of both.[1]

Interactions Between Law and Its Social Context

Implicit in all that has gone before in this chapter is the view that law and its social environment stand in a relation of reciprocal influence; any given form of law will not only act on, but be influenced and shaped by, the established forms of interaction that constitute its social milieu. This means that for a given social context one form of law may be more appropriate than another and that the attempt to force a form of law on a social environment uncongenial to it may miscarry with damaging results.

For present purposes, I shall employ simply the notion of a spectrum or scale of relationships, running from intimacy, at the one end, to hostility, at the other, with a stopping place midway that can be described as the habitat of friendly strangers, between whom interactional expectancies remain largely open and unpatterned. As typifying the intimate relationship, I shall take the average American family, with no servants, young children in the home, household chores to be apportioned, and members who are on reasonably good terms with one another. At the other end of the spectrum, I have in mind, not two individuals who are enemies, but two hostile nations not under the control of a superior political power that might contain their tendencies toward overt hostile action.

In attempting here to test the different forms of law against varying social contexts I shall begin with contractual law, by which, the reader will recall, I mean the "law" of the contract itself, not the state-made law of or about contracts. The reason for choosing contractual law as a starting point is that, in a sense, it stands halfway between customary law and enacted law, sharing some of the qualities of both. On the one hand, contractual law is like customary law in that its prescriptions are not imposed on the parties by some outside authority; they make their own law. On the other hand, contractual law resembles legislation in that it involves the explicit creation of verbalized rules for the governance of the parties' relationship.

If we start with the "intimate" end of the scale, it is apparent that contract is an instrument ill suited to ordering the relations within a functioning family. We are apt to put this in affective terms, saying that people united by affection would have difficulty in negotiating with one another and that any attempt to do so might disturb the harmony of the home. But the problem also has what may be called an *operational* aspect; the allocation of household responsibilities is affected by shifting and unpredictable contingencies: Someone becomes ill, one of the children falls behind in his schoolwork, father has to be away on a trip, and so on. No degree of contractual foresight would be equal to dealing in advance with all these permutations in the internal affairs of the family.

It seems a safe guess that not many married couples have attempted to arrange their internal affairs by anything like an explicit contract. In the few reported cases in which judicial enforcement of such contracts has been sought, the courts have denied relief. One court observed that "judicial inquiry into matters of that character, between husband and wife, would be fraught with irreparable mischief."[2] Another court remarked that if the parties were able to enter binding contracts regulating their internal relations this would "open an endless field for controversy and bickering and would destroy the element of flexibility needed in making adjustments to new conditions."[3]

If we move to the opposite end of the spectrum and consider contracts between parties standing in what I have called a *social relation of hostility,* a contractual regulation becomes, once again, not only difficult to negotiate, but also often an inept device for achieving the end sought. The simple way of explaining this is to say that hostile parties do not trust one another, and mutual trust is essential for both the negotiation and the administration of a contract. But the problem, once again, has what may be called an *operational* aspect. The negotiation of a contract of any complexity will involve an intricate fitting together of diverse interests. This, in turn, means that in the course of negotiations—in the stand he takes for or against some demanded concession—each party is compelled to make some disclosure of the internal posture of his own interests. This disclosure may be disadvantageous to him, especially if negotiations fall through. Thus, suppose that in negotiations looking toward a reduction in armaments between two hostile countries, Country A, to the surprise of Country B, seems quite ready to agree to a broad limitation on the production and use of Weapon X. Country B at once begins to ask itself such questions as "Why is that? Are they aware of some limitation on the effectiveness of Weapon X we do not know about? Or do they want us to give up producing Weapon X, which they fear, and divert our resources to Weapon Y, against which they perhaps have developed an adequate defense?" This necessity for some disclosure in order to achieve a successful fitting together of the parties' diverse interests is often inhibitive, not only in international relations, but in other fields as well, sometimes even in business deals. Perhaps the ultimate cure for it lies in the gradual and patient establishment of multiple ties of association between the parties, so that their social bond is not concentrated in one negotiation or one document. When that happens, however, the organizing principle of the parties' relationship is apt to cease to be contractual and become essentially one of customary law.

I should like now to turn to the middle ground of the spectrum of social contexts, the area I have previously described as "the habitat of friendly strangers, between whom interactional expectancies remain largely open and unpatterned." This is precisely the area where contractual law is most at home and most effective; it is also here, without much doubt, that the very notion of explicit contracting was first conceived.

We are prone to suppose that as we move away from relations of intimacy our freedom of expression and action becomes progressively restricted; with strangers we are "ill at ease"; it is only with close friends that we are free to say what we think and declare what we would like to have. But in fact, in dealing with intimates we are, often quite without knowing it, restrained by a host of unarticulated expectations—compelled, as it were, to act out roles tacitly assigned to us in previous encounters. As Simmel points out, it is often precisely the stranger who receives "the most surprising openness—confidences which would be carefully withheld from a more closely related person" (1950, p. 404). It is this "openness" of the relations between strangers that facilitates negotiation in a manner that would be impossible (and probably inadvisable) within an intimate group like the family.

All over the world the intimacies of the extended family, the tribe, and the country village have proved an obstacle to the establishment of dealings on a straightforward commercial basis. It is hard, for example, to hold a relative or a close friend to prompt payment of his account. Mair reports a general anthropological observation that the "pressures to give easy credit on a man setting up a store in his own village are apt to be so great that he cannot make a success of his business" (1965, p. 181). An enterprising American Indian tribe in the state of Washington is said to have encountered a similar frustration in attempting to engage in business enterprises on the reservation.[4] Perhaps the most interesting observation of this sort is contained in *The Irish Countryman,* by Conrad Arensberg. According to Arensberg, the practice in rural Ireland is for the customer of the local shopkeeper virtually never to pay off his account in full; indeed, this is something he would do only in a fit of anger. The standing unpaid account, reduced from time to time by partial payments, is regarded as symbolizing a bond of mutual trust—the customer gives his patronage, the shopkeeper extends his credit (Arensberg, 1937, pp. 155-162). Many Americans have observed a similar phenomenon: When one makes a purchase at the local store and, instead of charging it, as he usually does, offers to pay cash, this may be resented by the storekeeper. When one considers how common this tendency is to shy away from a purely impersonal businesslike relationship, it is no wonder that the pioneering merchants and traders seem everywhere to have been "outsiders"—the Jews in Europe, the Parsees in India, the Indians and Lebanese in Africa, the Chinese in the Pacific, and perhaps one could say, in the early days, the Yankees in North America. As some of the items on this list suggest, it might even appear that a difference in religion may at times facilitate the achievement of the kind of social distance essential for purely contractual relations.

It might be worth remarking here that sometimes the very success of a contractual relation has the effect of supplanting it by something akin to a two-party customary law. Those who renew contracts year after year and who thus become "intimates" are likely to have increasing difficulty in preserving an atmosphere of open negotiation; they become prisoners of the expectations created by past practice. This is, of course, especially likely to occur where a situation has developed in which it is not easy for the parties to find alternative sources for filling their needs, a situation approaching that of "bilateral monopoly."[5]

So much for the interactions between contractual law and its social context. Turning now to customary law, the first observation is that this form of law is at home completely across the spectrum of social contexts, from the most intimate to those of open hostility. That the family cannot easily organize itself by a process of explicit bargaining does not mean there will not grow up within it reciprocal expectancies of the sort that, on a more formal level, would be called "customary law." Indeed, the family could not function without these tacit guidelines to interaction; if every interaction had to be oriented afresh and *ad hoc,* no group like the family could succeed in the discharge of its shared tasks. At the midrange, it should be observed that the most active and conspicuous development of customary law in modern times lies precisely in the field of commercial dealings. Finally, while enemies may have difficulty in bargaining with words, they can, and often do, profitably half-bargain with deeds. Paradoxically, the tacit restraints of customary law between enemies are more likely to develop during active warfare than during a hostile stalemate of relations; fighting one another is itself in this sense a "social" relation, since it involves communication.

That customary law is, as I have expressed it, "at home" across the entire spectrum of social contexts does not mean that it retains the same qualities wherever it appears. On the contrary, it can change drastically in nature as it moves from one end of the spectrum to the other. At the terminal point of intimacy, customary law has to do, not primarily with prescribed acts and performances, but with roles and functions. The internal operations of a family, kinship group, or even tribe, may demand, not simply formal compliance with rules, but an allocation of authority, and a sense of trusteeship on the part of those who make decisions and give directions. In the middle area, typified by arm's-length commercial dealings, customary law abstracts from qualities and dispositions of the person and concentrates its attention on ascribing appropriate and clearly defined consequences to outward conduct. Finally, as we enter the area of hostile relations, a decided change in the general "flavor" of customary law takes place. Here the prime desideratum is to achieve—through acts, of course, not words—the clear communication of messages of a rather limited and negative import; accordingly, there is a heavy concentration on symbolism and ritual.

Resuming our analysis of the effects of social context on the different forms of law, there remains for consideration enacted law as exemplified in a statute. At the outset, it is apparent, I think, that the "home ground" of enacted law coincides largely with what we have already found most congenial to the organizing principle of contract, that is, with the middle area on the spectrum of social contexts—the region populated by friendly strangers, whose relations with one another generally stand open in the sense of not being prestructured by bonds of kinship or the repulsions of a shared hostility.

If enacted law and contractual law are alike in finding especially congenial the midpoint on the spectrum of social contexts, they also share an ineptitude for attempting anything like an internal regulation of the family. If a contract of the parties themselves is too blunt an instrument for shaping the affairs of a family, the same thing could be said with added emphasis if any attempt were made to impose detailed state-made regulations on the intimate relations of marriage and parenthood.[6]

Yet, as I have observed here, much of customary law

serves—and often serves well—the function of putting in order
the relations of kinsmen. What is the explanation for this special
quality of the customary law of family affairs? I think it is to be
found in the fact that customary law does not limit itself to
requiring or prohibiting precisely defined acts but may also
designate roles and functions and then, when the occasion
arises, hold those discharging these roles and functions to an accounting for their performances. This conception does not conflict with the analysis of customary law presented at the beginning of this essay. Stable interactional expectancies can arise
with reference to roles and functions as well as to specific acts;
a language of interaction will contain not only a vocabulary of
deeds but also a basic grammar that will organize deeds into
meaningful patterns.

It is important to observe that the very qualities of enacted law that make it an inept instrument for regulating intimate relations are precisely those which lend to it a special
capacity to put in order individuals' interactions within the
larger impersonal society. Within that wider context, the basic
necessity is to impose rules that will serve to set the limits men
must observe in their interactions with one another, leaving
them free within those limits to pursue their own goals. This in
turn means that the law must deal with defined acts, not with
dispositions of the will or attitudes of mind. The rule of law
measures a man's acts against the law, not the man himself
against some ideal perceived as lying behind the law's prescriptions.

What is involved here may be expressed as a distinction
between judging the person and judging the act.[7] In the ordinary affairs of life, these two forms of judgment are in constant
interaction. We judge what a man is by the way he acts; we evaluate his acts as expressions of what he is. We know that a man
sometimes has to act as he does "because that's the sort of person he is"; we also know that over a lifetime a man, to some
extent at least, makes himself the kind of person he is by a
multitude of decisions as to how to act in specific situations.

Primitive systems of law, including the common law of
England in its early period, accept without qualms this com-

monsense view of the matter and show but little concern to preserve a distinction between the man and his act. The jury was originally selected from the immediate vicinage so that they might know the litigants personally and perhaps even be acquainted with the facts of the controversy itself. Included in the criminal law were what have been called "crimes of status"—the crime, for example, of "being a common scold."

All of this has, of course, changed drastically. In a criminal trial today, personal acquaintances of the defendant would normally be excluded from the jury, evidence of past misconduct is inadmissible, and it is unthinkable that a witness, however well acquainted he might be with the defendant, would be allowed to tell the jury what kind of person he considers him to be.[8] The task of the jury is to determine as best it can just what act or acts the defendant committed and then to measure those acts against the prescriptions of the law.

This picture of a lean and sparing justice, deliberately averting its gaze from the man himself, becomes considerably clouded, however, when we consider what happens before and after the confrontation that takes place in open court. Before the case is brought to court, the defendant has to be arrested, and it would certainly be a rare policeman who routinely—and without taking into account the nature and circumstances of the offense—arrested every person he believed to have committed a crime. Certainly in dealing with minor offenses the police officer uses, and is expected to use, "judgment"; this judgment is inevitably affected by his perception of the kind of person the suspected party seems to be. When the case is brought to the prosecutor, he in turn is influenced in some degree by similar considerations in deciding whether to prefer charges. If he has the case set for trial, there will, in many routine cases, ensue a process that has come to be called "plea bargaining." This is a procedure by which the prosecutor and the defense attorney will attempt, with court approval, to reach an agreement by which the defendant will plead guilty to a lesser charge than that asserted to be justified by those representing the state. The outcome of this process is inevitably affected by opinions about the basic dispositions of the defendant. If the case goes to trial and the accused is found guilty, the question of the appropriate sentence has to be decided. In deciding that question, the judge will take into account what is known about the defendant himself, his past, and his probable future propensities. Similar considerations will, of course, determine the granting of parole or a pardon. When, finally, we consider that probably less than 10 percent of the criminal charges filed ever come to trial, the emphasis placed in open court on the act, rather than on the person of the defendant, will shrink in significance to the point where it may seem only a kind of symbolic tribute to the principle of judging the deed and not the man.

This symbolism is, however, of vital importance. If it were ever completely lost from view, the principle of legality, the rule of law, would become an empty sham. The apparent contradictions within the total processes of the criminal law are tolerable because it is generally perceived, at least by those directly concerned, that distinctive institutional roles are played by those who arrest, prosecute, defend, try, sentence, parole, release, and pardon—all of these roles being directed toward the discharge of differing functions. Whether these distinctions are always perceived by the public or by the accused himself is doubtful. There is, however, no question that any such elaborate division of function would be impossible within an intimate society; it presupposes large and impersonal processes.

When we view the matter in this light, it becomes apparent that in a complex modern society enacted law and the organizational principles implicit in customary law are not simply to be viewed as alternative ways of ordering men's interactions, but rather as often serving to supplement each other by a kind of natural division of labor. Generally, we may say that enacted law will default in complex relations of interdependence that cannot be organized by set rules of duty and entitlement; these situations are by no means confined to such as we would call "intimate" in any affective sense.[9] That they cannot be put in order by statutory enactment does not mean that they cannot, and do not in our own society, receive an effective ordering by silent processes that, manifested in a primitive society, would be called "customary law."

Much that is written today seems to assume that our larger society is enabled to function by a combination of the individual's moral sense and social control through the threatened sanctions of state-made law. We need to remind ourselves that we constantly orient our actions toward one another by signposts that are set neither by "morals," in any ordinary sense, nor by words in lawbooks. If this chapter has served to rekindle some appreciation of this fact, I shall be content.

Notes

1. In my book, *Anatomy of the Law* (1968), pp. 84-112, I have undertaken an analysis of the special virtues and defects of the common law system.

2. Miller v. Miller, 78 Iowa 177, 182, 42 N.W. 641, 642 (1889).

3. Graham v. Graham, 33 Fed. Supp. 936, 938 E. D. Mich. (1940). See, generally, Foote, Levy, and Sander (1966), chap. 2, pt. 2, pp. 297-366; note "Litigation between Husband and Wife," 1966, pp. 1650-1655; McDowell (1965), pp. 43-62.

4. A study by Colson (1953), reported in Max Gluckman (1965), 333-334.

5. The thesis of the study by Friedman, *Contract Law in America* (1965), might be stated as the tendency of contractual relations to convert themselves into something like customary law. However, Friedman's study does not, in my opinion, take sufficient account of the special qualities of the economic background of the phenomena studied; it should definitely have been called *Contract Law in Wisconsin*, not *Contract Law in America*. Another valuable study is Stewart Macaulay (1963).

6. I am not at this point, of course, referring to such problems as child abuse, compulsory education, and the like.

7. I have attempted to apply some of the implications of this distinction to the internal legal systems of voluntary associations in my article, "Two Principles of Human Association," (1969), especially pp. 17-19.

8. I am not attempting to deal here, of course, with expert testimony concerning the sanity of the defendant. It might be suggested, however, that the modern legal uses of psychiatry present some difficult problems when viewed in the light of the person-act dichotomy.

9. I have tried to show the inadequacies of formal legal rules and processes of adjudication for dealing with "polycentric" problems in "Collective Bargaining and the Arbitrator" (1963); see also Fuller (1965).

References

Arensberg, C. M. *The Irish Countryman: An Anthropological Study.* London: Macmillan, 1937.

Colson, E. *The Makah Indians: An Indian Tribe in Modern American Society.* Minneapolis: University of Minnesota Press, 1953.

Fitzmaurice, G. G. "The Law and Procedure of the International Court of Justice, 1951-54: General Principles and Sources of Law." *British Yearbook of International Law,* 1953, *30.*

Foote, C., Levy, R. J., and Sander, F. E. A. *Cases and Materials on Family Law.* Boston: Little, Brown, 1966.

Friedman, L. M. *Contract Law in America: A Social and Economic Case Study.* Madison: University of Wisconsin Press, 1965.

Fuller, L. L. "Collective Bargaining and the Arbitrator." *Wisconsin Law Review,* 1963, *3,* 18-42.

Fuller, L. L. "Irrigation and Tyranny." *Stanford Law Review,* 1965, *17,* 1021-1042.

Fuller, L. L. *Anatomy of the Law.* New York: Praeger, 1968.

Fuller, L. L. "Two Principles of Human Association." *Nomos,* 1969, *11,* 3-23.

Gluckman, M. *Politics, Law, and Ritual in Tribal Society.* Chicago: Aldine, 1965.

"Litigation between Husband and Wife." *Harvard Law Review,* 1966, *79,* 1650-1665.

Macaulay, S. "Non-Contractual Relations in Business: A Preliminary Study." *American Sociological Review,* 1963, *28,* 55-67.

McDowell, B. "Contracts in the Family." *Boston University Law Review,* 1965, *45,* 43-62.

Mair, L. P. *An Introduction to Social Anthropology.* Oxford, England: Clarendon Press, 1965.

Parry, C. *The Sources and Evidences of International Law.* Dobbs Ferry, N.Y.: Oceana Publications, 1965.

Parsons, T., and Shils, E. with the assistance of J. Olds. "Values, Motives, and Systems of Action." In T. Parsons and E. Shils (Eds.), *Toward a General Theory of Action.* Cambridge, Mass.: Harvard University Press, 1951.

Simmel, G. *The Sociology of Georg Simmel.* (K. H. Wolff, Trans. and Ed.) New York: Free Press, 1950.

Part 2

Comparative Perspectives

There are many points with respect to which different legal systems could be compared. Among them we might mention the degree of institutionalization of the system and (closely connected) the degree of underlying value consensus in the society (values, it may be recalled, being defined as normative conceptions of the ideal society, serving as guides to individual and collective action and as standards of judgment). At a different level of analysis, we might mention the following points of comparison: the degree of independence of the legal profession and its training and organization (matters discussed in a comparative perspective by Rueschemeyer); the extent to which the courts are differentiated from government bodies; the relative importance of adjudication and legislation (an important matter treated briefly in this book by Fuller and Rueschemeyer; but see, especially, Fuller, 1968, pp. 84-112); the method of selecting judges, whether appointment, election, or appointment with the approval of elective bodies; the extent to which the legal system is "cut loose" from formal ties with a particular religious tradition; the degree and kinds of differentiation within the legal system itself, including the legal profession; the degree to

91

which the system is uniform across a whole society; and the degree to which the system has become universalistic or still retains particularistic features.

The most important recent development in the theory of cultural and social evolution is the ordering of facts in terms of the four-function paradigm (Parsons, 1966, 1971, 1977). The primary criterion of evolutionary change, as opposed to structural change in general, is enhanced adaptive capacity. Small, homogeneous societies, such as ancient Israel or Athens, have been able to make important contributions, but, broadly speaking, these contributions have had to be more completely developed and institutionalized in much larger societies. Accordingly, one of the salient themes in Parsons' treatment of social evolution is the development of value systems and more specific structural mechanisms that make possible a substantial level of solidarity in religiously and ethnically heterogeneous *societies. As we have seen, law is functionally important both for overall integration and for goal attainment in all four functional subsystems (the pattern maintenance or fiduciary system, the integrative system or societal community, the goal attainment system or polity, and the adaptive system or economy).*

For integration, fundamental problems (whether clearly recognized or not) are fairness of the legal system and the degree to which it facilitates or requires broad religious and ethnic "inclusiveness." Thus, the cutting loose or emancipation of the legal system from too-close subservience to a particular religion is functionally important if it can be accomplished without loss of legitimation. In the same way, also important are the extension of the electorate in a democratic order and the relative autonomy of the courts from the government in the narrow sense. The legal profession and the courts must be fiduciary custodians of universalistic law.

For goal attainment, the most important thing is flexibility in the commitment and allocation of both human and nonhuman resources. For this flexibility, a high level of differentiation is required. In pattern-variable terms, "universalism" and "performance" must be institutionalized and sanctioned in a full-fledged legal system; "particularism" and "quality" in the technical pattern-variable senses must be redefined and reinte-grated in an overall normative order in which universalism and performance have become salient. Uniform universalistic laws make possible predictability of the courts and government and enable individual and collective units to negotiate many kinds of contract securely without having to establish beforehand par-ticularistic ties of kinship, marriage, or friendship. The range of markets is greatly extended.

These considerations enable us to understand the enor-mous importance Max Weber attached to the institutionaliza-tion of universalistic law. In Parsons' three-stage theory of social evolution, the development of universalistic law divides the third stage from the second. A relatively autonomous legal system, both in the cultural and the social sense, establishes greater "control," in the normative, cybernetic sense, over the inevitable play of economic and political interests, with their ever-present potentiality to be divisive and inimical to the gen-eral welfare.

It is important not to get stuck in an all-or-nothing con-ception of universalistic law: Either it works perfectly across the board or it is a sham façade. Sharlet's article shows that the legal system of the Soviet Union is definitely under the govern-ment (which in turn is not democratic in the usual sense), yet there are definite tendrils growing into a higher degree of legal autonomy. We have already noted that there is not necessarily anything "improper" or dysfunctional in the pursuit of unit interests. As Parsons notes in his contribution to this book, once universalistic values have been "spelled out" in more spe-cific laws, the very competition within and between various "sectors" of society creates a common interest in maintaining the consistency of the universalistic principle. Imbalances can occur, but they can be rectified through institutionalized mechanisms. Rueschemeyer points out, for example, that cor-porate producers have been able to shape the law in their inter-est; but now we see a newly activated movement to shift the balance in favor of consumers' interests. We should note, in passing, that when such movements are especially active there is a tendency toward dedifferentiation in that ideology tends to exaggerate the conflict *of interests and play down the fact that the conflicting parties may both be to a great extent performing valued functions and may therefore have legitimate interests.*

Fuller, Rueschemeyer, Yngvesson, and Kidder, in various ways, all bring out the evolutionary importance of social differentiation. Undifferentiated systems, by definition, are systems in which people tend to have "multiplex ties" with others, to use the term favored by Barbara Yngvesson. Undifferentiated systems also tend to lock people into their multiplex networks. As all these authors make clear, impersonal law, focusing on acts *rather than* persons, *tends to be inappropriate and unviable in such systems. This points up the fact that flexibility of human and nonhuman resources requires differentiation, and differentiation* with flexibility *in turn requires universalistic law and in the conditional sense makes it workable. Relatively formal sanctions also become possible to a greater extent.*

A very common theme is the strain produced by "impersonal" universalistic law. Among the authors of this book, this is expressed in the most extreme way by Robert Kidder. Surely, however, it makes a difference what the societal value system is and to what extent a system of universalistic law becomes institutionalized. The traditional value system of India (for example) stressed not equality but, in an extreme way, hereditary hierarchy and privilege. Both the "democratic" value system and the system of "impersonal" law, with juries selected in part because they do not *know the adversaries in court, are relatively new in India and must make their way against very strong conservative traditions and interests. Rita Simon's chapter on American juries (in the next section) shows that even in relatively extreme tests (that is, in nonroutine cases) American juries tend to take universalistic standards, "impersonality," and focus on* acts *for granted. Howard Haycraft, in his* Murder for Pleasure *(1951), points out, as others have done, that the detective novel has become a popular genre only in democracies, where rules of evidence count and where there is fairly widespread understanding of what constitutes "good" evidence. Agatha Christie and Edgar Wallace were banned in fascist Italy; in Nazi Germany, all foreign detective fiction was banned. De-*

tective story writers take it absolutely for granted that their readers—and average persons in democratic societies—are interested in pursuing all the available "evidence" to whatever conclusion may come, affecting no matter whom, so long as impartial justice be arrived at. What I am trying to indicate is that the perception of universalistic law is not the same for all peoples; culture makes a difference. We may reasonably assume that as time goes on it will be possible (not inevitable) for universalistic law to be less disruptive in India. Thus, although it is meaningful to regard universalistic law as "external" law wherever it has been introduced from the outside or even imposed by foreigners, it is perhaps less appropriate to label universalistic law "external" in general. On the other hand, the chapter by Hagan and Leon shows that even when universalistic law is accepted in principle, respect for law can vary according to the conditions of a society and according to different emphases of the societal value system.

Among the deficiencies and dangers that make universalistic law sometimes ineffective and always precarious are insufficient institutionalization of the relevant values, insufficient control of "selfish" interests incompatible with the public welfare, corruption of the legal profession and of the police, and abuse of political power. We could summarize or at least partially restate what has been said about relatively favorable cultural and social controls by saying that under certain conditions in historical evolution new societal values have crystallized out, particularly equality of opportunity, freedom from arbitrary power, and equality under law. Under these circumstances, deficiencies are to some extent remedied and dangers counteracted. The "need" for legitimation, which is operative in all social systems, becomes the "need" for a new kind of legitimation. The "need" for solidarity becomes a pressure for "inclusion" of religious and ethnic minorities. (In India, the outcastes now regard their age-old inferior status as illegitimate discrimination.) The legal system has a better chance to develop relative autonomy. Political power (hence, law enforcement), comes to be legitimated (or eroded) according to its legitimacy as measured in the light of the new values.

References

Fuller, L. L. *Anatomy of the Law.* New York: Praeger, 1968.

Haycraft, H. *Murder for Pleasure: The Life and Times of the Detective Story.* (2nd ed.) New York: Appleton-Century-Crofts, 1951.

Parsons, T. *Societies: Evolutionary and Comparative Perspectives.* Englewood Cliffs, N.J.: Prentice-Hall, 1966.

Parsons, T. *The System of Modern Societies.* Englewood Cliffs, N.J.: Prentice-Hall, 1971.

Parsons, T. "Comparative Studies and Evolutionary Change." In T. Parsons, *Social Systems and the Evolution of Action Theory.* New York: Free Press, 1977.

3　　　　　*Dietrich Rueschemeyer*

The Legal Profession in Comparative Perspective

Studying the legal profession is of interest from a number of perspectives. Here it is sufficient to spell out a few arguments why an understanding of the legal profession seems indispensable to the sociological study of the law. A first point is plain and simple: Beyond a certain level of complexity of the law, it takes professionally trained specialists to run legal proceedings in an orderly and effective fashion. The availability and the relation of these specialists to different parts of the population—to different occupational groups, classes, and castes and to people residing at various removes from the political and legal centers— determine to a large extent how well or badly the ideal of equality before the law is realized—if, that is, such an ideal exists at all in a society. But the part played by lawyers goes beyond assisting in the administration of existing law in the courts. In various ways, lawyers shape the substance of the legal order rather than merely apply it.

The ideal of a "rule of law, not of men" can never be fully realized, as we know from the arguments of legal realism and from numerous empirical studies of the law. To begin with, any workable legal order must give its judges, policemen, and other legal officers considerable leeway of discretion in applying rules to individual cases and unforeseen circumstances—so much leeway, in fact, that there have been serious doubts about the integrity of legal norms as universal rules. The reality of social change, always unpredictable to some extent, entails that adjudication can never be reduced to a mere application of existing legal norms to given cases. There is always the possibility of changing the norms in the process of adjudication—of *judicial legislation*. This element of rule change may in a given court decision be infinitesimally small, or it may be conspicuous, but the possibility can never be eradicated, even in countries that seek to codify legal norms as much as possible and put a high premium on bureaucratic orderliness. In legal systems such as the American one, where the record of judicial decisions defines more than in other systems "what the law is" and where parties and their lawyers play a more active part in court, rule making through adjudication is particularly important, and it is clear that not only judges but also attorneys and private parties appearing before them have a chance to shape the body of legal norms.[1]

Finally, much of the actual substance of a legal order is shaped directly neither by legislatures nor by the courts but by private parties who, with the help of legal counsel, enter contracts they expect to see enforced by the courts; yet these contracts may never reach the test of litigation because of uneven economic, political, and legal resources of the parties. The conditions laid down by monopolistic or quasi-monopolistic corporations in their relations with each other and with the multitude of other buyers and sellers of goods and services rest only indirectly on the legal machinery of the state but determine much of the actual legal framework of economic life. Hence the judgment of a major legal historian that "the true power of law lies in the unlitigated contract that defines, arranges, and delegates power over economic resources" (Murphy, 1964, p. 934). With these brief considerations, we have assembled a number of powerful reasons why the study of the legal profession must be an integral part of the sociological analysis of the law.

To be of theoretical rather than merely descriptive use, our understanding of the legal profession should be based on international comparison and should not confine itself to one country. Legal systems are closely related to the particular character of each society. Therefore, it would be difficult to decide which findings about the legal profession are of general significance and which are bound up with the peculiarities of the Japanese, the German, or the American legal and social order, if our investigations were limited to one country. Unfortunately, even our knowledge of the American bar is less than perfect, and there are only a few systematic studies about lawyers in other countries. If in this chapter I nevertheless try to raise a number of problems and develop ideas and hypotheses about the legal profession in a comparative perspective, I do so in the conviction that problem formulation may precede and stimulate research and that such comparative analysis is indispensable for a theoretical understanding of the functioning of law in society.

Variations in the Size of the Profession

A first impression of the varying roles lawyers play in different countries can be gleaned from comparative statistics about lawyers. A closer inspection of such statistics does reveal that there are severe problems of completeness and comparability; but even an analysis of these faults of the statistical evidence may lead to important insights and raise questions that are basic to any comparative study of lawyers.

The number of lawyers in proportion to the population varies drastically from one country to another. To a large extent, this is a reflection of differences in the degree of occupational specialization, in the level of overall wealth, and in the complexity of social institutions—interrelated factors that represent the socioeconomic development of a country. The demand for professional law work increases with differentiation of social structure and economic development. Thus, while Sierra Leone, Kenya, and Nigeria are reported to have fewer than 50 lawyers per million population, the United Kingdom, Australia, Canada, New Zealand, and the United States—the highly developed "old common law countries"—have more than 500 lawyers for every million inhabitants (Galanter, 1968-1969, pp. 204-206).

Table 1. Relative Number of Lawyers in Selected Countries, 1960, 1961.

Country	Lawyers per Million of Population	Country	Lawyers per Million of Population
United Kingdom	507	United States	1,595
Japan	70	Israel	1,523
Germany	366	Sweden	945

Source: Galanter (1968-1969, pp. 204-206). Galanter makes it clear that "extreme caution is appropriate in using" his much more comprehensive table, because "in some cases figures include nonpracticing law graduates, judges, prosecutors, retired persons; in others they do not"; in addition, a lag in population figures and differing age structures of different populations may add distortion.

Yet the comparisons in Table 1 suggest that there are considerable differences among countries that cannot be explained in terms of various aspects of socioeconomic development. If valid, these contrasts must be indications of fundamental differences among modern societies in the use of lawyers. Japan represents the most drastic exception from the pattern typical of more developed societies. A major explanation of its very small number of lawyers is, it appears, that law plays a lesser role in Japan than in any other highly developed society. "Traditionally," states Takeyoshi Kawashima (1963, p. 43), "the Japanese people prefer extrajudicial, informal means of settling a controversy." Stable social relations in Japan traditionally emphasize hierarchy, harmony, and a personal character; they are threatened both by open disputes and by impersonal legal-judicial means of settling them. Even in relations *between* solidary groups, where disputes are not as easily restrained, compromise and reconciliation rather than judicial decision are the preferred alternatives to unmitigated antagonism and the use of power and violence. It is remarkable that these attitudes and behaviors regarding law and dispute settlement have survived major changes in the social structures that gave rise to them.

The Japanese case illustrates an important generalization: "Law varies inversely with other social control" (Black, 1976, p. 107). No society is primarily ordered by legal norms maintained by legal sanctions. Nonlegal, informal norms, conventions, and customs are a major source of social order, and nonlegal sanctions—from admonition and ridicule to loss of reputation and disgrace—are important in all societies in exacting conformity with social norms. Societies vary considerably, however, in the extent to which there is agreement—in the elites or in the population at large—on the rules of social life; furthermore, the effectiveness of informal sanctions also varies, depending on such factors as the homogeneity or heterogeneity of subcultures within the same society or the deference to established elites. The relative importance of law as a means of social order and control in turn determines to a large extent the demand for services of legal specialists.

England is another country where the role of law and the work of the legal profession are limited by the effectiveness of nonlegal social controls. "In England," claim Abel-Smith and Stevens (1967, p. 1), "the law plays a less important role than in almost any other Western country. . . . The very nature of English society permits many things to be settled by custom or convention, political or social pressure, which in other countries would be settled by some enactment or judicial decision."[2] Since English lawyers in addition have largely concentrated on those disputes settled in court, an area of law that has declined in relative importance with the rise of the modern social service state, Abel-Smith and Stevens conclude that "most of the really important issues of modern society are not getting into solicitors' offices and barristers' chambers" (1967, p. 3).

If the United Kingdom has, nevertheless, a large number of lawyers compared to many other modern societies, especially in comparison to countries on the European continent, the explanation is at least in part found in the complexities of the common law, with its greater reliance on judicial precedent compared to civil law systems. E. J. Cohn, who has practiced both in Germany and in England, states, "A question which would require a common law practitioner to search in books of reference for one or several quarters of an hour could be solved by his continental colleague completely satisfactorily in as many minutes" (E. J. Cohn, 1960, p. 587).

The large number of lawyers in the United States can now be understood better—by applying the same considerations discussed earlier to the special conditions in this country. A highly developed society, it has a legal system that shares the complications of the common law with England but that is further complicated by strong decentralization, a less-than-perfect coordination of different jurisdictions, the judicial review of legislation and a specially strong tradition of judge-made law (see Huntington, 1966). Furthermore, the ethnic and regional heterogeneity of cultural traditions, egalitarian values militating against deference toward elites, and the fact that America's elites were from the beginning bourgeois elites with commercial interests rather than landed aristocratic elites suggest that law should play a prominent role as a means of social control in this country; and, indeed, "three great foreign observers—Burke, de Tocqueville, and Bryce—noted successively how legal-minded the Americans were" (Lerner, 1957, p. 429).

The characterization as "legal-minded" also seems to fit German society, although the sources of such orientations toward the law in political and socioeconomic history differ considerably from the American case. Yet the statistics typically quoted, including those in Table 1, indicate a drastic disparity in the number of lawyers. The more detailed comparison of the German and the American bar, however, shows that the figures usually reported about Germany are thoroughly misleading (Table 2). They include for the United States all "lawyers," but for Germany only lawyers admitted to court practice as attorneys, leaving out judges, prosecuting attorneys, and lawyers in government administration, as well as lawyers working in private employment who are not admitted to court practice. It so happens that, while three out of every four American lawyers are in private practice, only one quarter of the German legal profession fits this description, which for most Americans defines the meaning of the term *lawyer*. Once all German lawyers are taken into account, the size of the two professions in rela-

Table 2. Size of the Legal Profession and Its Major Subgroups
in Germany and the United States.

Group	United States, 1960		West Germany, 1961	
Graduates of law schools	*330,000-340,000		93,600	
Members of the bar (lawyers reporting to major law directory in the United States and those qualified by second state examination in Germany)	252,385		*57,000-59,000	
Lawyers in private practice (excluding syndic-attorneys)	192,353	Percent of whole bar 76%	13,000	Percent of whole bar 22-23%
Lawyers in judicial office	8,180	3%	12,000	20-21%
Lawyers in government service (including prosecuting attorneys)	25,621	10%	*18,000-19,000	30-33%
Lawyers in private employment	25,198	10%	*13,000-18,000	22-30%

Note: Starred figures are estimates. All figures are given for an indication of rough proportions only.

Source: Rueschemeyer (1973, pp. 32-33).

tion to population turns out to be much more similar: Instead of using more than four times as many lawyers, the United States has in fact only 30 to 40 percent more lawyers than Germany. The remaining difference can probably be explained by the more complex character of the American legal and political system.

The extremely important fact that at least half of the German lawyers are government-employed civil servants, judges, prosecutors, or administrators, in contrast to only 10 to 15 percent of the American bar will occupy us later. Before this discussion of some implications of the varying number of lawyers

is concluded, however, we have to raise explicitly a fundamental, yet very troublesome question: How is the term *lawyer*
defined in these statistics? Major omissions—such as that of 70
percent of the German lawyers—aside, the usual criterion is
some form of official certification as lawyer typically linked to
formal legal education. When compared to a definition in terms
of work performed, this definition is likely to err in two directions at the same time, and without detailed study of each
country it is very difficult to determine the extent of the error.

A definition in terms of certification includes in many
countries persons who are registered officially as lawyers but do
not practice law at all or do so only marginally. It is often asserted about the Latin American countries that many persons
holding law degrees do not in fact practice law. This pattern is
to be expected where the educational system does not differentiate law from training in the social sciences and business or
where legal studies serve as the conventional training of the
elites. As for the Latin American countries, the evidence is
mixed. Colombia, where less than one third of all law degree
holders practice law, contrasts with Chile where the proportion
of those never practicing is negligible (Lowenstein, 1970, pp.
30-32). Table 2 indicates that both in the United States and in
West Germany the number of law school graduates is considerably larger than the number of those who are registered as lawyers in a narrower sense. Even the latter group contains many
who engage in other activities than legal work. Thus the work of
many German lawyers in private employment and in government administration, where lawyers hold between two thirds
and three quarters of the higher civil service posts (Rueschemeyer, 1973, p. 35), bears little relation to the law. With some
exaggeration, Dahrendorf has called the German law faculties
the "functional equivalent of English public schools"—training
institutions for the country's elite (Dahrendorf, 1964). In many
countries, lawyers in private practice engage partially or even
primarily in pursuits other than the law, such as work in real
estate, insurance, or involvements in the business affairs of their
clients.[3] While all of these conditions lead to an overestimation
of the size of the legal profession, the legal training of the law-

yers not practicing law in a narrow definition is worth remembering when the overall demand for legal services is considered; it is likely to make some professional consultations unnecessary and shorten others considerably.

On the other hand, there are in most societies various categories of people whose work is quite closely concerned with the law, although they do not hold a certificate as a lawyer. Accountants, tax consultants, debt collectors, title insurance companies, architects, insurance salesmen, bankers, and union officials often in one country do work, as a minor or major part of their own specialized pursuits, that would be considered as the practice of law in another country. A fuller understanding of the division of labor between these different occupations and the forces that shape it is one of the most urgent tasks of the comparative study of legal practice. Disputes over "unauthorized practice of law" focus only on contested areas in the context of what has become established practice in a given country.[4]

Law work done by persons not officially recognized as lawyers is also a factor that explains the very small size of the official legal profession in some countries. In Japan's two-tiered system of legal education, university law departments train proportionately about as many students as American law schools, while the advanced Legal Training and Research Institute accepts only 500 students per year. Many of the law-trained individuals who did not graduate from the institute and who are not formally members of the bar nevertheless work as legal advisers or at any rate make incidental use of their training (McKay, 1977; Hattori, 1963). In addition, there are various specialized occupations concerned with legal work but not recognized as lawyers (Henderson, 1968-1969). Similarly, in England there are at least two groups worth mentioning here. "Some 16,000 (lay) magistrates had for generations administered criminal law and parts of the civil law on the cheap" (Abel-Smith and Stevens, 1967, p. 464), while professionally trained judges number only in the hundreds, including those who serve on administrative tribunals. In regard to the number of solicitors and barristers, it has been pointed out that the managing clerks of law

offices can be considered "functional equivalents of lawyers";
including law clerks working on the legal staffs of public and
private institutions, the number of these legal workers, estimated as at least 29,000, is larger than the total number of barristers and solicitors combined (Johnstone and Hopson, 1967,
pp. 360, n. 13, 401, 441).

Clearly these facts can go a long way in explaining the
comparatively small number of officially recognized lawyers in
Japan and England, although not enough is known about the
relative contribution of paralegal personnel and related occupations in other countries to come to a conclusive judgment. The
problems of a functional definition of law work must be resolved and conceptually adequate evidence must be made available before interpretations of the varying incidence of "lawyers" can be put on firm factual grounds. Socioeconomic
development, the relative importance of nonlegal social controls, and the complexity of the legal system are without doubt
major determinants of the demand for professional legal work.
For this conclusion, there are solid theoretical grounds as well
as persuasive, although partial, empirical analyses, but the
weight of each factor and the role it plays in a given country
cannot be determined without more adequate evidence and
analysis of who performs which legal services under different
socioeconomic and political conditions.

Lawyers in Premodern Societies

If lawyers are specialists dealing with the rules and procedures concerning governmental social control, they are a relatively recent figure in human history. Most simple societies were
neither wealthy enough to support such specialists, nor did they
have a need for complex rules governing the public use of coercion,[5] given their low level of structural differentiation and the
effectiveness of nonlegal social controls. Full-scale agriculture,
the development of towns with a substantial division of labor,
and the use of writing seem necessary conditions for the first
emergence of legal specialists. Beyond these general conditions,
there were two developments that were crucial for the appearance

of legal practitioners resembling the modern legal profession—the growth of market exchange and the rise of bureaucratic government. The same two developments and their interrelations also prove to be of great consequence in later phases for the areas of work, the organization, and the outlook of the legal profession in a given country and historical period.[6]

The importance of bureaucratic government and of market exchange are easily made plausible in theoretical terms. Bureaucratic centralization of power displaces other social controls (Diamond, 1971), creates formal and systematized legal norms, and provides the machinery for the enforcement of judicial decisions. The beginnings of Roman law go back to the Roman city-state, but it matured under bureaucratic rule in Imperial Rome. Broadly similar developments have been found in other historic bureaucratic empires (Eisenstadt, 1963). Bureaucratic rule favors the development of legal expertise, although primarily in the roles of administrator, judge, counselor to lay judges, and law teachers. The growth of private legal counseling may be stifled if various bureaucratic agencies become closely involved in the affairs of groups and institutions outside of the government proper. This seems to be the major explanation of the fact that ancient China never had a private legal profession.[7]

However, groups and institutions independent of the central bureaucracy may develop a strong interest in using the coercion machinery of the state for their own purposes. Agreements between them will be "consciously and rationally adapted to the expected reaction of the judiciary" (Rheinstein, 1954, p. 72), and this creates a commanding need for legal counsel loyal to the interests of private parties. Growth of market exchange seems to be the major factor encouraging such a development. Contractual market relations that are not embedded in kinship and communal ties and not directly protected and sponsored by political authorities, are vulnerable and in need of legal guarantees if they are to be viable in the long run. It is the conjunction, then, of bureaucratic rule establishing a body of legal norms as well as a functioning enforcement machinery *and* the need for legal guarantees in shifting and highly specific market exchanges separated to some degree from kinship and community controls that brings about the earliest development of a full-fledged legal profession.

The two broad conditions are interrelated in complex ways. On the one hand, some development of market exchange appears to be necessary for the emergence of bureaucratic rule. Significant segments of a society have to be freed from traditional fixations of personal and material resources to make a rational allocation of resources for the new forms of government possible (Weber, 1968; Eisenstadt, 1963). On the other hand, the bureaucratic rules have a strong interest not only in curbing the powers of tradition but also in keeping the new social forces under control. Eisenstadt concludes, from his analysis of many historic bureaucratic empires, "Broadly speaking, the rulers' general objectives in the legal field were to minimize the legal autonomy of traditional groups and strata (for example, the aristocracy and the urban patriciate) and to advance the development of more complex and differentiated legal institutions and activities. At the same time, however, the rulers wished to maintain control over these institutions and to keep them, as far as possible, from autonomous growth" (1963, pp. 137-138).

Imperial China and early modern England indicate the range of possible outcomes. In Imperial China, where private commerce and nonagricultural production were of low formal standing and subject to close supervision and competition by government bodies, a private bar never became established. By contrast, in England there were many obstacles and greater resistance to so strong and pervasive a role of central authorities, and an autonomously organized bar played in the seventeenth century a crucial role in the limitation of government (Eusden, 1958). In conjunction with other factors, to be sure, it was the relative timing of bureaucratization and commercialization that shaped these contrasting outcomes.

The administration of law in agrarian societies, supported by a limited development of market exchange and bureaucratic government, can be viewed as a special case of "partial modernization" (Rueschemeyer, 1976). This applies not only to the early historic states but also, in varying degree, to contemporary developing countries. Typically, there are serious discontinuities between the core of the official legal order, which has been rationalized to some extent, and the operating modes of many other institutions and groups—of family and kinship, of rural communities, or of landlord-peasant relations. Not only is the centrally espoused law often seen as an alien system imposed by distant authorities, but its rationales do not fit with the realities of a less commercialized, less individualistic, and less specialized life. While it certainly would be wrong to think of peasant communities as harmonious and solidary groups, relations within them are highly personalized, cover a broad spectrum of mutual concerns, and, in contrast to passing and specialized contractual relations, derive a measure of stability from this personal and multifunctional character. Rights and obligations are, in addition, often tied to birth and to membership in given, "ascriptive" collectivities and are less subject to individual agreement. Relations between such groups and, generally, contractual relations not embedded in traditional social controls often constitute occasions for extreme distrust and for exploitation. "The specific ethics of the marketplace is alien to [feudal strata]. Once and for all they conceive of commerce, as does any rural community of neighbors, as an activity in which the sole question is who will cheat whom" (Rheinstein, 1954, p. 194). And legal roles—of partner to a contract, litigant, legal counsel, and judge—are only very tenuously differentiated from one's personal status in the broader system of privilege, wealth, and power.

These conditions, which can be observed in eighteenth-century Prussia (Rueschemeyer, 1973, pp. 147-153), as well as in nineteenth-century Egypt (Ziadeh, 1968) or in contemporary India (B. S. Cohn, 1959, 1965; Kidder, 1973, 1974), have pervasive consequences for the administration of justice and the role of lawyers. Litigation often does not serve the resolution of a conflict but constitutes just another means to fight the opponent. Interminable delays are common and force a settlement favorable to the party that has the resources to outwait the other. "In societies in which the law on the books does not reflect fairly accurately the community's accepted and operative values . . . individuals turn to law and lawyers when their behavior and their values are not those that are generally accepted. The law and the lawyer provide official sanction for such deviant behavior" (Von Mehren, 1965, p. 1184).

The administration of justice under these conditions tends to be shot through with particularistic favoritism. Lawyers are as important for their personal connections and influence as for their knowledge of the law. They find themselves in the precarious role of mediating between different worlds, subject to contradictory expectations and pressures but also, because they can play one world against the other, in a position to take advantage, to cheat, and to exploit.[8]

In these same conditions we also find the explanation for formal divisions of legal practitioners into different occupational subgroups, which is characteristic of most traditional and transitional societies. Such divisions, of which the English distinction between barrister and solicitor is the best-known example surviving in more developed countries, give the authorities greater control over at least part of the bar. At the same time, a chain of interconnected roles reduces the moral distance between subcultures to be bridged by any one practitioner. The bases of such subdivisions are many. Distinctions between advocates in court, counsel outside of court, and advisers close to the party who help approach the official lawyer ("touts," in India), as well as those between specialists in different traditions of law, where disparate legal systems exist side by side, combine in various ways with differences in the social background, the type of training, and the clientele of various groups of lawyers. That this diversity of private practitioners has in modern societies largely given way to a unitary profession with functional specialization in different areas of law attests to the generally closer integration between law and the social order under modern conditions.

Some Contrasts Between Modern Societies

Modern industrial societies are vastly more complex than agrarian societies. The correspondingly greater problems of integration and the special needs for predictability and flexibility

give a much broader scope to the use of contract and bureaucratic organization. Therefore, the role of law as a means of
social control is much larger in modern societies. At the same
time, prevailing attitudes and values give more support to legal
forms of regulation and dispute solution, and the discontinuities
discussed earlier have a much reduced impact on the administration of justice.

However, there are substantial differences among more
developed countries. As we have seen, problems of integration
transcending the effectiveness of nonlegal social controls are not
equally prevalent in all countries at similar levels of socioeconomic development. Furthermore, law work is not necessarily done by lawyers, and the relative role of the different
branches of the legal profession varies considerably from one
country to another. It appears that much of these variations can
be explained by the relative importance for social integration of
centralized administration, public *and* private, and of decentralized contractual agreements. Furthermore, the different
paths of development, including the relative phasing of advances
in bureaucratization and commercialization, have created historical traditions and organizational structure that may resist
the pressure of later changes. There are multiple ways of dealing
with the same functional problems, and not all functional problems are dealt with equally well under different conditions.

The complexity of the resulting patterns can be appreciated if we consider that in the USSR *and* West Germany
roughly similar percentages—just over half—of the lawyers work
in government employment as judges, prosecutors, government
administrators, and law teachers, while the corresponding percentages for the United States and England are much lower—not
more than 15 percent.[9] If one naively conceives of the USSR as
a monolithic political-administrative organization, it must come
as a surprise to find that nearly half of all Soviet lawyers in
cooperatively organized private practice are advocates or are in
the service of economic enterprises. The fact is that even this
highly centralized socioeconomic system involves transactions
and disputes between individuals and organizations for which
contractual agreements, legal regulations, and litigation are
necessary tools.[10] At the same time, it seems clear that legal

work for private parties flourishes most where the regulative role of government is largely indirect, where routine administration, including the administration of justice is differentiated from the political process, and where social integration is achieved in large measure through market exchange, autonomous voluntary associations, and contractual relations in general. Freedom of contract within wide limits and the institutionalization of formal, impersonal modes of conflict settlement generate high levels of demand for partisan legal expertise. This is illustrated by the high proportions of American and English lawyers in private practice and private employment.

If, however, the distribution of lawyers among the different branches of the profession is largely a function of the relative importance of bureaucratic coordination and decentralized decision making by individuals and organizations, how can we explain that West Germany, a capitalist society with a market economy, has nearly as high a proportion of its lawyers in government employment as the Soviet Union? Here the legacy of the past is of major importance. As in other continental European countries, bureaucratic rationalization of government, rather than autonomous entrepreneurial activities, spearheaded the modernization of society. University legal education was primarily devoted to the training of royal judges and administrators, and the government regulated and narrowly circumscribed the role of private legal counsel. From 1793 to 1879, Prussian attorneys in private practice had a status similar to that of civil servants. Until recently, lawyers had a virtual monopoly on higher civil service posts in government administration. By contrast, American public administration developed relatively late, when different relevant professions had emerged and government operations required a wider variety of specialized expertise. Thus American government lawyers typically work as legal specialists side by side with other professionals. In litigation, German judges play a far more dominant role than their counterparts in this country (Kaplan, Von Mehren, and Schaefer, 1958), and the systematization of legal norms through statutory enactment, another product of central bureaucratic rule, has simplified the work of attorneys in and out of court.

Thus a strong involvement of German lawyers in government, in the diffuse and varied roles of administrators and in the specific ones as judge, prosecutor and legal counsel, corresponds to a more narrowly delimited part played by advocates in court.

Equally important for the character of the legal profession in a country is the form and scope of its involvement with private business, the major consumer of legal services in capitalist countries. Until the late nineteenth century, legal services for business focused largely on litigation even in the economically most advanced countries. This changed with such developments as the growth of large and variously interrelated corporate bureaucracies, increasing taxation affecting a large variety of business decisions, government regulation of various aspects of the economy, and the rise of labor unions, employers associations, and labor law. The legal profession responded to these changes in different ways, conditioned by past work patterns, organization, and outlook, and the response made for lasting differences in the division of labor within the profession and between the bar and other business-related professions.

More than in any other country, the bar in the United States became involved in these matters as well as in related business decisions beyond the immediate legal sphere. Unencumbered by a strong professional organization or government control and in their outlook akin to the new dominant groups, American lawyers were well prepared for this expansion, their elite having shaped and continuing to shape, through argument before appellate courts, a legal order favorable to capitalist business (Horwitz, 1977; Hurst, 1950, 1960; Twiss, 1942). In the process, large law firms with internal specialization grew up. The bar in large cities became intensely stratified, corresponding to the differential wealth and prestige of the clientele and to very uneven legal education (Carlin, 1962, 1966; Ladinsky, 1963). The development of house counsel employed in law departments within corporations was slow, limited by the growth of large law firms, although the proportion of privately employed lawyers is now growing.

In Germany, employment of lawyers in business corporations is more common than in the United States (Table 2), although little is known about the early development of house counsel and more diffuse roles of lawyers in business. Business-employed lawyers were rather sharply separated from the regular bar in private practice and seen with antagonism by its more conservative elements. In addition, private practitioners lost much law-related business to other professions such as tax consultants and accountants. These shifts in the division of labor with other occupations were accelerated during the National Socialist regime by the expulsion of Jewish lawyers and the change toward an administered economy.[11] However, the comparative reserve of many German lawyers toward the world of business has deeper roots in a strong civil service orientation of long standing that is grounded in past history as well as in contemporary patterns of education and recruitment (Rueschemeyer, 1973).

That English lawyers have a relatively minor involvement in business matters and other potentially relevant concerns in modern society has already been noted. Part of the explanation seems to lie in the resistance to court reform that has "led a large segment of the industrial and commercial community to abandon the courts and establish their own tribunals for settling disputes" (Abel-Smith and Stevens, 1967, p. 459). While such tendencies are found in all modern societies,[12] they seem particularly strong in England. Abel-Smith and Stevens suggest that part of the explanation lies in the tremendous respect for the judiciary in Britain and the powerful interests of the senior branch of the profession, the bar from which the judiciary is recruited, in the continuation of inherited and favorable arrangements (Abel-Smith and Stevens, 1967, pp. 460-468). The very strong institutionalization of an established pattern has prevented adjustments to changing conditions.

While the virtually exclusive concentration of Indian lawyers on litigation may in part be a consequence of importing traditions and work patterns of the English legal profession and in particular the English bar ("Lawyers in Developing Countries," 1968-1969; Kidder, 1973, 1974), a much more limited role of lawyers than that of the American bar is the modal pattern in most countries. Thus the wisdom of using the activities of American lawyers as a yardstick for policy recommendations in other countries (for example, Lowenstein, 1970; Von Mehren, 1965) may be questionable, quite aside from more general doubts about the value of American models for legal assistance in developing countries (Trubek and Galanter, 1974; see also Goldstein and Donaldson, 1977, for a critical analysis of "exporting professionalism" in medicine).

The Bar and the Dominant Interests

Lawyers tend to be associated with the dominant interests in a country—the more so, the more successful the lawyers are. The technically most interesting as well as the most lucrative legal work derives from the problems of the upper strata and the most complex organizations in a society. This work often involves confidences as well as interest representation not easily trusted to counsel whose basic loyalty to the client is in doubt. These considerations explain why in most bars there is considerable internal stratification, although even the run-of-the-mill lawyer tends to work for middle-class, not lower-class, interests, if for no other reason than the cost of his services. Looking at the matter from a different angle, it would be surprising if access to the enforcement machinery of the state were equally available to all citizens rather than being aligned with the general structure of power, status, and privilege. This hypothesis remains basically valid even if there are great variations between countries in the inequality of access to legal services.

The particular articulation of the role of the legal profession with dominant interests can take many different forms, in part because of varying alliances and antagonisms between different dominant groups, and it shapes the public leadership exercised by the bar. The classic picture of the nineteenth century was an alignment, especially of the bar in private practice, with the rising commercial and industrial interests, a tendency that led in countries such as Prussia to countervailing attempts of the royal government to keep the bar under close government control. In developing countries, lawyers were often leaders of national anticolonial movements representing at the same time liberal causes of reform, although they typically lost much of their leadership when national autonomy was established and problems of socioeconomic development had to be faced (Ziadeh, 1968; "Lawyers in Developing Countries," 1968-1969). The political role of lawyers is generally greater where class differences and antagonisms are subdued by nationalist and ethnic or racial sentiments or where the party structure and the legal framework of electoral politics discourage class-based politics. Under these conditions, the particular affinity of law work and politics favors election of lawyers as political representatives.[13]

The actual influence of lawyers as public leaders depends on the comparative power and influence of other elite groups. Thus the impact of the bar's elite on public affairs in this country was largest before the Civil War when large corporations, other organized interests, and a stronger government bureaucracy had not yet developed, and in the Soviet Union lawyers exert whatever influence they have through the pursuit of specialized legal work only (Barry and Berman, 1968). Alignment with dominant interests and a professional concern with procedural rather than substantive justice also explain why modern revolutions typically have been hostile to the legal profession and often tried to abolish professionally trained and autonomously organized partisan counsel. If this role was invariably reinstituted, this proved that partisan counsel is indispensable for legal forms of conflict settlement, but the relatively brief interruptions constituted a break of continuity and meant that alignments with the previous status quo were severed or at least modified.[14]

Law as a Profession

"The practice of law is a profession." This statement makes multiple claims—that legal practitioners are competent in their field, that they are loyal to their clients' interests while at the same time devoted to the legal order, that the profession as a group will ensure competence and service orientation through organized self-regulation, and that therefore lawyers deserve trust, respect, and a comfortable income as well as autonomy from lay control and protection against lay competition. As in other professions, these claims and assurances are offered as a solution to the dilemma posed by expert services: While important interests are at stake, the nonexpert client has no way of judging and controlling the services he receives. The "bargain" offered as a solution to the dilemma is highly favorable to the professions. It gives them a monopoly over their claimed area of work and freedom from lay control, as well as handsome material and nonmaterial rewards. Whether the interests of the clientele or of the wider society are safeguarded depends on the informal and formal controls within the profession.

Recent writing (for example, Freidson, 1970; Rueschemeyer, 1964) has been critical of the functionalist model of professional autonomy. This was paralleled by more widespread discontent with professional privileges, which has a history of recurrent eruptions in this country. Professional self-regulation often functions primarily to protect the reputation of the professions and gives little assurance to the clientele and the wider public. The privileges of the professions do not rest so much on the fulfillment of an assumed "bargain" between a group of practitioners and the wider society as on the power and influence inherent in expertise, on the general privileges of upper-middle-class groups, and on the political gains made by professions as interest groups. In a historical and comparative perspective, the model of professional self-regulation represents by no means the only arrangement for the delivery and the control of expert services (Johnson, 1972; Rueschemeyer, 1973, pp. 13-19). In modern societies, bureaucratic controls exercised by client organizations or governmental bodies are of particular importance, and the political function of the model of professional autonomy and self-regulation is precisely to fend off such limitations of the professions' freedom and power.

The professional independence of lawyers has a hard core that rests on two foundations. First, their knowledge of legal norms and procedures is indispensable for dealing with some integration problems in all modern societies, including the most politically centralized ones. Second, the requirements of dispute settlement give a certain independence to roles with loyalty both to the parties of a conflict and to the legal framework as well as the public policy it serves. Yet either side of this delicate balance may put the independence of legal practitioners into jeopardy. The clients of lawyers, typically drawn from the advantaged strata, are often more knowledgeable about their problems and certainly less incapacitated than the doctor's patients. Furthermore, organizations as clients often command tremendous resources. Under certain conditions, client influence may undercut the public-service commitments of lawyers and subvert the interests of justice and public policy. Conversely, public controls over the legal profession may become so powerful as to endanger the lawyer's service to individual rights and conflict settlement. A cohesive culture and organization of the bar can help to counterbalance these forces even if, and perhaps especially if, it also supports socioeconomic interests of the profession.

"In the United States, the state's control over the lawyer is weak and diffuse.... one danger is that the lawyer will tend to neglect the interests of society in favor of the exclusive interests of his clients.... the urge to professionalize ... is necessary precisely because state control is so weak that internal (psychological, social, and professional) controls are of grave importance"; in the Soviet Union, "the need for professionalism arises out of precisely the opposite phenomenon. Here state control is so unlimited and (at least potentially) so unrestrained that the lawyer is gravely tempted to neglect the interests of his clients in order to advance the interests of society ... the lawyer needs professionalization as a bulwark against interference with what he considers proper application of his skill in a professional manner" (Friedman and Zile, 1964, pp. 35-36). Compared to the situation of the American bar at the turn of the century and the Soviet bar immediately after the revolution and under Stalinism, professionalization has served in both countries some of those purposes, although the differences are still far too great to speak of a convergence of patterns.[15]

The varied and diverse character of legal work raises difficult problems for the attainment of professional autonomy and self-realization. The second of the two major bases of professional independence, grounded in the requirements of conflict settlement, supports primarily the independence of judges and lawyers in private practice, especially those concerned with litigation, and extends only to a lesser extent to legal practitioners employed in government and business. If these branches of the profession are separated from each other with little overarching solidarity and if in addition many tasks are met in legal departments of public and private organizations rather than by the bar in private practice, the potential for outside control over large parts of the bar increases considerably. This is illustrated by the patterns of legal work in the USSR and in Germany in contrast to the United States.

The American bar, on the other hand, comprises so much diversity that strong professional self-regulation is difficult to attain. American lawyers, those in private practice as well as the minority in other employment but with strong orientations toward the bar in private practice, are involved in very different types of work, develop loyalties to different clienteles, and occupy correspondingly different positions in the internal stratification of the bar as well as in the structure of power in community and nation. Not surprisingly, this heterogeneity is reinforced by diverse social backgrounds and the very uneven professional training generally characteristic of education in this country. These conditions are particularly strong in the larger cities (Carlin, 1962, 1966; Handler, 1967). They strain professional solidarity, reduce identification with the profession, make the bar more open to outside influences especially from the world of business, and severely limit the possibilities of professional self-regulation, informal as well as formal (Rueschemeyer, 1964, 1973).

A strong legal profession can be a counterbalancing element protecting justice and equity as well as individual freedom against overwhelming government control and one-sided private power. Yet the conditions for this are very complex and vary from country to country. Aside from a mix of public regulation, client influence, and autonomous professional self-regulation, it is above all broad access of the lower strata to legal advice and service that would strengthen such a mediating role.

One implication of our brief review is that the role of the bar is closely related to a country's political and socioeconomic structure. Autonomous action of the bar can modify the impact of these conditions, but it is unlikely to alter them fundamentally on its own.

Notes

1. See Horwitz (1977) for an important historical study that stresses the role of the judiciary. Twiss (1942) analyzes for a later period the very important role played by legal counsel in developments of constitutional law. That certain parties have a much better chance to "play for rule gain" while others cannot afford to sacrifice a given case for such strategies is stressed by Galanter (1974).

2. They point out that constitutional norms, including the protection of civil liberties, rest on political and social rather than legal guarantees, that administrative law developed late and to a limited extent only, and that labor relations disputes rarely are settled by adjudication.

3. Carlin reports the extent of the latter to be substantial for the bar in New York City (1966, p. 8) and among individual practitioners in Chicago (1962, pp. 114-115). For Chile, see Lowenstein (1970, pp. 30-31).

4. One of the few good analyses of parts of the problem is given by Johnstone and Hopson (1967). The following generalization gives a glimpse of some of the forces involved: "It appears axiomatic in the United States that whenever a particular task or combination of tasks performed by lawyers grows to mass volume proportions and the mass demand promises to continue, laymen will eventually take over performance of these tasks unless deterred from doing so by unauthorized-practice laws. In part this results from more efficient lay specialization and standardization and more aggressive advertising and solicitation. But in part, too, it results from lawyers' reluctance to counter lay competition by cutting fees or increasing quality" (pp. 157-158). It should be noted that lawyers in most other countries have a narrower field of work than American lawyers in private practice. Some of the underlying conditions are discussed for England by Abel-Smith and Stevens (1967) and for

Germany, where the areas of work claimed by the bar are broader than in England yet narrower than in the United States, by Rueschemeyer (1973).

5. The implied definition of law goes back to Max Weber (Rheinstein, 1954). For a discussion of criticisms of such a "coercive definition," see Gibbs (1968).

6. In this and the following section, I rely in part on ideas and materials developed more fully elsewhere (Rueschemeyer, 1973, chaps. 1 and 5). On the development of private legal counsel, see Schwartz and Miller (1964) and Rueschemeyer (1973, pp. 1-7).

7. On the marginal role of private legal counseling, see Wigmore (1928, p. 178) and Ch'ü (1965, pp. 284-285). On the Chinese bureaucracy's involvement in the legal sphere, see Eisenstadt (1963, especially appendix, table 1, pp. 404-411). On the absence of full-fledged private legal counsel in classical Hindu law, see Rocher (1968-1969).

8. The primary cause of these discontinuities is probably found less in particular attitudes, occupational traditions, and cultural values than in the peculiar structural arrangements and in the opportunities they open to the different participants. Thus they will be found under comparable circumstances in more developed countries, too. Kidder has applied insights about litigation as protracted negotiation rather than dispute settlement and about strained lawyer-client relations gained in India (1973) to the relations between lawyers and poor as well as radical clients in the United States (Kidder, 1977).

9. See Barry and Berman (1968, p. 11) for the USSR. In the late 1960s, there were an estimated 101,000 lawyers in the USSR, or about 440 for every million inhabitants. Lawyers working for government enterprises have been counted in the 40 to 50 percent "assisting individuals and organizations in the exercise of their legal rights and representing them in civil and criminal litigation" (Barry and Berman, 1968, p. 11). For Germany and the United States, see Table 2 of this chapter; for England and Wales, see Johnstone and Hopson (1967, p. 360, n. 13), and Abel-Smith and Stevens (1967, pp. 342, 443, 444, 462).

10. "Most of the work of the Soviet advocate consists of giving legal advice and legal representation to individuals in civil matters. . . . Generally the subject matter involved . . . is about

the same as that in most American civil cases—personal injury litigation, contractual claims, inheritance disputes, family law problems, and the like . . . [though of course] there are no cases involving corporation-shareholder relations since no economic organizations in the USSR issue stock. . . . advocates sometimes represent state economic enterprises in contract disputes" (Barry and Berman, 1968, p. 13). However, Soviet advocates cannot represent clients before administrative agencies, and their role in court proceedings is more limited than that of the American attorney, a contrast similar to differences between the United States and Germany (Barry and Berman, 1968, pp. 14-15; see also Kaplan, von Mehren, and Schaefer, 1958).

The main functions of "jurisconsults" in economic enterprises are "(1) to advise and represent management in legal matters connected with the enterprise's relationships with superior and subordinate organizations, other enterprises, and individual workers; (2) to give legal advice to labor unions, comrades' courts, and other groups in the enterprise; (3) to 'visa,' or certify as legal, internal regulations issued by management; and (4) to report to the enterprise's superior agencies any violations of law committed by the enterprise" (Barry and Berman, 1968, p. 18). The role of the jurisconsult is closely related to the independence of enterprises. "When managerial independence has been stressed and the role of contracts between state enterprises enhanced, as in the period since 1955, jurisconsults have gained substantially in numbers and importance" (Barry and Berman, 1968, p. 18).

11. For brief analyses of the German bar in the "Third Reich," see Willig (1976) and Rueschemeyer (1973, pp. 179-183).

12. See, for instance, Macaulay (1963) on the limited use of formal contracts by American business firms.

13. Lawyers have the largest representation in political life in the United States. The two major explanations seem to lie in the closer linkage between legal offices and the political process and in the fact that voting is in this country less class-based than in many other modern societies. For a comparative analysis of these determinants of the political role of lawyers in the United States, Canada, Great Britain, Australia, and West Germany, see Rueschemeyer (1973, pp. 71-75). See also Pedersen (1972). Of the large literature on lawyers in American politics, see Schlesinger (1957) and Eulau and Sprague (1964).

14. In the classic revolutions of France and Russia, we find intense hostility toward the bar in private practice and attempts to radically restructure legal services. The German National Socialists also displayed intense hostility toward lawyers (Willig, 1976). Extensive "purges" of the bar accompanied the American Revolution as well as the rise of the royal bureaucratic government in eighteenth-century Prussia (Rueschemeyer, 1973, pp. 149-150, 156-157).

15. On the American bar, see Hurst (1950), Pound (1953), and Auerbach (1976). On the very interesting changes of the Soviet bar in the two generations since the revolution, see Hazard (1960), Berman (1963), Friedman and Zile (1964), and Barry and Berman (1968) as examples of a much larger literature. On the much stronger, although not complete, convergence in organization and outlook between the German and the American bar since the nineteenth century, see Rueschemeyer (1973, chap. 5).

References

Abel-Smith, B., and Stevens, R. *Lawyers and the Courts: A Sociological Study of the English Legal System, 1750-1965.* London: Heinemann, 1967.

Auerbach, J. S. *Unequal Justice: Lawyers and Social Change in Modern America.* New York: Oxford University Press, 1976.

Barry, D. D., and Berman, H. J. "The Soviet Legal Profession." *Harvard Law Review,* 1968, *82,* 1-41.

Berman, H. J. *Justice in the USSR: An Interpretation of Soviet Law.* (rev. ed.) Cambridge, Mass.: Harvard University Press, 1963.

Black, D. *The Behavior of Law.* New York: Academic Press, 1976.

Carlin, J. E. *Lawyers on Their Own: A Study of Individual Practitioners in Chicago.* New Brunswick, N.J.: Rutgers University Press, 1962.

Carlin, J. E. *Lawyers' Ethics: A Survey of the New York City Bar.* New York: Russell Sage Foundation, 1966.

Ch'ü, T. *Law and Society in Traditional China.* The Hague: Mouton, 1965.

Cohn, B. S. "Some Notes on Law and Social Change in India." *Economic Development and Cultural Change*, 1959, *5*, 79-93.

Cohn, B. S. "Anthropological Notes on Disputes and Law in India." *American Anthropologist*, 1965, *67* (6, pt. 2), 82-122.

Cohn, E. J. "The German Attorney—Experiences with a Unified Profession." *International and Comparative Law Quarterly*, 1960, *9*, 580-599.

Cohn, E. J. "The German Attorney—Experiences with a Unified Profession." *International and Comparative Law Quarterly*, 1961, *10*, 103-122.

Dahrendorf, R. "The Education of an Elite: Law Faculties and the German Upper Class." *Transactions of the Fifth World Congress of Sociology*. Vol. 3. Louvain: International Sociological Association, 1964.

Diamond, S. "The Rule of Law Versus the Order of Custom." In R. P. Wolff (Ed.), *The Rule of Law*. New York: Simon & Schuster, 1971.

Eisenstadt, S. N. *The Political System of Empires*. New York: Free Press, 1963.

Eulau, H., and Sprague, J. D. *Lawyers in Politics: A Study in Professional Convergence*. Indianapolis: Bobbs-Merrill, 1964.

Eusden, J. D. *Puritans, Lawyers and Politics in Early Seventeenth Century England*. New Haven, Conn.: Yale University Press, 1958.

Freidson, E. *Profession of Medicine: A Study of the Sociology of Applied Knowledge*. New York: Dodd, Mead, 1970.

Friedman, L. M., and Zile, Z. L. "Soviet Legal Profession: Recent Developments in Law and Practice." *Wisconsin Law Review*, 1964, 32-77.

Galanter, M. "Introduction: The Study of the Indian Legal Profession." *Law and Society Review*, 1968-1969, *3*, 201-217.

Galanter, M. "Why the 'Haves' Come Out Ahead: Speculations on the Limits of Legal Change." *Law and Society Review*, 1974, *9*, 95-160.

Gibbs, J. P. "Definitions of Law and Empirical Questions." *Law and Society Review*, 1968, *2*, 429-446.

Goldstein, M. S., and Donaldson, P. J. "The Professionalization of Medicine in Thailand." Paper presented at 72nd annual meeting of the American Sociological Association, Chicago, September 1977.

Handler, J. F. *The Lawyer and His Community. The Practicing Bar in a Middle-Sized City.* Madison: University of Wisconsin Press, 1967.

Hattori, T., assisted by R. W. Rabinowitz. "The Legal Profession in Japan: Its Historical Development and Present State." In A. T. Von Mehren (Ed.), *Law in Japan: The Legal Order in a Changing Society.* Cambridge, Mass.: Harvard University Press, 1963.

Hazard, J. N. *Settling Disputes in Soviet Society: The Formative Years of Legal Institutions.* New York: Columbia University Press, 1960.

Henderson, D. F. "Japanese Lawyers: Types and Roles in the Legal Profession (Abstract)." *Law and Society Review,* 1968-1969, *3,* 411-413.

Horwitz, M. J. *The Transformation of American Law, 1780-1860.* Cambridge, Mass.: Harvard University Press, 1977.

Huntington, S. P. "Political Modernization: America vs. Europe." *World Politics,* 1966, *18,* 378-414.

Hurst, J. W. *The Growth of American Law: The Law Makers.* Boston: Little, Brown, 1950.

Hurst, J. W. *Law and Social Process in United States History.* Ann Arbor: University of Michigan Law School, 1960.

Johnson, T. J. *Professions and Power.* London: Macmillan, 1972.

Johnstone, Q., and Hopson, D., Jr. *Lawyers and Their Work: An Analysis of the Legal Profession in the United States and in England.* Indianapolis: Bobbs-Merrill, 1967.

Kaplan, B., Von Mehren, A. T., and Schaefer, R. "Phases of German Civil Procedure." *Harvard Law Review,* 1958, *71,* 1193-1268 and 1443-1472.

Kawashima, T. "Dispute Resolution in Contemporary Japan." In A. T. Von Mehren (Ed.), *Law in Japan: The Legal Order in a Changing Society.* Cambridge, Mass.: Harvard University Press, 1963.

Kidder, R. "Courts and Conflict in an Indian City: A Study of Legal Impact." *Journal of Commonwealth Political Studies,* 1973, *11,* 121-138.

Kidder, R. "Formal Litigation and Professional Insecurity: Legal Entrepreneurship in South India." *Law and Society Review,* 1974, *9,* 11-37.

Kidder, R. "Radical Lawyers." In J. Gerstl and G. Jacobs (Eds.), *The Politics of Skill.* Cambridge, Mass.: Schenkman, 1977.

Ladinsky, J. "Careers of Lawyers, Law Practice, and Legal Institutions." *American Sociological Review,* 1963, *28,* 47-54.

"Lawyers in Developing Countries With Particular Reference to India." *Law and Society Review,* Special Issue, 1968-1969, *3,* 191-468.

Lerner, M. *America as a Civilization.* New York: Simon & Schuster, 1957.

Lowenstein, S. *Lawyers, Legal Education, and Development: An Examination of the Process of Reform in Chile.* New York: International Legal Center, 1970.

Macaulay, St. "Non-Contractual Relations in Business: A Preliminary Study." *American Sociological Review,* 1963, *28,* 55-66.

McKay, R. B. "Japan: Streets Without Crimes, Disputes Without Lawyers." *Japan House Newsletter,* 1977, *24* (9).

Murphy, E. F. "The Jurisprudence of Legal History: Willard Hurst as a Legal Historian." *New York University Law Review,* 1964, *39,* 900-943.

Pedersen, N. M. "Lawyers in Politics: The Danish Folketing and United States Legislatures." In S. C. Paterson and J. C. Wahlke (Eds.), *Comparative Legislative Behavior: Frontiers of Research.* New York: Wiley, 1972.

Pound, R. *The Lawyer from Antiquity to Modern Times.* St. Paul: West, 1953.

Rheinstein, M. (Ed.). *Max Weber on Law in Economy and Society.* Cambridge, Mass.: Harvard University Press, 1954.

Rocher, L. " 'Lawyers' in Classical Hindu Law." *Law and Society Review,* 1968-1969, *3,* 383-402.

Rueschemeyer, D. "Doctors and Lawyers: A Comment on the

Theory of the Professions." *Canadian Review of Sociology and Anthropology*, 1964, *1*, 17-30.

Rueschemeyer, D. *Lawyers and Their Society: A Comparative Analysis of the Legal Profession in Germany and in the United States*. Cambridge, Mass.: Harvard University Press, 1973.

Rueschemeyer, D. "Partial Modernization." In J. J. Loubser, R. C. Baum, A. Effrat, and V. M. Lidz (Eds.), *Explorations in General Theory in Social Science: Essays in Honor of Talcott Parsons*. New York: Free Press, 1976.

Schlesinger, J. A. "Lawyers and American Politics: A Clarified View." *Midwest Journal of Political Science*, 1957, *1*, 26-39.

Schwartz, R. D., and Miller, J. C. "Legal Evolution and Societal Complexity." *American Journal of Sociology*, 1964, *70*, 159-169.

Trubek, D. M., and Galanter, M. "Scholars in Self-Estrangement: Some Reflections on the Crisis in Law and Development Studies in the United States." *Wisconsin Law Review*, 1974, 1062-1102.

Twiss, B. *Lawyers and the Constitution: How Laissez Faire Came to the Supreme Court*. Princeton, N.J.: Princeton University Press, 1942.

Von Mehren, A. T. *Law in Japan: The Legal Order in a Changing Society*. Cambridge, Mass.: Harvard University Press, 1963.

Von Mehren, A. T. "Law and Legal Education in India: Some Observations." *Harvard Law Review*, 1965, *78*, 1180-1189.

Weber, M. *Economy and Society*. (G. Roth and C. Wittich, Eds.) New York: Bedminster, 1968.

Wigmore, J. H. *A Panorama of the World's Legal Systems*. St. Paul: West, 1928.

Willig, K. C. H. "The Bar in the Third Reich." *American Journal of Legal History*, 1976, *20*, 1-14.

Ziadeh, F. J. *Lawyers, The Rule of Law and Liberalism in Modern Egypt*. Stanford, Calif.: Hoover Institute on War, Revolution and Peace, 1968.

4

Barbara Yngvesson

Law in Preindustrial Societies

Law in preindustrial society has traditionally been the domain of study of anthropologists, and several recent overview articles of anthropological research in this field are available (Nader, 1965; Moore, 1969b; Nader and Yngvesson, 1974; Collier, 1975). To avoid repetition of points made elsewhere, I will discuss in this chapter not what has been accomplished in this field but rather the ways in which anthropologists have approached the subject, with a view to examining basic assumptions and suggesting ways in which future research might be directed.

The first section of this chapter focuses on two conflicting assumptions that have underlain anthropological studies of law during the past several decades. First there is the assumption that under normal circumstances the force of moral obligation is sufficient to guarantee the fulfillment by individual members of society of their obligations toward one another. Ideally, there should be little or no need for law, in the sense of physical force administered against deviant individuals by the group as a whole. It is assumed that these ideal conditions

128

existed in preindustrial social contexts and that they still exist in some relatively isolated areas. With industrialization and the assumed anomie accompanying it, moral obligation is no longer sufficient to guarantee conformity, and physical enforcement of certain rules, carried out by the state in the interests of society as a whole, becomes necessary. Second, there is the assumption that self-interest (rather than moral obligation) is a strong motivating force for or against conformity to social rules in both industrial and preindustrial societies. In both, rules are enforced to advance the interests of particular individuals or groups (rather than society as a whole), and a variety of social control mechanisms, including physical force, may be used to this end.

In the second section of this chapter, case materials collected in the course of my own research are analyzed with a view to exploring the validity of these assumptions in a village that is characterized by some social features that might be considered "preindustrial" but that nevertheless is very much a part of the modern industrialized world.

Finally, on the basis of this analysis, I suggest that while the façade of social control may differ in preindustrial and industrial societies, the actual mechanisms of control are linked to social variables—overlapping versus compartmentalized roles, difficulty versus ease of exit, wide versus narrow support network—rather than to "primitive" versus "modern" differences that the focus on industrialization implies. I suggest that this shift in emphasis can affect our research topics as well as our understanding of ways in which legal change can be sought.

The Basis of Order: Moral Obligation and Self-Interest

Anthropological studies of law, whether among nomadic, egalitarian peoples, such as the Nuer of the Sudan (Evans-Pritchard, 1940) or "urban tramps" of Skid Road (Spradley, 1970), or among settled, highly stratified peoples, such as the Barotse of (then) Northern Rhodesia (Gluckman, 1967), are shaped by each writer's assumptions about the basis of order in society. Many anthropologists assume that order is based on the com-

mitment of individuals at all levels of the social hierarchy to
society in its present form. Social rules are accepted because it
is through them that peace and general prosperity are guaranteed. Conflict, stemming either from excessive interest in ac-
quiring goods and/or power at the expense of others or from
the inability of individuals to fulfill competing (but legitimate)
demands on them of contradictory (but valid) social rules, is
perceived to be present but to be damped by an awareness that
it is ultimately against the interest of society as a whole and
thus of the individual. To this extent, conflict is perceived as
aberrant by anthropologists with this concept of social order.
Various legal mechanisms come into play as a means of controlling conflict when it occurs, and in this sense law is viewed not
only as equal to social order but also as a process for restoring
the proper balance between individual needs and social order.
Judges, for example, act in the interests of society to chastise,
to give sermons on proper role fulfillment, to reconcile, or to
punish and isolate if the individual is too much of a threat. Less
overt forms of social control (divination, gossip) act to mask
contradictions in social rules and to reaffirm shared values.[1] A
healthy society is one in which conflict is masked or suppressed,
in which all affirm (and, it is strongly implied, believe in) the
same values, and that at least in this sense appears to be harmonious.

On the other hand, law is viewed by a number of anthropologists more as a political tool, used by individuals and groups
to advance or maintain their own interests vis-à-vis those of
other individuals and groups. Ideological systems—legal rules,
principles of social organization[2]—are seen as closely linked to
material interests, and social values are assumed not to be
shared but to be fought over. From this perspective, judges act
less to uphold the interests of society as a whole than to maintain the position of a ruling group: "A courtroom decision or a
legislative act is a gesture which often glorifies the values of one
group and demeans those of another. . . . It demonstrates which
cultures have legitimacy and public domination, and which do
not. Accordingly it enhances the social status of groups carrying
the affirmed culture and degrades groups carrying that which is

condemned as deviant" (Gusfield, 1969, pp. 309-310). Covert social control mechanisms, such as gossip and divination, act to test out public opinion, to shape and pattern issues over which there is controversy and that, for political reasons, cannot yet be aired in public.[3]

These approaches, reflecting in general terms greater or lesser indebtedness to Durkheim, on the one hand, and Marx, on the other, are familiar to students in the social sciences. However, the extent to which Durkheim has molded studies of law in what have variously been called "primitive," "tribal," "preliterate," "early," or "preindustrial" societies is less generally recognized. Redfield wrote, some years ago, in an article entitled "Primitive Law" (1964) that "the most obvious general conclusion about primitive law is that there is not much of it. . . . On the whole, people do what they are expected to do and what . . . they find it expedient to do. . . . In undisturbed primitive societies, as Durkheim put it, the consciences of individuals are uniform and strong. Human impulses are the same as everywhere else, but there is less need for a state-enforced legal system" (Redfield, 1964, p. 21). And Gluckman, in a series of articles and books spanning the period from 1954 to 1972, which have provided such perceptive insights into the role of legal institutions, state enforced and otherwise, in "tribal" societies, nevertheless focused heavily on the overlap in these societies of the "natural, the social, and the moral orders" and on the moral force that social rules exert on members of a group. Among such peoples, he suggested, conflict and dispute stem not so much from "naked self-interest" as from a failure to fulfill social obligations, obligations of kinship, affinity, and coresidence. Because all share an interest in maintaining the social order, these disputes can be settled amicably by elders or councilors, who point out the lack of fit between an individual's behavior and that of an (ideal) reasonable incumbent of his or her social position. Among the Lozi, for example, "It is a supreme value that villages should remain united, kinsfolk and families and kinship groups should not separate, lord and underling should remain associated," and this value shapes the disputing process in such a way that the emphasis is not on "winning" but

on pointing out wrongdoings to both sides with a view to reconciliation (Gluckman, 1967, pp. 21, 49). The most serious disputes are a consequence not of self-interest, but of contradictions in the social order itself, which lead individuals to
pursue legitimate, but conflicting, courses of action. In such
situations, where no clear resolution is possible, ritual is used to
heal breaches and reaffirm group unity.[4]

Gluckman's own research (1967) among the Lozi,
Griaule's work (in Forde, 1954) among the Dogon, Radcliffe-
Brown's analyses (1922) of Andaman Islander and Australian
Aborigine social organization, Evans-Pritchard's (1940) and
Fortes's (1945) analyses of the Nuer and Tallensi, and many
other analyses of tribal life have been used as a basis of support
for this approach. Thus Evans-Pritchard wrote of the Nuer that
"I have never heard of a Nuer stealing a cow from a fellow
tribesman merely because he wanted one." "Stealing" means
simply that one has taken without permission and by stealth
but does not imply one should not have taken. "Within a tribe,
an abductor of cattle always considers that he is taking what is
owing to him. It is a debt (ngwal) which he is settling in this
way, because the man who owes him cattle has not repaid them
of his own accord. The legal issue, therefore, is whether he is
right in assuming a debt" (Evans-Pritchard, 1940, p. 165). Thus
law, for the Nuer, is "a moral obligation to settle disputes by
conventional methods" (p. 168). Law in this sense only functions effectively within a village or camp, or between residents
of nearby camps, where everyone counts, in one way or another, as a kinsman, and where multiple ties, related to economic support, defense needs, and ritual obligations, link and
cross link the same individuals, reiterating their dependence on
one another in a variety of symbolic and practical ways. As the
radius in which the parties to a dispute widens, however, these
multiplex[5] ties decrease, and the moral obligation to settle (that
is, the rule of law, in Evans-Pritchard's sense) decreases accordingly. In these wider groups, "The club and the spear are the
sanctions of rights. What chiefly makes people pay compensation is fear that the injured man and his kin may take to violence" (Evans-Pritchard, 1940, p. 169).

In sum, this view of preindustrial social order stresses the predominance (if not the exclusive importance) of a strong identification by individuals with group sentiments; the notion of an isolable "moral person" in tribal society is essentially denied.[6] "The wrongs righted are wrongs against kinship groups, the claims are pressed by kinship groups, and the liability of the individual is to his kinship group" (Redfield, 1964, p. 22). Self-interest is portrayed as playing some role in the behavior of kinsmen toward one another (that is, they conform because of their dependence on one another and out of fear of losing support), but there is a strong tendency to view kin as in good faith following the dictates of custom or at least as doing so without any evident application of physical force by the group to which they belong. This situation is contrasted with that involving nonkin (or people considered not to be kin), who are portrayed as motivated primarily by self-interest, and to be controlled by fear of (physical) retaliation. Among such people, in tribal society, there is no law, only self-help and the rule of force.

There is a curious parallel, among writers of this school, between the relations posited among groups of nonkin in tribal society and the relations posited for citizens of a modern industrial state. Maine's thesis that industrialization brought with it "the gradual dissolution of family dependency, and the growth of individual obligation in its place" (Maine, 1894, p. 168) suggested the breakdown of the "moral force" exerted by kinship obligation and the consequent reliance on physically enforced contractual agreements between individuals. Implicit is the assumption that between individuals in industrial society, as between nonkin in tribal society, self-interest takes precedence over joint commitments, and in both contexts individuals are seen as being constrained in their pursuit of self-interest primarily by the application or the threat of physical force. In tribal society, this force is depicted as being privately controlled (by competing kinship groups) and applied without regard to a more abstract concept of "justice," while it is portrayed as being a legitimate function of the state, applied in the interests of society as a whole, in industrial contexts. The notion that a kind of idyllic group unity that existed, and still exists, in many "primitive" communities, has been lost with industrialization, leaving us with a kind of "stripped-down" human nature where only tooth and claw would reign, but for the imposition of a state-enforced legal order, is a marked characteristic of the classic early studies of "primitive law," as well as of many later works.[7] Implicit is both a fascination with and longing for the unity that has been lost, combined with a (more explicit) satisfaction with the progress we have achieved in replacing the particularistic, "survival of the fittest" relations between tribes and other groups of nonkin in tribal society, with a broadly based legal system in which legal officials are neutral representatives of society at large rather than partial members of specific kinship groups.

There are many problems in this thesis, although ethnographic materials indeed point to marked differences both in social organization and social control mechanisms in preindustrial and industrial contexts. The predominance of kinship as an ideological framework linking individuals and groups in the former contexts is a widely reported ethnographic fact. This is true both of politically centralized societies, such as the Barotse, and politically decentralized groups, such as the patrilineal Nuer or Tallensi, or the Tonga, among whom the lineage system is absent but who are "knit together by the spread of kinship ties from locality to locality, and the intertwining of kinship ties within any one locality" (Colson, 1953, p. 210). In modern industrial contexts, in contrast, the (ideological) basis for social integration has been replaced by others. The heavy reliance on a national, codified system of laws, physically enforced by specialized state officials, and supported with courts and prisons, in industrial contexts, and the absence of these features in most or at least in many preindustrial contexts, is also an ethnographic fact. However, the assumption that the rules and principles of kinship organization have a "binding moral force" that makes more formal (physical) enforcement of rules unnecessary in preindustrial society, that somehow "custom constrains" and self-interest is damped in these contexts, more than in industrial society, is questionable. This in turn raises questions about the basis of the industrial-preindustrial (or tribal-modern) contrast.

Much has been written during the past two decades or so about what Van Velsen (1964) has termed "the politics of kinship," and these analyses suggest, not that individual identity in tribal society is simply social (kinship) identity writ small, but that individuals in preindustrial contexts are as much motivated by self-interest as individuals in technologically more advanced contexts and that kinship rules are used for purposes of advancing that interest. As Leach (1961, p. 305) suggested, "What the social anthropologist calls *kinship structure* is just a way of talking about property relations which can also be talked about in other ways." This approach essentially turns on its head the idea, advanced by Gluckman and others, that position in space somehow "concretizes" and legitimizes social structure and gives it enduring quality.[8] Rather, it is suggested that the social (kinship) structure legitimizes position in space and places it within a meaningful explanatory framework. The framework is explanatory, however, only of a social and political order that is being endorsed by a particular individual or group, not of a system with timeless validity, and the version presented will depend to some extent on the political status of the person describing it. Thus Evans-Pritchard, for example, describes how genealogies are "telescoped" by the Nuer, omitting political nonentities (1939, pp. 213-215), and Leach illustrates ways in which the Burmese Kachin vary their accounts of myth in such a manner as to validate the status of the individual who tells it. He suggests that native descriptions of social structure, as presented in myth and ritual, should be taken not as in fact socially and politically "true" but as a fiction, an "as if" account, the function of which is to uphold vested interests (Leach, 1954, p. 265). Similarly, principles of kinship and descent can be used to validate claims by one person on another, but this need not mean that the individual in question is under a "moral" obligation to fulfill the claim. In her analysis of Lango property disputes, Moore (1969a, p. 397) suggests that "descent gave a [Lango] man a position as a legitimate claimant to the assets and assistance of his close agnates for particular purposes. . . .

But there is a difference between contingent claims and absolute rights. There could easily be claimants with higher priorities." Moore suggests that among people such as the Lango, where the same individuals interact with one another in a number of different guises—not only as kinsmen, for example, but as coresidents of a village—each of which carries a series of potential rights and obligations with it, a number of different elements in an individual's social personality[9] may have to fit if he is to receive requested support. She contrasts this with the more typical Western single-interest tie situation where "a man may sue another as the holder of a negotiable instrument; it is not relevant to his rights as holder where he lives, whom he sees often, what he does for a living, or whether he is faithful to his wife" (Moore, 1969a, p. 396).

The research of these authors and others suggests that in many preindustrial contexts, kinship is a political language through which claims and obligations of individuals on and toward one another are expressed. But this simply provides an overall framework for explaining and rationalizing behavior; it is not the only, or even necessarily the primary, basis for pursuing a course of action. Rather, what is most marked about the relations of persons in preindustrial society is the complexity of the strands linking them to one another and the constraints on action which this implies, since *the consequences of action in any one field will spill over into a number of others*. One result of this is what Moore (1972) has called the "principle of expanding disputes." In societies where complex ties link the same set of individuals, the borderline between public and private disputes may be blurred, and what starts out as a family quarrel may become a basis for confrontation between members of important political units in the community. Whether or not this occurs is at least in part related to the desirability of confrontation for the individual or individuals involved, but the potential for escalation is part of the social structure and can have marked effects on the ways in which disputes are handled. Another important consequence of multiplex relationships on dispute processing is that *relationships* seem to be more the focus of attention than *acts*. This does not mean that acts are unimportant, but that they tend to be viewed in context, within certain limits. Until that limit is reached, acts are defined and explained in such a way that the political system remains intact: Kin borrow; they do not steal.

Case Studies: Rock Island

To illustrate some of these points, I will describe and analyze the handling of two cases in a small Atlantic fishing community, Rock Island, where I lived for fifteen months in the late 1960s.[10] These cases are of interest because they provide examples of processes through which conflicts between private individuals become, or fail to become, issues of public interest, and illustrate as well the use of subtle and informal mechanisms for sanctioning deviants, thus laying bare the actual workings of "moral pressure" among people who are closely linked by long-range, multiplex ties. They suggest that while "custom," in the form of overlapping roles and cross-cutting ties, may constrain, there is a cutoff point, and that to understand mechanisms of social control and conflict management in such societies, a long time span is critical. Disputes may simmer for years before they surface, if in fact they do surface, and during this period subtle political pressures can be exerted by both sides to influence the ways in which the conflict is defined and how it is to be handled.

The Grocery Store Thefts. The Stevens family sold their grocery store to the Mores, who moved to Rock Island from the mainland (Mrs. More's mother was a native islander). The store was located in the Stevens' house, and the Stevens continued to live there after the sale. During the next four years, according to the Mores, goods and money disappeared steadily from the store. They purchased new locks and bolts for the store, but the thefts continued. They hesitated to take any public action because "people on this island are all relatives and friends," but various people were suspected—mostly, they maintained, outsiders or people who were known to drink and hang around. Finally, after four years of the thefts, the Mores' daughter (who lived on the mainland) and a son-in-law (who also lived on the mainland but who was the son of an islander) sat up one night and caught the thieves: Mrs. Stevens and her two daughters. Their husbands knew nothing of what had been going on. Mrs. Stevens offered to pay back the money and settle informally, but Mrs. More said that too much money was involved, and the police were notified. Both parties in the case were assigned a lawyer, and the case went to court. The Mores claimed $2,000 in damages, but the three women only admitted to taking $200 worth of goods, and that was what the Mores were finally awarded (islanders claim this was because they did not have a good lawyer). The women received suspended jail sentences.

People on Rock Island expressed great surprise that the Stevens had been involved in the thefts, when asked by court officials investigating the case. Mrs. Stevens was one of the prominent Carlisle family, which islanders had considered honest. One of the daughters in the case had been treasurer for the local Red Cross, a position that involved some prestige. After the discovery of the thefts, however, the social standing of the family changed radically. The Carlisle family is now said to have a "stealing trait" that was inherited by the mother and daughters, and it is said that the mother had never been so careful to distinguish between "mine" and "yours" as a child. The daughters' husbands, who had been co-owners of a fishing boat, sold it shortly after the trial and joined other teams as crew. It is also said that, while they "used to have a drink together once in a while" even before the thefts were revealed, it became much worse afterward.

One of the daughters left Rock Island at about the time I arrived, and moved to the nearest mainland city, ostensibly because of trouble with her lungs; but a friend of hers reported that she had in fact left because she "didn't feel at home" on the island any longer. Mrs. Stevens is now in her seventies, and is said to "take in men": A salesman who comes to the island every once in a while is said to spend time at her house. I have seen this woman walk alone along an island road, and people do not greet her or stop to talk to her. "Everyone knows what they did. Every time I meet her, I know she did this. They are frozen out here" (statement by an informant, 1968).

The Deviant Mechanic. This case has been in progress since at least 1955-1956 and is still unresolved. Albert Cooper (a descendent of Edward Cooper and a fifth-generation fisherman) is a self-trained mechanic and has been repairing old island trucks since he was a teenager (he is now forty). He can frequently be seen near the store, working on a truck, pausing to chat with young people as they pass along the road. He is very popular with children, particularly with young girls, who enjoy hitching rides on the back of one or another of the trucks he is currently working on. The island is quite long, and he often offers to take a group of children in one of the trucks to Pebble Beach, a favorite spot on the far northern tip of the island. Some of the younger girls (eight to nine years old) say that he is teaching them to swim.

During the time I was on the island, girls in the twelve to thirteen age group began complaining that Albert was pestering them to go swimming out at Pebble Beach and that he insisted there that they bathe without swimsuits. He had apparently been doing this for several years, but the children had not previously found it objectionable. They said that when they refused to go with him, he became very angry. The daughter of an informant stated that when she was in school (in 1955) similar problems had arisen with Albert.

In 1968 all the girls over twelve on the island decided to stop talking to him, and their parents did not object; but I was told that it was the girls' decision, not the parents'. At the time I left, the island's two nine-year-old girls were friendly with him and sometimes accompanied him to Pebble Beach.

My principal informant for this case stated that the parents had known about the situation all along, yet did nothing. They simply said, "He is that way" or "It is an illness" and appeared interested in Albert's behavior but took no action. Another informant explained that fishermen were familiar with Albert's ways: "They have known him since he was a child and have seen how he ran naked [in the rocky uninhabited areas of the island]." At the time I left Rock Island, several mothers were expressing concern about the situation, but there was no indication that they were planning to take action against Albert.

Although no overt action was being taken against Albert in this particular situation, open objection to other deviant behavior on his part was expressed by members of the community. I was told that infidelity is "judged severely" by the fishermen, yet Albert, who was married, had more or less openly established a liaison with another woman. I heard this commented on critically, and it was impossible to miss the open distaste with which they were regarded when they appeared in public together. More serious from the fishermen's point of view was his public dissent from the general stand of the fishing community with respect to a forest preserve proposed by the government for a large portion of the island's land area. The dissent was noted and criticized publicly by a politically prominent but socially "fringe" member of the community during an island council meeting.

Albert has openly expressed the opinion that people should be free to do and say as they wish and makes it clear that he finds conventional opinions and behavior distasteful. After an Island Council meeting, a fisherman mentioned that only one person opposed the island's stand on the preserve. His twelve-year-old daughter said immediately, "That must have been Albert—he's always against everything."

To understand the handling of these cases, it is important to keep in mind both the closeness and the diversity of the bonds linking most Rock Islanders to one another, and relative to this, the loose nature of the bonds linking islanders to the mainland. The island is in fact linked economically (through the activities of its fishermen) and politically (through its local government structure) to the nation of which it is a part, but in contrast to this is the paucity of person-to-person links with mainland people. On the island itself, however, the network of kinship and marriage ties is dense. Of the island's 314 inhabitants, only 56 were born elsewhere. Of the remaining 258 people, 194 are either descended from or married to descendants of 3 men who settled on the island in the eighteenth century. Several generations of inmarriage among this group have resulted in a situation in which, as one islander describes it, "everyone is related to everyone else." An additional factor binding islanders to one another and separating them from the mainland economy is the relative paucity of marketable skills, other than fishing, among the present generation of fishermen. While today's children are receiving the same education that mainland children receive and are taking advantage of the options this provides for exit from the island, if desired, earlier generations have not had this advantage. A third factor is a shared ideological commitment to social, political, and economic equality among members of the fishing community. There has been a long tradition there of mutual support and dependence on one another and of independence from, and even hostility toward, the mainland. An aspect of this commitment to egalitarianism and supportiveness of one another is a voiced ideal that everyone in the community is committed to its welfare (rather than to their own personal welfare, if this is at the expense of the community as a whole) and that all community members are honest and trustworthy. Any minor problems that might arise can be resolved amicably and in private. In contrast, however, outsiders (people not born on the island) are said to frequently cause public dispute.

In spite of the ideal that members of the fishing community do not precipitate public disputes, the two cases I have described are not atypical. In these, as in several others, persons born on Rock Island were engaged in activities on the borderline or beyond the border of behavior considered "normal" by islanders. Yet in both the activities persisted for several years without any formal recognition that a "case" existed, although they were discussed widely on the island during this time, and in one case children (structural outsiders)[11] were used as a sanctioning device. In the first example, a formal case ultimately developed and charges of theft were brought against three islanders; in the second, however, the "case" is still in process after twenty years, and it is not clear whether it will ever in fact be formalized.

Several factors influenced the ways in which these two cases were defined and handled on the island. The extreme flexibility of island categories of person and deviance meant that a wide formal leeway existed for labeling behavior as "normal" or "deviant." For example, islanders maintain that theft, property damage, and sexual molestation are deviant acts, but there is ambiguity as to which kinds of actions can be labeled "theft," and so on. "Taking the property of another" is sometimes defined as "theft," but the same behavior may also be defined as "borrowing" or "failure to distinguish between what is mine and yours." Whether an act is defined as theft or borrowing depends, in part, on whether the person taking the property is defined as an "islander" or an "outsider."[12] This is complicated by the fact that the concept "outsider," while usually applied to persons not born on the island, is sometimes manipulated to include persons born on the island who deviate too far from community norms and who may have an "outside" ancestor. In the first case described, four years of "borrowing" were ultimately translated into charges of theft, and the three island women were prosecuted at a mainland court. But the women had been socially reclassified before they even went to trial. They were not "really" islanders, but outsiders, and their descendants have been known since that time as the "Carlisle group," after the maternal kin of the mother, from whom the "thief trait" is said to be inherited. It is unclear whether a mainland ancestor was in fact present in this case, but in two other similar cases a "thief trait" was attributed to mainland ancestry, and the offenders were reclassified as outsiders on these grounds. The second case was more complex, owing to the strong political position of the offender, Albert Cooper. Almost a third of Rock Island's population is descended from Edward Cooper, one of the three fishermen-farmers who settled on the island in the eighteenth century. For generations, the Coopers have been among the island's most successful fishermen and among the fishermen, the island's principal landowners. Together with the descendants of the other two settlers, to whom they are closely linked by marriage, the Coopers present a formidable group. Partly because of this situation, the only systematic sanctioning of Albert's behavior was carried out by schoolgirls whose action, as children, did not formally count. Yet as the case description indicates, there were several grounds on which Albert's behavior could be attacked. His opposition to the community stand on the forest preserve was a sensitive issue at a time when many Rock Islanders were concerned about the decline of the island as a fishing community and about attempts by the national government to increase its attractiveness to summer tourists, through measures such as the preserve. The islander who seemed to be taking most advantage of this situation (by a public verbal attack on Albert) was a politically ambitious fisherman who had been encroaching on the generations-long political supremacy of the Coopers for several years.

Thus in both these cases, the long period of informal discussion was a time when a (potential) offender's behavior could be assessed in the light of (1) what was expected of him or her, as an individual whose patterns of behavior had been known and accepted in the community for many years and (2) what could be tolerated given his or her structural position on the island and the political and economic context in which the actions were being carried out. In Albert's case, many people simply said, "He is like that," remembering his behavior as a child. Beyond this, his position as a "real" islander with deep roots made it difficult to take action against him without alienating a large segment of the island population. Many years of gossip about his behavior provided not only a means for venting hostility but also acted as a kind of political sounding board for those who wished—for various reasons—to oppose his behavior in public.

Thus on Rock Island, actions of individuals are assessed in much more complex terms than that of an "ideal" role model to which each person is expected to conform, and "moral pressure" is a complex process involving visible physical elements. Actions by an offender or against an offender are often explained and rationalized in terms of expectations linked to status as a kinsman and islander, or as an "outsider." But social identity—as a "real islander," as a somewhat odd individual, as a political obstacle to another ambitious islander—seems to have greater influence on what is actually done about an offender and on whether his actions are defined as deviant than does his formal island status, and this identity is, at least in part, shaped by the gossiping that inevitably follows any behavior that might be interpreted as "borderline." Moral pressure is in part exerted by the gossiping, which may reach the object of the gossip but which also consists in gestures and actions that clearly indicate one's acceptance into or exclusion from the community. Because these actions are relatively covert, however, and because the time span involved in the recognition and sanctioning of deviance is often long, one might well assume that an intangible "moral pressure" is at work. Yet among people for whom the exit possibilities are limited, for the reasons discussed earlier, this kind of pressure can be considered comparable to physical exclusion (such as imprisonment), and does in fact lead to self-exile in some cases (as in the store theft case).

Conclusions: Cooperation, Competition, and the Social Context of Disputes

Analysis of case materials from other village and tribal contexts where people are socially and economically dependent on kin and neighbors to whom they are linked by complex ties, suggests that the dominant features of conflict management on Rock island are not unique. These analyses[13] suggest that while ties of kinship, marriage, coresidence, and neighborhood may well act to constrain both potential offenders and complainants so that public dispute is muffled or avoided and so that when it does occur disputes are processed with a view toward compromise settlements and reconciliation, this is only one aspect of conflict management in these contexts. Reconciliation attempts, whether in private or in a moot, court, or other public forum, may be only one stage in a much longer-range dispute, which can terminate in a win-or-lose judgment or in physical exclusion. Which of these options is chosen is often influenced by political factors, but the justification for the option is usually phrased in terms of well-known rules defining the rights and obligations of kinsmen toward one another. Thus Collier (1973, p. 179), discussing property disputes between kin in Zinacantan (Mexico), states: "Zinacanteco kinsmen who prefer to avoid dispute have an adequate mechanism for handling potentially conflicting claims, but those who wish to quarrel have a rich language of contradictory principles at their command. Thus we find it argued that all siblings should share equally in the parent's property; that sons should share equally but should get more than daughters; that respectful sons deserve a larger share than disrespectful sons. . . . The fact is that these principles do not govern Zinacanteco inheritance, but only serve as justifications for a claim to property." People who value continued cooperation appeal to an elder in property disputes, with a view to a compromise solution; others, more interested in economic gain than in maintaining cooperative relations with kin, can appeal their cases to the town hall, where win or lose decisions are possible (Collier, 1973, pp. 56-61, 178-179).

What this suggests is that, as Nader (1965) indicated a decade ago, studies of "primitive law" should focus not only on ideology, on what people *say* they do and feel, as expressed in legal rules, judicial sermons, and the norms of kinship, but on what people *do* when involved in disputes with their fellows. What people do, in tribal as well as in modern industrialized contexts, is to create flexible rules, which provide an ideological framework within which a range of political options can be pursued. Pressing for an either/or, take-all or lose-all outcome in an adjudicatory setting is one of these options; another is compromise; a third is avoidance and/or taking no action at all. Any of these may be defined as "winning," or as part of a winning strategy, by one or both of the participants, depending on their time perspective.[14]

Compromise seems to be most common in contexts where the exit possibilities are limited (and thus where people feel some "moral pressure" to compromise with their fellows) and/or in contexts where people are linked in multiplex relationships with considerable time depth, which they wish to preserve. Where exit possibilities are limited, more powerful individuals or groups may be able to force a compromise solution that is to their advantage, regardless of "right" or "wrong."[15] When multiplex relationships are involved, "right" or "wrong" are often defined, at least initially, with this in mind. Dispute management in these contexts tends to be subtle. Diffuse sanctioning (that is, conducted through many social channels) may take the place of or at least precede a more focused response to a perceived offense; the process tends to be longer range; and it is masked by an ideology that underlines social commitments of individuals to one another, rather than the rights of individuals vis-à-vis one another. In contrast, when conflict occurs in relationships that are single-interest and perceived as replaceable, there is less concern with the consequences of action on the relationship of victim to offender. In contexts where many of the relationships in which any given individual is involved are of this type—that is, where relationships are typically compartmentalized rather than overlapping—the basis for an evaluation of questionable behavior as deviant or normal is restricted, and the opportunities for diffuse sanctioning are limited. Likewise, the chances that a private quarrel will expand into a major political dispute are slim. In such contexts, response to behavior perceived as deviant, if it occurs, will typically be rapid and overt. Data on the third option, nonaction or avoidance, are limited and are difficult to collect in any systematic way, but the use of such a strategy in both compartmentalized and overlapping relationships has been analyzed.[16]

While the more subtle, compromise-oriented approach to dispute processing may be more typical of preindustrial contexts and the more aggressive pursuit of rights at the expense of relationships may be more typical of urban industrialized contexts, the literature in legal ethnography suggests that the important variables for understanding dispute management are social and political variables, not the implied primitive-modern contrast that a focus on industrialization suggests. Careful studies of dispute management in preindustrial societies indicate that the perception of self-interest as (kin) group interest in these contexts fails to account for the long-range management of some quarrels that are initially handled by avoidance and compromise, or the short-range strategies of some litigants who seek zero-sum solutions for disputes with kinsmen and neighbors. Similarly, studies in urban industrial contexts suggest that many quarreling individuals prefer to compromise (at least initially) and define self-interest and personal gain in much broader terms than those of winning a case in a zero-sum contest in court. Studies by Macaulay (1963) and Ross (1975), for example, suggest that for store managers and for business-men in the automobile industry, both the voluntary and forced (through legal intervention) exit that leads to termination of a relationship with a customer or business associate may be less desirable, economically and otherwise, than a compromise that guarantees ongoing interaction. For quarreling neighbors or hus-bands and wives in crowded urban ghettos, both court and dis-putants alike are aware that escalation into a public dispute brings more loss than gain, but there is often no alternative, since low-level, compromise-oriented services are unavailable.[17] Even in cases where preservation of a relationship is of little consequence, such as most consumer complaints against manu-facturers or department stores and tenant complaints against landlords, the experience of plaintiffs such as these in small-claims courts throughout the country has made it increasingly evident that going to court is more likely to produce loss than gain. For these litigants, as for those in the many rural hamlets described by anthropologists, "winning" is often related to being powerful enough (in terms of numbers, economic re-sources, or political influence) to persuade the other side to alter its stand, and to be in a good position to participate in the process of fashioning the rules within which interaction takes place. This may occur in court (Galanter, 1974) or over a bar-gaining table, but it assumes not only that single individuals per-ceive self-interest in broadly defined terms but also that groups perceive the difficulty of functioning without the cooperation or at least the tacit compliance of others with whom they share some common interests and a degree of mutual dependence.

These studies suggest that the focus, in future studies of law and society, should be not so much on the differences be-tween law in industrial and preindustrial contexts as on the im-pact of social and political variables (overlapping-compartment-alized roles, difficulty-ease of exit, wide-narrow support network) and of legal options, on the way a population manages conflict. This requires not only a broadening of the social con-text within which dispute processing is observed but also a broadening of our time perspective on dispute management.

Tribal and urban, village farmer and city tenement dweller are all part of the modern, industrialized world. Quarrels that begin in a village hamlet may terminate in an urban court, and it is important both to follow this development and to take note of how it is explained, if the disputing process is to be understood. Rock Islanders can take to court repeated offenders who refuse to respond to local pressure; kinsmen in Zinacantan can mediate through a hamlet elder or press their case in an urban tribunal. For these people and others, improved communications and ease of exit have placed powerful tools in the hands of some and have loosened the hold of established mediators, elders, and other traditionally powerful individuals and groups in the community. In other industrialized countries, however, much of the population is facing a situation in which both local and higher-level alternatives for processing disputes have been reduced. In many urban areas of the United States, for example, high mobility and role compartmentalization have contributed to a situation in which there is little basis on which low-level "community" mechanisms for dispute management can function. At the same time, centrally controlled, highly bureaucratized courts are becoming increasingly inaccessible to, or at least nonfunctional for, a large part of the population, due to expense, delay, and the inability of court officials (or the specialized intermediaries through whom access to the courts is often controlled) to deal meaningfully with the conflicts that come before them. In addition, while mobility is high, the actual possibilities of exit are restricted today in countries, such as the United States and Sweden, for example, where high technological development and narrow occupational specialization have contributed to the growth of widespread credit-rating networks and "recommendation" networks (Danzig and Lowy, 1975, pp. 680-681). Thus, while for some inhabitants of the industrialized world options have expanded, for many others a lack of options for handling conflict, through the formal legal system or otherwise, is having serious social and political consequences. Research in these areas can both contribute to our understanding of the impact of law in society and serve as a basis for action with a view to legal and social change.

Notes

1. Gluckman (1967, 1961, 1963b, 1965a, 1965b, 1972), Turner (1957), Fortes and Evans-Pritchard (1940), are among several anthropologists who have dealt with some of these issues.

2. I am using the concept "ideology" to mean a set of beliefs, believed to be valid, which shape the ways in which people interpret the world and understand their own actions and those of others, and which are used to justify and legitimatize these actions (Bernstein, 1976, pp. 107-108).

3. While Quinney (1969) and Chambliss (1975) represent the more extreme forms of this position, the approach has also influenced anthropological studies such as those by Gulliver (1971, 1973), Moore (1972), Peters (1972), Collier (1973), and Epstein (1974).

4. A particularly clear analysis of this position is in Gluckman (1965b, chap. 6).

5. A relationship is "multiplex" when it serves many interests. Gluckman (1967, pp. 18, 19) used the term in describing Barotse society, where "With his kin a man holds land and chattels; he produces goods in cooperation with them and shares with them.in consuming these; he depends on them for insurance against famine, illness, and old age; he forms with them religious communities tending the same ancestors; they are responsible for the main part of his education; he seeks his recreation with them."

6. Read (1967) presents a clear but oversimplified analysis of individual and social identity among one group in New Guinea, but see Geertz (1973, pp. 360-411) for a more complex and convincing discussion of what the concept of person entails in another village context.

7. Moore (1972, pp. 56-75) presents a detailed critique of this approach, while Colson (1974, pp. 31-60) provides a careful and balanced consideration of anthropological assumptions about the basis of order.

8. See Gluckman's (1965a, pp. 113-139) discussion of this.

9. The concept "social personality," as Moore uses it, includes various facets of an individual related to each of the positions he or she occupies in society. In this paper, I will use the

concept "social identity" to include social personality in Moore's sense, as well as more ephemeral qualities related to reputation and demeanor over a period (possibly brief) when a case is being dealt with (see also Collier, 1973, pp. 82-90).

10. One of these cases is also dealt with in an earlier publication (Yngvesson, 1976), where dispute processing on this island is discussed in detail. See also Yngvesson (forthcoming), where issues discussed on pp. 144-148 of this chapter are also considered.

11. By virtue of their youth, the schoolgirls are able to take retaliatory action without eliciting the political response that adult sanctioning would bring. They are "only children" and in this sense outsiders, not full participants in the community. But as Peters (1972, p. 158) points out, this kind of externality is a fiction, since youth groups such as these often act as the sanctioning arm of the adult community.

12. See also Firth (1951, p. 196), Read (1967, p. 204), and Moore (1972, p. 68).

13. See, for example, Moore (1972), Collier (1973), Starr and Yngvesson (1975).

14. Galanter (1974, pp. 100-103) points out that powerful litigants who frequently use courts for dispute management can afford to lose some rounds, with a view to longer-range gain. Likewise, compromise or nonaction may be one step in a longer-range strategy.

15. Leigh-Wei Doo (1973) describes the problems and inequities of forced compromise for Chinatown residents, and Murphy (1967) describes the ways in which experienced corporate litigants armed with lawyers force "compromise" settlements on inexperienced, unrepresented litigants in Washington, D.C., small-claims courts.

16. See Yngvesson (1976) for a discussion of nonaction in an isolated village; Felstiner (1974) discusses avoidance in technologically complex, rich societies.

17. See Nader (1975, pp. 163-165), Yngvesson and Hennessey (1975), Danzig and Lowy (1975), Danzig (1973), Felstiner (1974), and Yngvesson (1975).

References

Bernstein, R. J. *The Restructuring of Social and Political Theory*. New York: Harcourt Brace Jovanovich, 1976.

Chambliss, W. J. (Ed.). *Law in Action*. New York: Wiley, 1975.

Collier, J. F. *Law and Social Change in Zinacantan*. Stanford, Calif.: Stanford University Press, 1973.

Collier, J. F. "Legal Processes." In B. J. Siegel (Ed.), *Annual Review of Anthropology*. Stanford, Calif.: Stanford University Press, 1975.

Colson, E. "Social Control and Vengeance in Plateau Tonga Society." *Africa*, 1953, *23*, 199-212.

Colson, E. *Tradition and Contract: The Problem of Order*. Chicago: Aldine, 1974.

Danzig, R. "Toward the Creation of a Complementary, Decentralized System of Criminal Justice." *Stanford Law Review*, 1973, *26*, 1-49.

Danzig, R., and Lowy, M. J. "Everyday Disputes and Mediation in the United States: A Reply to Professor Felstiner." *Law and Society Review*, 1975, *9* (4), 675-694.

Doo, L.-W. "Dispute Settlement in Chinese-American Communities." *American Journal of Comparative Law*, 1973, *21*, 627-680.

Epstein, A. L. "Introduction." In A. L. Epstein (Ed.), *Contention and Dispute: Aspects of Law and Social Control in Melanesia*. Canberra: Australian National University, 1974.

Evans-Pritchard, E. E. "Nuer Time Reckoning." *Africa*, 1939, *12* (2), 189-216.

Evans-Pritchard, E. E. *The Nuer*. Oxford, England: Clarendon Press, 1940.

Felstiner, W. L. F. "Influences of Social Organization on Dispute Processing." *Law and Society Review*, 1974, *9* (1), 63-94.

Firth, R. *Elements of Social Organization*. London: Watts, 1951.

Forde, D. (Ed.). *African Worlds*. London: Oxford University Press, 1954.

Fortes, M. *The Dynamics of Clanship Among the Tallensi*. London: Oxford University Press, 1945.

Fortes, M., and Evans-Pritchard, E. E. "Introduction." In M. Fortes and E. E. Evans-Pritchard (Eds.), *African Political Systems*. London: Oxford University Press, 1940.

Galanter, M. "Why the 'Haves' Come Out Ahead: Speculations

on the Limits of Legal Change." *Law and Society Review,* 1974, *9* (1), 95-160.

Geertz, C. "Person, Time and Conduct in Bali." In C. Geertz, *The Interpretation of Cultures.* New York: Basic Books, 1973.

Gluckman, M. "African Jurisprudence." *Advancement of Science,* 1961, *74,* 1-16.

Gluckman, M. "The Reasonable Man in Barotse Law." In M. Gluckman, *Order and Rebellion in Tribal Society.* New York: Free Press, 1963a.

Gluckman, M. "Gossip and Scandal." *Current Anthropology,* 1963b, *4* (3), 307-316.

Gluckman, M. *The Ideas in Barotse Jurisprudence.* New Haven, Conn.: Yale University Press, 1965a.

Gluckman, M. *Politics, Law and Ritual in Tribal Society.* Oxford, England: Blackwell, 1965b.

Gluckman, M. *The Judicial Process Among the Barotse of Northern Rhodesia.* (2nd ed.) Manchester: Manchester University Press, 1967.

Gluckman, M. "Moral Crises: Magical and Secular Solutions." In M. Gluckman (Ed.), *The Allocation of Responsibility.* Manchester: Manchester University Press, 1972.

Gulliver, P. H. *Neighbours and Networks: The Idiom of Kinship in Social Action Among the Ndendeuli of Tanzania.* Berkeley: University of California Press, 1971.

Gulliver, P. H. "Negotiations as a Mode of Dispute Settlement: Towards a General Model." *Law and Society Review,* 1973, *7,* 667-692.

Gusfield, J. R. "Moral Passage: The Symbolic Process in Public Designations of Deviance." *Social Problems,* 1969, *15,* 175-188.

Leach, E. R. *Political Systems of Highland Burma.* Boston: Beacon Press, 1954.

Leach, E. R. *Pul Eliya: A Village in Ceylon.* Cambridge, England: Cambridge University Press, 1961.

Maine, H. S. *Ancient Law.* (15th ed.) London: Murray, 1894.

Macaulay, S. "Non-Contractual Relations in Business: A Preliminary Study." *American Sociological Review,* 1963, *28,* 55-66.

Moore, S. F. "Descent and Legal Position." In L. Nader (Ed.), *Law in Culture and Society*. Chicago: Aldine, 1969a.

Moore, S. F. "Law and Anthropology." In B. J. Siegel (Ed.), *Biennial Review of Anthropology*. Stanford, Calif.: Stanford University Press, 1969b.

Moore, S. F. "Legal Liability and Evolutionary Interpretation: Some Aspects of Strict Liability, Self-Help and Collective Responsibility." In M. Gluckman (Ed.), *The Allocation of Responsibility*. Manchester: Manchester University Press, 1972.

Murphy, T. "D.C. Small-Claims Court—The Forgotten Court." *D.C. Bar Journal*, 1967, *34*, 14-17.

Nader, L. "The Anthropological Study of Law." *American Anthropologist*, 1965, *67* (6, part 2), 3-32.

Nader, L. "Forums for Justice; A Cross-Cultural Perspective." *Journal of Social Issues*, 1975, *31* (3), 151-170.

Nader, L., and Yngvesson, B. "On Studying the Ethnography of Law and Its Consequences." In J. J. Honigman (Ed.), *Handbook of Social and Cultural Anthropology*. New York: Random House, 1974.

Peters, E. L. "Aspects of the Control of Moral Ambiguities: A Comparative Analysis of Two Culturally Disparate Modes of Social Control." In M. Gluckman (Ed.), *The Allocation of Responsibility*. Manchester: Manchester University Press, 1972.

Quinney, R. (Ed.). *Crime and Justice in Society*. Boston: Little, Brown, 1969.

Radcliffe-Brown, A. R. *The Andaman Islanders*. Cambridge, England: Cambridge University Press, 1922.

Read, K. E. "Morality Among the Gahuku-Gama." In J. Middleton (Ed.), *Myth and Cosmos*. Garden City, N.Y.: Natural History Press, 1967.

Redfield, R. "Primitive Law." *University of Cincinnati Law Review*, 1964, *33*, 1-22. Reprinted in P. Bohannan (Ed.), *Law and Warfare*. Garden City, N.Y.: The Natural History Press, 1967.

Ross, H. L. Paper delivered at Research Colloquium, Law and Society Association, Buffalo, N.Y., June 5-7, 1975.

Spradley, J. *You Owe Yourself a Drunk*. Boston: Little, Brown, 1970.

Starr, J., and Yngvesson, B. "Scarcity and Disputing: Zeroing in on Compromise Decisions." *American Ethnologist,* 1975, *2* (3), 553-566.

Turner, V. *Schism and Continuity in an African Society.* Manchester, England: Manchester University Press, 1957.

Van Velsen, J. *The Politics of Kinship: A Study in Social Manipulation Among the Lakeside Tonga.* Manchester: Manchester University Press, 1964.

Yngvesson, B. "Case Worker as Culture Broker: Court and Community in the Ghetto." Paper delivered at annual meeting of the American Anthropological Association, San Francisco, November 1975.

Yngvesson, B. "Responses to Grievance Behavior: Extended Cases in a Fishing Community." *American Ethnologist,* 1976, *3* (2), 353-373.

Yngvesson, B. "The Reasonable Man and the Unreasonable Gossip: On the Flexibility of (Legal) Concepts and the Elasticity of (Legal) Time." In P. H. Gulliver (Ed.), *Essays in Memoriam Max Gluckman.* Leiden, The Netherlands: E. J. Brill, forthcoming.

Yngvesson, B., and Hennessey, P. "Small Claims, Complex Disputes: A Review of the Small Claims Literature." *Law and Society Review,* 1975, *9* (2), 219-274.

5

Robert L. Kidder

Western Law
in India
External Law and Local Response

"The judges' anxiety to clear the file, to show quick disposal of cases, and to stick to the technicalities of the law as distinct from what the justice of the case demands, are responsible for many a wrong decision. . . . Litigation has come to be regarded, and rightly so, as a sort of gambling. . . . The lawyer is mostly responsible for this uncertainty. . . . In fact, the greater the lawyer's ability to confound and confuse the judge and the true issues in the case, the higher the fee that he commands. . . . But the worst feature of the system of administration of justice now prevalent is the wholesale demoralization of the people. The law courts are largely responsible for the constantly diminishing respect for truth" (Prasad, 1926, pp. 109-114).

Why does this quote sound so familiar? How could this Indian lawyer's half-century-old lament sound so much like that of a "law and order" candidate for mayor in Philadelphia in the 1970s or like a man-on-the-street interview in present-day Chicago? In law, as in so many other areas, we need to see past the assumption that "East is East and West is West, and never the

twain shall meet." Like many of his contemporaries, the lawyer
just quoted saw the courts and judges of colonial India as in-
advertent sources of moral decay. Americans have expressed
very similar feelings about American courts and judges, those
"bleeding heart liberals" who keep encouraging crime and de-
pravity by freeing known criminals on "technicalities."

In spite of the obvious differences between American and
Indian culture, there are strong parallels between the Indian
reaction to "Western law" and reactions to it wherever it has
come to prevail. We have much to learn from a study of the
ancient strong embrace between Indian society and Western
law. Such study bears lessons about the American experience
with law also because the most powerful characteristics of Western law give it the same relationship to all societies regardless of
culture.

What has the Indian experience been? The answer is—one
of the longest periods of colonial rule and contact with law in
modern history.

History of Western Law in India

To attempt a brief history of anything in India is to court
disaster because of the diversity one must ignore. However,
some background is needed here to give us a shared context for
discussion.

Western law in India means British law (and, more lately,
Anglo-American law). As the British began, late in the eighteenth century, to develop colonial control in India, their concern for the development of commerce led them to conclude
that some regulation of the local population was needed. They
took on this task to ensure a level of tranquility sufficient to
protect their trading activities.

As colonial control spread inland from early coastal enclaves, their realm gradually enveloped larger and larger populations. Law in these areas, before the British, was typically
administered by various princes whose small kingdoms expanded and contracted with periodic feuds and wars. In addition to their law, a host of village, caste, familial, and regional

tribunals functioned as law courts with very narrow jurisdictions.

As British involvement grew from simple trade relationships to the more complicated structure of full colonial rule, colonial motives and actions became more complex. Churches found fertile ground for Christian conversions. This new interest coincided with the spread of educational institutions for Indians. At the same time, utilitarianism in England became a philosophy administrators wanted to test in India (Stokes, 1959). The utilitarian influence on English law had a counterpart in the colonial attempt to establish that law system in India. To the British, India before their arrival appeared chaotic, lacking law, the victim of capricious and unscrupulous rajas. As colonial involvement in Indian society grew, the law took on the combined ideological qualities of utilitarianism and imperialism—a civilized society bringing rational order and peace to a supposedly backward region. By the nineteenth century, the law was no longer just a tool for the protection of private commerce. It had become a crusade in a "heathen" land.

But it was not a crusade to turn Indians into Englishmen. Rather, the British goals were to (1) create an instrument with which Indians could fairly and rationally enforce their own norms and values and (2) adopt acceptable procedures for regulating relations between colonial administrators and subjects. In the view of administrators, there was no need to impose British standards of conduct. What they needed was a means to protect people who wished simply to follow the practices of their ancestors. The British sought to substitute the calm, reasoned approach of the court for the bloody solutions of feud, intimidation, and war.

Throughout the nineteenth century, the interdependence of English and Indian colonial law grew. Proposed reforms in English law were tried first in India. Appeals from Indian courts led to precedents proclaimed by the Privy Council in London for all of English law. As interdependence grew, so did the institutions of colonial Indian law. The number of lawsuits outpaced the rate of territorial expansion because Indians began seeing the courts as a resource to be used rather than shunned. As business grew, so did the legal profession. From a handful of English lawyers and judges at the beginning of the nineteenth century, the profession gradually became filled with Indians. At first these were merely self-taught facilitators who found the courts crowded with neophytes in need of advice. Step by step, educational and apprenticeship restrictions were introduced, creating a multitiered body of legal advisors and advocates (Schmitthener, 1968-1969).

The system grew mostly in response to local disputes. Most of the lawyers' and judges' time was taken up with land litigation, inheritance disputes, marital arrangements, and caste relationships. Both the British then, and social scientists since then, were awed by the rate of litigiousness of Indian society. A polyglot society of artisans, merchants, and peasants, presumably unsophisticated about "Western" institutions and presumably wedded to their own strange values and institutions, flooded the courts in the nineteenth century and have continued to do so ever since (Cohn, 1959). By most standards, India became one of the most litigious populations in the world under British rule. India's legal profession became one of the largest in the world while rising to a position of prestige and influence in colonial society. And the lawyers' principal source of income was civil litigation, although some also earned reputations as champions of oppressed colonial subjects against unfair administrators.

The "Gift" of Law: A Closer Look

What was happening here? Was there some crying social need that the British accurately identified? Were they right in claiming that they could help local people live by local standards? Was the creation of Pax Britannica a resource for the maintenance of traditional Indian values? Were Indians flooding the courts because the British had successfully incorporated the true meaning of local culture into a rational legal system?

The logic of the British approach would lead to the conclusion that these questions were simply different ways of asking the same thing. But the answers to them are not identical.

The popularity of the courts, if it proved anything, was far from proving that Indians were seeking status quo solutions to their disputes.

Features of Colonial Law. Consider what the British asked the typical Indian villager to accept. The list will not sound alien to most readers. Many of us now take it for granted that, without these characteristics, there is no "law." First, all persons were to be treated equally before the law. Status differences were not to influence the outcome of decisions. Second, the purpose of the courts was to deal with isolated "cases" of conflict in which clear-cut rights and duties would be established by investigation of only those events "relevant" to the pending case. In other words, the principle of *contract* was to replace the principle of *status* in determining the obligations of people toward each other and toward government. For example, the idea of land *ownership* was enforced in place of complex communal relationships (Cohn, 1961, pp. 614-618) as a means of isolating tax revenue responsibility and proprietary privilege with respect to the means of agricultural production.

Third, courts made final, enforced decisions. This meant that cases were always treated as involving a right and a wrong party. Court personnel had to "find" the "truth" in each case and award justice to the right party. The court's decision was to be coercively enforced. The British assumed that a "just" solution was one that rewarded law-abiding behavior. In the prevailing utilitarian view, they expected rewards and punishments to produce compliance with the customary laws, which they would enforce for the good of all.

Fourth, rules of evidence restricted the contents of testimony made on a litigant's behalf. Those rules multiplied the effects of the narrow definitions of contractual rights and duties. For example, if a lawsuit involved a charge of trespass, a defendant could not raise his daughter's marital difficulties with the plaintiff's son as a defense unless it was an issue directly related to the issue of ownership. Even if the marriage was the true source of conflict, the trespass was the only issue that could be debated.

Fifth, justice was to be "blind." Judges had to be either

Englishmen or Indians born and raised far from the scene of their jurisdiction. They must not be related to any of the litigants. They must have no interest (other than the preservation of their profession's standards) in the outcome of the case. In other words, the judge should be aloof, a total stranger to the parties and issues raised in his courts.

Sixth, while judges were to be blind, lawyers were to be myopically one-sided. As principal performers in the adversarial drama, they were supposed to use their privileged professional status to present an unashamedly biased interpretation of both facts and law. The "experts" in this system were thus routinely seen disagreeing with each other on almost every salient point.

Seventh, the substance of the law was to be drawn from prevailing Indian custom. This meant a search for a single, exhaustive definition of that custom and the careful recording of "precedent" to which judges should refer in making decisions. Previous judicial decisions should be the basis for subsequent decisions. Judgments made in one locale should be consistent with those in other areas. Above all, the courts should not seem capricious, nor should they impose English standards of conduct on Indians.

Indian Responses. If the purpose of these policies was to guarantee truth, justice, and the revitalization of Indian custom, they failed. Almost every account of Indian responses to this "Western" institution carries the same message: Courts were the object of rampant abuse and manipulation. Every trick in the book is described in detail: perjury, falsification of evidence, procedural manipulation in order to stalemate opponents with delay, and bribery of court personnel. Touts stirred up conflict in the villages and then brought the opponents to lawyers who paid for this service. People's cynicism about the quality of English justice was only matched by their ambivalent, gambler-like hopes for personal success. Litigants were pictured either as innocent dupes of an alien system or as conniving aggressors grabbing for fortunes from their inexperienced opponents.

Where did the British go wrong? The answer is that they produced the same clash between "Western law" and local custom as can be seen wherever Western law prevails. Cohn notes

(1959) that the characteristics I have just listed were diametrically opposed to the essential elements of local community practice, especially to their ways of handling conflicts. As a procedural standard, "equality of all before the law" violated the caste-organized principles of Indian social structure. These statuses were, according to Cohn and others, essential to an understanding of obligations and standards of conduct. They could not be ignored in court without creating a strong sense of injustice. Too many "normal" decisions were contingent on status. Likewise, the idea of contract, with its strict definitions of right and duty, did violence to the complexity of local relationships, especially concerning rights to land. The attempt to treat land as an object to be owned created a scramble for ownership among all the elements that had previously participated in agrarian communal life. British insistence on finality, the conclusion of a case by a declaration of a winner, violated the preferred option of compromise. By providing an arena where all-or-nothing decisions were promised, the British created the atmosphere for speculative litigation. People formerly obliged to negotiate their claims under the watchful eyes of a whole community could now file a suit and manipulate the more remote machinery of justice to their own aggressive ends. Restrictive rules of evidence violated the complex fabric of local relationships by allowing only proximate events to be mentioned in debate. The many strands of long-running disputes could be only partially captured within the narrow confines of a lawsuit. The result was that court decrees, rather than settling disputes, often added to the many already existing devices used by disputants to pursue their opponents.

To many, "blind" justice meant capricious justice. How, they asked, could a stranger to the community ever detect perjury or sense the complexity behind the apparent "facts" of a case? Whether English or Indian, most judges appeared either arbitrary or naive when they accepted as "truth" testimony about events, customs, and relationships known intimately to everyone in court except the judge. Blinded by professional hauteur and tied down by restrictive rules of evidence, judges could only find succor in the maintenance of courtroom decorum, the preservation of careful records, the pursuit of "professional" standards, and the intellectual excitement of legal debate.

The word *lawyer,* for many people, became synonymous with the word *scoundrel.* Colonial administrators often wrote their most eloquent prose in reports on the deviousness, unscrupulousness, and greed of the lawyers who seemed to profit from the abuse of English justice. They saw lawyers as sharks swimming in troubled waters. Indians generally shared this view. Even those who hired lawyers saw them as untrustworthy, but temporarily necessary, evils. Many saw lawyers as the source of most conflict. People were not bad, it was said, but their lawyers "put them up" to the evil tricks being played in court.

Law and Custom. To return to a point I made earlier, the British were committed to a common law ideal, which meant that, wherever possible, they should let local custom govern official actions. Their intent was not to change local custom, but to preserve it. But, as Galanter (1966, 1972) shows, the inherent logic of the English system paradoxically changed what it was designed to preserve. The first question facing a judge hearing rival claims from impassioned litigants is "What is local custom here, and how does it apply to this case?" Reasoning from their own relatively unified and catalogued body of common law, colonial court administrators set about the task of "finding" local custom, recording it, and then codifying it for use in the courts. What they wanted was an authoritative source a judge could use to separate true claims of custom from false.

At first, they employed local "experts" whose literacy and high social standing were assumed to guarantee accurate and impartial knowledge of local custom. Slowly, this use of experts yielded to reliance on a growing body of precedent and the simplistic assumption that ancient scriptures could provide definitive statements on local custom. As Galanter (1966, p. 160) says, ancient texts on customary Hindu law (the *Dharmasastra*) had never before operated as support for general legal decrees. Their influence had been by example, like the influence Paris fashion designers have on clothes sold in American department stores. When the British began using these scriptures as the basis for judgments about local disputes, they transformed Indian custom the way a freezer preserves fish. Form was preserved, but the living relationship between the elements was eliminated.

In dealing with disputes over caste privilege, for example, the courts relied on ancient statements about caste hierarchy. In doing so, they ignored the complexity of the multifaceted relationships that had developed around the caste principle. This complexity was produced by the ever-changing economic fortunes of localized groups. Caste subsets could rise to power and sink into near-slavery on the waves of very isolated economic conditions. Caste had not been a centrally administered system of monolithic stratification. Colonial court insistence on common law standards for proof of custom locked people into relationships, such as caste, making them less flexible than they had been under pre-British conditions (Galanter, 1968a, 1968b). By shutting off access to older, more familiar sources of mobility within the caste system, the British opened the arena of mobility action to entrepreneurs whose techniques and rationales caught opponents by surprise. Status and prestige claims that would have been maneuvered and negotiated within traditional authority channels were transformed by legalistic language and the opportunities for legal maneuvering that the courts offered. This pattern of British action and Indian response affected marital and inheritance arrangements, land use agreements, and the development of criminal law.

In retrospect, the British "gift" had features of both control and chaos. The courts were heavily used. Disputing which had been carried on through mediation and a hodgepodge of caste, village, familial and territorial tribunals now flowed into the courts, producing constant pressure to expand the system. But only remote higher courts could preserve their reputations for integrity, because few people had direct experience with them. In courts they had experienced, people saw truth and justice as victims of judicial shortcomings. They saw their customs distorted beyond recognition by simplistic judicial routines of interpretation. Court became a place where the only way to

support truth was by lying, a place where "the winners lose, and
the losers are dead" because of the debilitating effects of litigation on family finances, personal integrity, and reputation.

Explaining the Indian Experience

With such a negative image, why were the courts so heavily used? If people mean it when they say, as they have for
more than a century, that court must be a last resort, that one
should do everything to avoid court, that only thieves and
troublemakers go to court, then why do so many persons liti-
gate? Galanter is on target when he says (1966, p. 162) that "A
modern system [of law] breaks the tie of law with local and
group opinion; this can be liberating for the dissenter and the
deviant." When a court system such as the one introduced into
India becomes available, it becomes a rival to any local authority. It fundamentally alters the options available to people.
Where, in the past, a local malcontent might have had to accept,
at least temporarily, the decision of a village council, he could
now file a lawsuit. This would drag everyone into an alien arena
where he would have "nothing to lose." Even though the
colonial ideal was to support local custom, rigorous rules of evidence made it nearly impossible for a judge to sort out factual
assertions of "troublemakers" from those of village authorities
so that custom could be accurately invoked. Shifting coalitions
of family, caste and village politics meant that relationships and
obligations were often ad hoc rather than customary.

We should remember, too, that this period of legal development was also a period of economic change in India. The
British did not provide markets and productive support systems
only for themselves. Development of railway and communications systems, urban centers, and the spread of governmental
jurisdiction, unified monetary and metric systems all contributed to an expanding range of economic options for Indians
seeking release from prior economic subjugation. The courts
became a scene of confrontation between those arguing for a
status quo that preserved their hereditary privileges and those
insisting on changes consistent with their efforts at self-improve-

ment. Because of the law's insistence on ancient custom, these lawsuits were often carried on as battles of interpretation over ancient custom.

Caste groups, for example, went into court to argue for an end to indignities imposed on them as low caste. Their position was that ancient wars had led to their degradation from lofty status and that their more recent economic successes proved their worthiness to be restored to high status. The vague documentation of ancient history made such arguments at least plausible, although these groups did not always succeed (Hardgrave, 1969).

In what I have written so far, there appears to be a paradox. One argument is that the courts ossified Indian society by insisting on ancient standards of conduct. The other is that courts opened the gates to dissenters and deviants, those local troublemakers least devoted to community harmony. Did the courts support the status quo, or did they open new opportunities to those brash enough to defy local authority? Or is there some way they could have done both?

Unfortunately, there is no way to test whether social change and mobility would have been faster or slower without the courts. They were too intimately linked with the rest of the colonial experience to be separately assessable. Both deviants, or "troublemakers," and established members of local elites used the courts in battles over status and privilege. But the overall impact of these battles on the rate of change is difficult to assess. What we can say is that the courts produced a pattern of distortion in the customs and relationships they were intended to preserve. The terms of conflict were altered by the new judicial presence. An element of chance now faced local disputants. An escape through court action became a real alternative for those with reason to resist local authority, as well as for those seeking to solidify unstable but advantageous definitions of local authority. Judicial decrees supporting the status quo could not support it, because the strategies and alliances needed to win produced important changes in local relationships. Even where entrenched privilege was upheld in court, the means of preserving that privilege was altered. By offering the chance for total victory in place of the traditional necessity to compromise, courts gave local conflicts a new urgency. The potential for loss or gain promised to be much more total than in traditional tribunals.

So the courts were a central element in changing the terms of "traditional Indian society." And this process of change was associated with the court's reputation as the center of treacherous dishonesty, capricious "justice," and immorality.

Comparison: Authoritarian Versus Common Law. Paradoxically, we can understand the fate of Britain's "live and let live" legal policy better if we compare it with a more authoritarian episode of imposed "Western" law. Bolshevik legal intervention in Soviet Central Asia (Massell, 1968) during the 1920s was designed to *change* local custom. The Soviets wanted to revolutionize Moslem society so that it could play a role in the industrialization of the country. To do this, they designed a plan, including the development of a completely new legal system, which would generate conflict among the Moslems. They created new courts, originally staffed by cadres from Moscow, and passed laws specifically designed to incite Moslem women to rebel against their slavelike status in the Moslem family.

The series of events that followed showed the ability of this system to produce conflict and change, but it did not match the Soviets' expectations. At first, there was feigned compliance with the new laws. Prominent leaders, for example, hired prostitutes to pose as their wives in mass ceremonies of unveiling. This was followed by a period during which women in growing numbers actually did take advantage of their "modern" legal status, especially in urban areas. The result was widespread divorce. For the women, this meant destitution, because family was the only traditional source of support, and Soviet authorities had inadequate resources to support women cast off by their families. Prostitution was their only economic alternative, and it grew to epidemic proportions. In reaction, Moslem men took violent revenge against women. Groups of men slaughtered wayward women in the streets, sometimes even disemboweling pregnant women. Many women finally returned to their families begging forgiveness. The rest remained prostitutes.

One Soviet response to this extreme reaction was to pull back and let local persons fill some of the positions in Soviet courts. While they hoped these would be persons versed in Soviet doctrine, they could not assure this. Men who had been judges under the traditional Moslem legal system thus infiltrated the Soviet system. These were locals well versed in the complexity of local custom and intrigue. The Soviets thus lost control of judicial decision making even as they gained the stability of local expertise. Still committed to their traditions rather than Soviet theory, these locals co-opted the Soviet courts, turning them into instruments for the preservation of the practices the Soviets wanted to destroy. Instead of Sovietizing Moslem law, the Soviets faced the Moslemization of their own system.

The British and Soviet models could hardly be more different at the level of intentions. But there are revealing similarities in the results of both systems. The Soviets were promoting conflict. The British sought ways to *reduce* conflict. The Soviets intended to eliminate local custom and make people into productive Soviet citizens. The British worked for the *preservation* of custom as a way of reducing conflict. For them, change was the enemy.

In spite of these differences, both powers lost control over the forces they had unleashed. And the loss of control was similar in both cases. Massell says that the Soviets lost control because they could not reconcile their use of the law to violate respected standards of conduct with the need to legitimize their own authority (Massell, 1968, p. 225). As I have shown, British law had unorthodox impact. It liberated many of those whose local reputations were tarnished by "immoral," unconventional actions and aspirations. The act of filing suit was itself widely regarded as a gesture of insolence, of irreverence. Even today, people try to clothe their legal action in legitimacy by saying their opponents "dragged them to court." As in the Soviet case, old relationships became unreliable, so new ones were developed. Although Indians did not co-opt the courts through official positions, as in the Soviet case, they did turn the courts to their own purposes through evasion, manipulation, subversion, and infiltration of lower-level court jobs. The net effect of much Indian litigation is to engage courts as additional agents in prolonged episodes of conflict that are periodically suspended by temporary compromises (Kidder, 1973).

We cannot measure how much additional conflict was generated by either the Soviet or British courts. But both systems made conflict more overt and altered its consequences. In this sense, both systems were agents of substantial social change, and both systems "got out of hand." How could two legal systems with such different philosophical bases and administrative procedures produce such similar results? The answer lies in certain shared characteristics that make up the essence of what is usually meant by the difference between "Western" law and "traditional" law.

For one thing, both the British and Soviet systems were centralized. While a common law tradition theoretically gave greater flexibility to the British Indian courts, the problems of evidence alluded to in the beginning of this chapter pressured colonial administrators to search for more certain, unqualified definitions of custom. The resulting rigidity stirred up the same kinds of alienated manipulative responses as those faced by the Soviets who began with more rigid statutes. The existence of externally determined legal agendas produced alienation, whether the intent was to alienate or not.

Secondly, both systems were designed with external economic and political considerations in mind. The Soviets had a clear-cut plan for the future of Soviet society, and the legal system was to abet the necessary economic transition. The British, while not planning for a specific new society, were concerned about maintaining a colony-wide atmosphere within which commerce and production could thrive. Efforts expended on behalf of the legal system had to be justified as contributing to the strength of the empire. So the agendas of Soviet and British-Indian courts were determined not only by local needs or local conflicts but also by economic and political policy needs defined by remote but influential actors.

Thirdly, both systems relied heavily on outsiders for routine administration. The Soviets sent cadres from Moscow, and the British sent judges and lawyers from London. In both cases, policy makers set criteria for employment according to gener-

alized, external standards—either "correct" political training
(Soviet) or "professionalism" (British colonial). The individual's
standing in the local community, his familiarity with local relationships and customs, and his reputation as local problem
solver counted *against* anyone seeking jobs in these systems. In
both cases, as people at the center began to see the need to employ locals, they tried to find those locals most different from
their peers. They still wanted people who would make decisions
following the external standards.

External Versus Internal Legal Systems. Both British and
Soviet systems were *external* to the communities whose affairs
they were designed to regulate. The British experience in India
demonstrates a general feature of the relationship between custom and law. Stanley Diamond (1973) calls that relationship
cannibalistic. By saying that law "cannibalizes custom," Diamond is emphasizing that "law" develops at the expense of
local custom, that "law" feeds on that custom and replaces it
with a new entity that bears only a faint, hollow resemblance.
In the Indian case, the difference is between the vital, changing
customs of local communities and the codified, inflexible body
of "custom" the British designated as law. Galanter summarizes
this same tendency: "In a modern system, there is a strong and
persistent tendency toward the replacement of local and popular law by official lawyer's law" (Galanter, 1966, p. 161).
India's experience with British law demonstrates the principle
that a community's customs cannot be separated from the
method of their enforcement without fundamentally altering
the effect (and therefore the meaning) of those customs in the
community.

What Galanter calls a "modern" legal system and what
Diamond calls simply "law," I am calling *external* legal systems.
Victor Li (1971) made the external-internal distinction to distinguish two legal models operating in modern China. The external model—a centrally administered, formalized legal system—
closely resembles "Western" law. But its impact on Chinese
society is marginal, compared to the internal model. This one
involves almost no use of the state's coercive power. Instead,
people's compliance even with central authority depends on

promoting community authority over individual choice. Law at the level of the local unit (neighborhood, work team, commune) is kept simple. Lawyers are never involved. Procedures are chosen to suit the case and the community. They need not be formally "just," only politically effective, pragmatic. While the state encourages this program, it does not intervene in the decision making. Appeal of decisions at this level is rare. The state's authority pervades the process because of the constant emphasis on political consciousness. The process of local decision making itself serves the goal of politicization, but not by imposing procedural restraints. The potential chaos of autonomy is checked by the intense program of political education. Local variation is not "cannibalized" by any system of legal standardization. Instead of using law either to protect local custom or obliterate it, the Chinese are using their protection of local autonomy as a means of mobilizing individuals. So there is broad-based participation in local decisions about responses to centrally stimulated change. Because one's own local group is the agent of so much social control and change, there is less alienation from mechanisms used. The potential for alienation is there in the tension between internal and external systems, but it is not directed against the internal forms.

The Indian experience with British law is best characterized as a clash between external and internal legal models. The fact that Indian culture differs from British culture is beside the point. I have shown elsewhere (Kidder, 1973) that Indian complaints about the inadequacies of a universalistic legal system are practically identical to the complaints one hears from litigants in the United States and Great Britain. Like Americans and Englishmen, Indians are struggling with the gap between the *legal culture* of centralized, bureaucratized legal authorities and the constantly changing, negotiable basis of local relationships. And, like Americans and Englishmen, Indians respond ambivalently, both condemning the system's impersonality and mystery (and expense) and manipulating the system to their own advantage. The "Western" law mentioned in the title is better understood as *external law*. Its key features, as itemized earlier, are all elements that, within the British colonial system, were produced by the dual remote pressures of operating an empire and a rationalized legal system.

On their face, the features of the British system seem designed to protect the individual. But protection of the individual promotes the interests of professionalism and colonialism. Steadfast promotion of the individual as the subject and object of legal action produces friction, if not outright rebellion, between individuals and the "traditional" or local communities that lay claim to their loyalties. Wherever the state steps in on behalf of the individual, there is a usurpation of the authority of local arrangements. The Soviets tried to use this inherent tension as a tool of policy. The Chinese have done just the opposite, removing the tension from the shoulders of communal units by telling individuals not to look to the state to bail them out of unwanted local obligations. The British plan in India was deceptive. It appeared to promote community values by defending the rights of individuals. But, by denying local autonomy over disputes and rule infractions, the British gutted local communities of one of their most important functions. They did not understand that the locus of community values (or custom) is the community, not the individual. Their system emasculated long-established devices for the assertion and development of community values and stifled the development of new devices to meet changing circumstances.

Independence and External Law

I have discussed colonial India at length here because little has happened since independence in 1947 to change basic elements of the picture. Indian law has remained *external* in spite of occasional attempts to "cleanse" it by a return to ancient practices. The persistence of externality is more than just the inertia of a stagnating society. It is part of a worldwide trend toward centralization that, under present economic and political conditions, seems irreversible. The political forces that won India's independence opted for the continuation of central control. To them, chaos and chronic inequality seemed to be the only alternatives.

The grip that "Western" law has had on India was not loosened by independence. If anything, liberation intensified the process of centralization, because the new government handed itself the task of rapid social and economic development. Within two years of independence, India adopted a constitution that guaranteed fundamental rights such as those in the United States Bill of Rights, spelled out the division of power among governmental bodies, and went into great detail about the government's responsibility to promote the transformation of Indian society into a unified, modern, secular state. It assigned government the task of ending caste and economic inequality, and it prescribed that the legal system was to be the vehicle for the transformation. Castism and religious favoritism were outlawed in the name of individual rights.

By 1956, India had adopted uniform codes of domestic law that prescribed "enlightened" standards for Hindu marriage, family relationships, and inheritance practices. These codes were meant to apply to all parts of India, and they were to be administered by the completely unified court system headed by the Supreme Court in New Delhi.

The legal profession has continued to experience the pressure for standardization. Today the only route into legal practice is through law college and qualifying examinations. Even the lowest courts are now staffed by judges who must earn law degrees and pass special qualifying examinations.

All such developments are extensions of the *external* legal model in spite of the departure of the British. The agendas of secularism, nationhood, and swift economic development produce pressure to circumvent or deride local "traditional" preferences. Castism, communalism, the dowry system, and arranged marriages are disparaged in favor of more "enlightened, modern, democratic" practices. Government must offer scholarships and special privileges to formerly deprived caste groups in order to redress ancient inequalities.

The Search for Internal Model Alternatives. As Galanter has shown (1972), one recurring theme of reaction against the external model has been the promotion of pre-British ideals of legal structure. Important elements of the independence movement, including Mahatma Gandhi, broke with the proponents of the centralized secular state. They argued instead for a return to village-based autonomy and self-sufficiency, including the elimination of centrally administered law.

From time to time since independence, people of this persuasion have pressed for the restoration of *panchayat* justice. Their model has been a romanticized version of India before the corruption of colonial rule. As *panchayats,* local village councils would preside over the hearing and dispositions of local conflicts. With their prestige as elders, these councils would cause litigiousness to evaporate. The goal was to provide all those features that are lacking in the present court system—cheap, efficient, popular conciliatory justice. The goal, in other words, was an internal legal model. The substance of solutions to disputes was not the main issue; the method of administration was.

Government finally responded to these wishes by establishing judicial and administrative *panchayats* for the villages. However, both were parts of government's pursuit of better economic performance through increased citizen participation. But this external agenda meant that the *panchayats* became simply an added layer of officialdom in the external system. The courts not only were left intact but were given the power to review *panchayat* decisions. Instead of insisting on a consensus as the basis of *panchayat* action, government took the majority-vote approach: Members were elected, not chosen by seniority; their decisions were treated as binding if supported by a bare majority. Each of these features transformed a traditional revival into an experiment in modern development. There is little evidence that these *panchayats* were ever allowed to be more than a channel for downward dissemination of official policies (Galanter, 1972, p. 9). No serious attempt has ever been made to restore local authority to the level of autonomy it is thought to have once enjoyed.

Externality and Civil Liberties. So "Western" law has become rooted in Indian society and shows no signs of yielding to any more indigenous system. But there have been changes in India's approach to law, particularly since the declaration of emergency in 1975. And those changes reflect an important distinction that needs to be made between different kinds of external legal models.

Like all complex legal systems, India's does not deal only with relationships between citizens. It is also deeply involved in supervising the relationships between citizens and government. Long before independence, India's courts developed a reputation as the Indian subject's only meaningful defense against arbitrary administrative action. Unlawful land seizures, unjust taxation, unjustified arrest, and arbitrary denial of service were all grievances that people could and did take to court. And the courts did serve as a check against administrative excess. This became even more acutely obvious during the long years of struggle for independence. Courts were often petitioned during those years on behalf of imprisoned freedom fighters. The drastic measures adopted by beleaguered police officials were subjected to judicial scrutiny, and many cases resulted in wholesale releases of detainees.

The constitution written after independence contained very careful provisions for the preservation of this judicial autonomy. The higher courts were given the power of judicial review and were empowered to entertain writs against government excess or nonperformance. Selection of judges was kept strictly apolitical, aloof from politicians and bureaucrats alike.

And these libertarian facilities were enthusiastically used. During the quarter century between 1950 and 1975, the Supreme Court of India ruled more pieces of central and state legislation unconstitutional than the U.S. Supreme Court has in its entire history (Gadbois, 1977, p. 22). A new legal specialty has arisen around the higher courts—the writ petition lawyer who handles nothing other than challenges to government actions.

In having this separate, highly independent judiciary, the governmental structure of India, both before and after independence, has differed from that of the Soviets. The Indian model contains a degree of pluralism within the external model that was almost totally lacking in the Soviet approach. For the Soviets, courts were not just channels for the downward dissemination of *legal* culture. They were explicitly treated as agents of a unified approach to planned change. In India, by contrast, the legal system has been external not only to local communities, but also to government itself. As apolitical agents of legal interpretation, the judges' isolation has been from both the masses and the political elites.

One result has been that government officials develop the same kinds of complaints about judicial naiveté that one hears among villagers. In his annoyance with judicial protection of property rights, for example, Nehru complained of judges "living in an ivory tower, unconnected with the world, unconnected with social developments, social forces, and everything that is happening, and thereby getting isolated from what is happening, from the facts of life" (Gadbois, 1977, p. 24). Like Franklin Roosevelt during the Great Depression, Nehru saw this "ivory tower" isolation as a barrier to important government economic reforms. Although the polarity is reversed, we hear the same kind of complaint today against federal judges whose "dream world" actions include court-ordered busing to achieve racial integration.

The history of relations between courts and the government since independence has been one of continuous conflict, particularly over property rights and the government's attempt to modify them in the pursuit of socialized development. The repeated stubborn refusal of the Supreme Court and state high courts to accept government initiatives has created growing friction, with the result that the courts were the prime target for "emergency" reforms between 1975 and early 1977. Several steps, including constitutional amendments, were taken to reduce the courts' power to interfere with reform programs. And the conservative "slant" of the judges themselves was alluded to as the primary fact making these changes necessary.

In March 1977, the government that took these authoritarian measures was toppled. In its place came a new regime pledging the restoration of judicial autonomy and the power to overrule government actions. This government was elected not on the strength of its commitment to economic development, but on its pledge to reverse the authoritarian trend.

The important question for this chapter is not whether one government or the other will survive, but what does this struggle reveal about the varieties of external law? Again comparing the British and Soviet models, we can see that the Soviet system was much more authoritarian. It was not a system that provided the Moslems with protection against the decisions of Bolshevik administrators. It was aimed exclusively at producing change by interference in domestic relationships. By contrast, a libertarian approach prevailed in India, where the goal was status quo maintenance. Social reform legislation was not a frequent part of the colonial program so the judicial frustration of administrative actions was not so frequently a source of tension in India.

But independent India has given itself a demanding agenda of social reform that is mandated in its constitution. And politicians have directly linked their own authoritarian initiatives with the need to move more quickly than judges and precedents have permitted. The dilemma of any Indian government that does not simply abandon the stated goals of social and economic reform is how to make reform legislation acceptable to judges whose constraints come from legal tradition, community values (custom), logic, precedent, and restrictive rules of evidence and procedure. This is a tension that is not likely to vanish in India, regardless of who governs.

But it is a tension between two external legal models. The authoritarian "emergency" attack on the courts was not an attack on their alienation from the masses, although periodic attempts were made to enlist mass support for reform by alluding to that alienation. Rather, courts were assailed for their alienation from the executive branch of government. Because they are both external models, they will continue to provoke moral condemnation and reaction among proponents of local values, and their contents will be distorted by contact with the limitless variations of localized conflict and compromise. People will continue to use courts, and local courts will continue to have a reputation for dishonesty, immorality, manipulation, delay, and expense. This will continue because the courts will still be the outsiders stepping in rather than the insiders lending their good offices.

An alienated reaction is the fate of all external model

systems, including America's. The imposition of an alien set of values—call them Western, modern, or revolutionary—does not produce this pattern. Rather, it is produced and reproduced throughout the world because external law lacks the fine tuning that gives internal model procedures the feeling of familiarity and responsiveness, although not necessarily fairness in a universalistic sense. Much of this sentiment against the external model is sheer romanticism—a form of forgetfulness about the potential for oppressive, exploitative, arbitrary action in internal-model proceedings. There is the implied belief that a return to internal forms could be accomplished without the sacrifice of individualism and egalitarianism that are among the products of the external model. The internal model can be cheap, quick, and recognizable even as it keeps people "in their place," whether this be as sharecroppers in Alabama or untouchables in South India.

But people's failure to appreciate the negative side of the internal model does not negate the analysis of their reactions to the external model. External legal systems are alien regardless of the "ethnic purity" of their practitioners and regardless of the degree of autonomy they grant to judges. And they are alien to those who feel abused by them as well as those who use them to their own advantage. The development of external systems, enlightened as we may feel they are about the value of the individual and the importance of "justice," always involves a sacrifice. The Indian experience with British law shows that sacrifice to be essentially the same as we find wherever external models of law have developed.

Conclusion

The power of the external model to provoke moral outrage and cynicism is obvious well beyond the borders of India. Almost every American generation has experienced the ritual of police and court reform when the "abuses" of existing procedures become too obvious to tolerate. While most reforms have had the net effect of increased centralization and professionalization (hence, increased externalization), some have been designed to restore simpler, more personalized, more pragmatic procedures (the internal model).

Most recently, this has taken the form of proposals to bolster urban neighborhood solidarity as a means of fighting crime. Proponents of this plan hope that if authority is taken from police and courts and returned to urban communities the greater simplicity of their actions will reduce crime and improve the atmosphere of trust in American cities. If past experience (including India's *panchayats*) is any guide, this hope is ill founded. It is unlikely that law can go internal as long as so many other facets of American life remain external, noncommunal. The small-claims courts, for example (see Yngvesson and Hennessey, 1975), were created in the belief that American law could be simplified and personalized for the "average citizen." They were supposed to offer inexpensive, uncomplicated, quick solutions to the "small" problems faced by ordinary people. Instead, they were transformed into tools of businessmen who used them as collection agencies for unpaid bills.

To recover the purity and simplicity of the internal model, revivalists would have to find ways to protect internal processes from external interference, whether from political or governmental manipulators, economic interests, or professional groups. A hands-off attitude would have to prevail generally, as it does now specifically for isolated groups such as the Amish, who have been given wide latitude to govern themselves. The Amish, of course, are very minimally integrated into mainstream American society. Most urban Americans are much more thoroughly integrated in ways that draw their attention and loyalties away from the urban "neighborhood." With the dual liabilities of low internal solidarity and continued pressure from competing external interests, the urban "community" seems an unlikely candidate for internal-model legal reforms.

Similarly, whatever India's future may hold, it is not likely to include a return to ancient forms of communal self-government. Too many features of Indian society have grown beyond the confines of communal self-sufficiency. Too many people have vested interests in avoiding the parochial constraints of locally based relationships. The issues that remain for debate concern the form of the external model that will prevail. That debate is by no means finished.

References

Cohn, B. S. "Some Notes on Law and Change in North India." *Economic Development and Cultural Change,* 1959, *5,* 79-93.

Cohn, B. S. "From Indian Status to British Contract." *Journal of Economic History,* 1961, *21,* 613-618.

Diamond, S. "The Rule of Law vs. the Order of Custom." In D. Black and M. Mileski (Eds.), *The Social Organization of Law.* New York: Seminar Press, 1973.

Gadbois, G. H. "The Emergency: Ms. Gandhi, the Judiciary, and the Legal Culture." 1977. Mimeograph available from author at the department of political science, University of Kentucky, Lexington, Ky. 40506.

Galanter, M. "The Modernization of Law." In M. Weiner (Ed.), *Modernization.* New York: Basic Books, 1966.

Galanter, M. "Changing Legal Conceptions of Caste." In M. Singer and B. S. Cohn (Eds.), *Structure and Change in Indian Society.* Chicago: Aldine, 1968a.

Galanter, M. "The Displacement of Traditional Law in Modern India." *Journal of Social Issues,* 1968b, *24,* 65-91.

Galanter, M. "The Aborted Restoration of Indigenous Law in India." *Comparative Studies in Society and History,* 1972, *14,* 53-70.

Hardgrave, R. L. *The Nadars of Tamilnad: The Political Culture of a Community in Change.* Berkeley: University of California Press, 1969.

Kidder, R. L. "Courts and Conflict in an Indian City: A Study in Legal Impact." *Journal of Commonwealth Political Studies,* 1973, *11,* 121-139.

Li, V. "The Evolution and Development of the Chinese Legal System." In J. Lindbeck (Ed.), *China: Management of a Revolutionary Society.* Seattle: University of Washington, 1971.

Massell, G. J. "Law as an Instrument of Revolutionary Change in a Traditional Milieu: The Case of Soviet Central Asia." *Law and Society Review,* 1968, *2,* 179-228.

Prasad, R. "The Profession of Law and What It Means." In M. S. Mani, *The Pen Pictures of The Dancing Girl.* Salem, India: Srinivasa, 1926.

Schmitthener, S. "A Sketch of the Development of the Legal Profession in India." *Law and Society Review,* 1968-1969, *3* (2-3), 337-382.

Stokes, E. *The English Utilitarians and India.* Oxford: Clarendon Press, 1959.

Yngvesson, B., and Hennessey, P. "Small Claims, Complex Disputes: A Review of the Small Claims Literature." *Law and Society Review,* 1975, *9,* 219-274.

6

John Hagan
Jeffrey Leon

Philosophy and Sociology of Crime Control

Canadian-American Comparisons

Although sociologists in recent years have shown considerable interest in the "societal response to crime," this interest usually has been circumscribed by national boundaries. The difficulties of gathering cross-national data make this situation understandable. Yet, if we are to improve our knowledge of variations in societal reactions to crime, cross-national comparisons will be of obvious value (Turk, 1977). This chapter draws on material from Canada and the United States to examine alternative North American responses to crime. Our concern is with such issues as how a society's efforts to control criminal behavior may be influenced by national values, historical conditions, and economic constraints. Our argument is that under different social conditions alternative societal strategies may be adopted to accomplish quite similar goals. However, before embarking

on this discussion, we must first introduce the concepts that
will form the background to our comparative analysis.

Two Models of the Societal Response to Crime

Packer (1964) has conceptualized societal responses to
crime in terms of "due process" and "crime control" models of
law enforcement. These models differ most conspicuously in
the rights they accord to individuals confronted by agencies of
the criminal law. The due-process model has its roots in the Enlightenment. Emphasis is placed here on the notion of John
Locke and others that the law can be used effectively in defense
of "natural" and "inalienable rights." Accordingly, the due-
process model is much concerned with exclusionary rules of evidence, the right to counsel, and other procedural safeguards
thought useful in protecting accused persons from unjust applications of criminal sanctions. Where errors are to be made in
law enforcement, advocates of the due-process model probably
are known best for their preference that guilty persons go free
before innocent persons are found guilty.

In contrast, the crime-control model receives philosophical support from the conservative reaction to Enlightenment thought. Influential here are the arguments of Edmund
Burke and others that civil liberties can have meaning only in
orderly societies. Thus, the crime-control model places heavy
emphasis on the repression of criminal conduct, arguing that
only by ensuring order can individuals in a society be guaranteed personal freedom. It is for this reason that advocates of
crime control are less anxious to presume the innocence of
accused persons and to protect such persons against sometimes
dubious findings of guilt. It is not that the crime-control model
favors the unfair treatment of individuals but rather that it is
willing to openly tolerate a certain amount of mistreatment
when the measures involved are seen as necessary, at least
symbolically, for the maintenance of social order. Individual
"rights" here assume a discretionary status in the hands of the
authoritative figures who control them

The Anglo-American democracies with which we are

most familiar tend formally more toward the due-process than the crime-control model just described. Nonetheless, the distinction between these models is one of degree. With this in mind, one Canadian social scientist notes that the "approach which is truest to our experience and most in keeping with our capabilities is that of Edmund Burke, not John Locke. Canadians— neither their judges, nor their politicians—are creatures of the Enlightenment" (Russel, 1975a, p. 592). Similarly, in the following pages we will argue that Canada, more than the United States, tends toward a crime-control model. Our interest is that these alternative societal strategies derive from a dissimilar set of societal conditions, yet are consistent with a quite similar set of goals: the establishment and maintenance of legal order. We are here using the concept of "legal order" to refer to any political organization that utilizes consensual and coercive mechanisms in the form of a "legal system" to regulate hierarchical relationships between authorities and subjects (see Turk, 1969, pp. 30-51; 1977, p. 32). We argue that for those at the top of the legal order—authorities—the consequences of the differing American and Canadian responses to crime may be much the same; however, for those at the bottom—subjects—the consequences of these alternative strategies seem to be significantly different. The purpose of this chapter is to provide a framework within which these possibilities can be discussed.

The United States and Canada in Comparison

We must begin with some sense of the possible societal differences that distinguish the United States and Canada. Classic Canadian-American comparisons are found in the works of Clark (1942, 1962, 1976) and Lipset (1963, 1964, 1968). Central to both authors' work is the proposition that "Whereas the American nation was a product of the revolutionary spirit, the Canadian nation grew mainly out of forces of a counterrevolutionary character" (Clark, 1962, pp. 190-191). Three factors are included among the counterrevolutionary forces that have influenced Canada: (1) the movement of British loyalists to Canada during and after the American Revolution; (2) the role

played by the Church of England and the Roman Catholic
Church in providing Canada with a set of hierarchical and traditionally rooted control mechanisms; and (3) the threat posed to
Canada's frontier expansion by parallel frontier activities in the
United States (Lipset, 1968, chap. 2). Each of these factors is
said to have had a conservatizing effect on the values of Canadians as contrasted with Americans.

Thus, various authors, in different ways, have called attention to the relatively more conservative values of Canadians.
Clark (1962, p. 191) speaks of the "forces of conservatism"
that emerged in the Canadian response to its frontier experience. Naegle (1964, p. 501) describes a "conservative mold"
that makes Canada "a country of greater caution, reserve, and
restraint." Vallee and Whyte (1971) speak of a Canadian "conservative syndrome," consisting of "a tendency to be guided by
tradition; to accept the decision-making functions of elites . . .
[and] to put a strong emphasis on the maintenance of order
and predictability."

Porter (1967, p. 56) links this Canadian conservatism to
the nation's two charter groups, noting that "English and
French Canadians are more alike in their conservatism, traditionalism, religiosity, authoritarianism, and elite values than the
spokesmen of either group are prepared to admit." However, it
is probably Lipset (1968, p. 51) who most explicitly links these
values differences to the events that shaped American and Canadian history: "Once these events had formed the structure of
the two nations, their institutional characters were set. Subsequent events tended to enforce 'leftist' values in the south and
'rightist' ones in the north."

Lipset (1963, 1964) conceptualizes these value differences in terms of four dichotomized variables, the first three of
which are adopted from Parsons: achievement-ascription, uni-
versalism-particularism, self-orientation-collectivity-orientation,
and egalitarianism-elitism. Lipset compares four English-speaking democracies—the United States, Australia, Canada, and
Great Britain—concluding that the four nations can be ordered
respectively in terms of the four polarities and that Canada patterns itself most after Great Britain. Thus, in Lipset's terms, the

Canadian value system is more ascriptive, particularistic, collec-
tivity-oriented, and elitist than is the case in the United States.
Evidence presented by Lipset in support of these conclusions
includes crime and divorce rates and levels of educational advancement. Both Lipset's evidence and conclusions have pro-
voked significant debate.

One measure of the intensity of the response to Lipset's
work is the judgment of Davis (1971, p. 16) that "The Lipset
concept of American ... and Canadian Society ... is so laced
with invalid claims and ideological blind spots that it is a waste
of time to refute it." Nonetheless, Davis goes on to argue that,
contrary to the American values portrayed by Lipset, "The
United States is a hierarchical, racist society." Davis further suggests (p. 19) that "After the first world war, the Americans
quickly displaced Britain as the primary influence on Canadian
society—a trend that was reinforced by the rapid decline of
Britain itself to a satellite status within the American orbit."
Thus Davis argues that Canada has assumed the role of a "hinterland" in relation to the American "metropolis," making
Canada "a pale reflection of American stratagems and American
drift." The result, according to Davis (p. 19), is "not only
second-class status, but also 'homogenization.' "

Similarly, Horowitz (1973, p. 330) argues that the view
presented by Lipset denies "the idea of class struggle and racial
conflict in American society," and that the older British or "imperial connection" to Canada is now replaced by a continental
or "American connection" (p. 346) that is hemispheric in scope
(see also Horowitz, 1966, 1970). Using various types of data,
including crime statistics, Horowitz (1973, p. 340) concludes
that "the differences between Canada and the United States, at
the level of values, are better framed in terms of cultural lag
than in terms of polarized or reified value differences" (see also
Truman, 1971). According to Horowitz, American imperialism
is supplanting British colonialism, and consequently the "cultural gap" is closing.

It may be instructive to briefly consider the evidence
Horowitz uses in reaching the specific conclusion (1973, p. 341)
that "The data on criminality and homicide reveal marked

tendencies toward closing the 'cultural gap.' " Canadian and
American statistics on rape, robbery, breaking and entering, and
theft are provided for one year only, 1966, and murder statistics are provided for Canada only, 1954 to 1970. It should be
apparent that data on the same crimes from *both* countries and
from at least *two* points in time are necessary to draw inferences about "closing the cultural gap." The data presented by
Horowitz, then, cannot speak properly to this issue. In a later
section of this chapter we examine the type of data that *is* required to address this issue.

Meanwhile, we should note that the most recent attempt
to deal with the debate between Lipset and his critics reveals
that the issues involved are as much semantic as empirical. Thus,
according to Hiller (1976, p. 140): "It could be argued that the
urbanization and industrialization of societies has contributed
to a *homogenization of values* among them. If this were so, we
might expect statistics of behavior patterns to be increasingly
similar. However, such a similarity might never be verified as
long as structural and cultural differences (such as divorce laws,
norms of family size, norms of remarriage) confound the meaning of our statistics. . . . Perhaps differences in the organization
of the Society (for example, forms and styles of government)
will help to perpetuate societal distinctions in spite of some
value convergence."

A difficulty with this argument is that it simultaneously
seems to affirm and deny societal differences. Apparently,
Hiller is arguing that values can converge, while norms, structures, and cultures remain different. Depending on how one defines these terms, this may or may not be true. However, the
significant issue would seem to be the type of differences that
actually distinguish societies, specifically Canada and the United
States, at different points in time. Thus, as Clark notes (1976,
p. 53), "It may be that Lipset was quite wrong in the criteria he
used but, even if he was, that in no way establishes the fact that
differences in the value systems of the two countries did not
exist. To resolve such an issue involves an examination of the
structure of the American and Canadian societies, something
that Horowitz does not attempt." The remainder of this paper

is devoted to such an examination in the area of Canadian and American attempts to deal with crime. Our interest is in how the differences discussed by Lipset and Clark may correspond to these two societies' responses to crime and their respective efforts to establish and maintain legal order.

A Historical Overview

It obviously is impossible to thoroughly discuss American and Canadian history in a paper devoted primarily to issues of crime and legal order. Nonetheless, salient aspects of the two nations' histories can be highlighted and related to the issues that confront us. Salient points of comparison are introduced in the works of the late Canadian historian Harold Innis and developed further in the more recent works of Clark.

Innis (1927, 1933, 1954), and later Clark, were convinced that the interplay of geographical, cultural and economic forces was quite different in the two nations. Each argued that Canada and the United States adopted rather different strategies of national development. Clark's most recent statement of this position emphasizes that these alternative strategies derived from differing conditions of expansion. The resources in the southern part of the continent were accessible and exploitable without large-scale state intervention: "Such was the case of the coastal fisheries off the Atlantic seaboard . . . the farmlands of Virginia, Massachusetts, New York, and, with the discovery of the Cumberland Pass, of Kentucky, or the coal fields of western Pennsylvania or the iron fields of northern Michigan" (1975, p. 55).

In contrast, Canadian resources were harder to reach and more difficult to develop. There was the persistent problem of transporting raw staple products out of the country (first fur; later lumber; and finally wheat, pulp, paper, and minerals) and moving manufactured goods back in (Innis, 1956). Furthermore, there was the challenge of fishing the continental shelf; the fur trade steadily receded further and further into the interior; until the peninsula of Western Ontario was reached, farm land was limited to Prince Edward Island, the Annapolis, Saint

John, and Saint Lawrence Valleys; and the minerals to be mined
were hidden away in the Precambrian shield and in the rock-
bound interior of British Columbia. Development of these areas
required large-scale organization, long lines of communication
and transportation, and extensive state support (Clark, 1975).
These initial problems served in Canada to encourage and legitimate state intervention and control (Innis, 1956; see also Risk,
1973).

Added to this, the difficulties of developing Canadian resources also made the northern nation vulnerable to attack from
the south. Outlying settlements in New Brunswick, upper
Canada, and the eastern townships all faced serious threats of
American absorption (Clark, 1962, p. 189). This problem became of added concern with the westward movement (R. C.
MacLeod, 1976).

In the East, Canada frequently had handled such problems of law, order, and sovereignty with the military: "Thus
about the fur-trading posts of New France, in the agricultural
settlements of New Brunswick and Upper Canada, and in the
shanty towns of Irish canal workers the army played an important role in maintaining order. . . . [and] in the isolated fishing
settlements of Nova Scotia, policing was a function of the
navy" (Clark, 1962, p. 191; see also Clark, 1942). Although the
military was to play a crucial role in the Canadian West as well,
early on it was determined that a more effective strategy would
need to be developed to make frontier development financially
feasible.

Thus, R. C. MacLeod (1976) notes that by the 1870s the
American government was spending over $20 million a year
alone fighting the Plains Indians. At the same time, the *total*
Canadian budget was just over $19 million, and every available
part of this budget was committed to providing the essential
railway transportation emphasized by Innis. In financial terms,
"It is not an exaggeration to say that the only possible Canadian
West was a peaceful one" (R. C. MacLeod, 1976, p. 3). So it was
that the North-West Mounted Police (NWMP) became an essential part of Sir John A. MacDonald's famous "National Policy"
for Canada.

Much of the efficiency of the NWMP derived from the fact that it "enjoyed powers unparalleled by any other police force in a democratic country" (R. C. MacLeod, 1976, p. x). This "temporary" force, which later became permanent, was to consist of men trained both as soldiers and police. Their mission was to prevent crime and disorder from developing (as it did in the United States) to the point where only military action could bring it under control. A key to accomplishing this goal was a fusion of the traditionally divided police and administrative functions. Thus the Mounted Police were given not only the usual powers to apprehend offenders but also administrative powers to act as magistrates. Furthermore, they were to carry out their responsibilities under the explicit direction of the executive branch of the federal government. In understatement, R. C. MacLeod concludes (1976, p. 163) that "A permanent federal police force was a long step ... [toward] direct government involvement in the life of the citizen." Clark (1976, p. 6) aptly describes these conditions of Canadian development as constituting a "closed" frontier.

On the other hand, in the United States, local authorities were free to develop their own law enforcement policies or to ignore the problem altogether (Quinney, 1970, p. 55). Inciardi (1975, p. 88) notes that "The American frontier was Elizabethan in its quality, simple, childlike, and savage. . . . It was a land of riches where swift and easy fortunes were sought by the crude, the lawless, and the aggressive, and where written law lacked form and cohesion." As previously indicated, the American frontier was nowhere more savage than in its treatment of the Indians. In Clark's terms, the American West amounted to an "open" frontier. The opposition of the terms *open* and *closed* in Clark's description of American and Canadian frontier conditions makes explicit the contrast between order and freedom in the two experiences. Thus, "In the United States, the frontier bred a spirit of liberty which often opposed efforts to maintain order. In Canada, order was maintained at the price of weakening that spirit" (Clark, 1962, p. 192).

This historical concern for order is again apparent when the Canadian response to political crime is examined. The historian McNaught (1975) makes this point in reviewing four famous challenges to the political structure of Canada: the cases of Lount and Matthews for their parts in the Mackenzie rebellion of 1837; the execution of Louis Riel in 1915; the cases of eight leaders and other participants in the Winnipeg General Strike of 1919; and the government response to the "Quebec Crisis" of 1970. McNaught (1975, p. 139) sees in these cases a pattern of "firm action and succeeding lenience which seems to characterize our basically conservative political-judicial tradition." His explanation of this pattern draws once more on the Burkean theme in Canadian politics, concluding that (p. 138) "the basically British belief that both liberty and justice are impossible without order lies at the heart of the Canadian political tradition and of the manner in which our judicial process has dealt with cases of a clearly political nature."

These impressions are once more confirmed by the historical development of various legal institutions in Canada. It is interesting to note that while in the United States jurisdiction to enact criminal law resides primarily with individual states, in Canada the British North America Act assigns the federal government jurisdiction over criminal law and procedure, resulting in a more orderly, centralized, and unified set of criminal statutes (Laskin, 1969). The first Criminal Code of Canada was enacted by Parliament in 1892 and has remained largely unchanged for more than eighty years. The code was based in large part on Sir James Stephen's English Draft Code, which, ironically, was never adopted in England. Although the code was minimally revised in 1953 (McLeod and Martin, 1955), Mewett (1967, p. 735) concludes that "tampered . . . and tinkered with, it remains the monument of the eminent Victorian, Sir James Stephen."

Nor have the procedural provisions associated with the Canadian criminal law been a lively body of legislation.[1] Mewett (1967, p. 724) notes that "the procedural rules still stem very largely from the Criminal Procedure Act of 1869 with little judicial development." This slowness of change may result in part from the differing character of Canadian and American efforts to avoid the arbitrary or inequitable exercise of state

powers. American civil liberties, including the right to due
process and to equality before the law, are constitutionally entrenched in the American Bill of Rights. Through the American
doctrine of judicial review, individuals and minorities look to
judges and the courts as the guardians of their constitutionally
protected liberties. In contrast, Smiley (1975, p. 89) notes that
"the term *entrenchment* has no accepted meaning in Canadian
constitutional law or practice" and (p. 100) that "when we
begin to inquire carefully into those institutions of Canadian
Society under the direct control of the bar and the bench we
will find less than a total commitment to humane values" (see
also Russel, 1975b). Similarly, McWhinney (1965, p. 69) notes
that "the theory of the judicial slot machine is still powerful in
a country whose jurisprudence is dominated, as Canada's is, by
the worst rigors of Austinian formalism." Thus, the Canadian
approach places its ultimate constitutional faith in the supremacy of Parliament. Bruton (1962, p. 108) reminds us that this
faith must ultimately rest on a belief in the self-restraint of a
parliamentary majority: "Consequently faith in parliamentary
supremacy as a protection against arbitrary government becomes faith that the majority can be depended upon not to
work its will in arbitrary ways."

In 1960, the Canadian Parliament was thought to have
supplemented, and perhaps even supplanted, its guardian role
with the passage of "An Act for the Recognition and Protection
of Human Rights and Fundamental Freedoms"—in short, the
"Canadian Bill of Rights." It can be argued that the late appearance of the Canadian Bill of Rights itself signals a fundamental
historical difference in concern for due process protections in
Canada. However, of possibly even greater significance are recent decisions of the Supreme Court of Canada that indicate a
reluctance to construe the Canadian Bill of Rights as authority
for a court to interfere with the substantive content of legislation enacted by the Federal Parliament, including the Criminal
Code of Canada (see Tarnopolsky, 1975b).[2] Such an interpretation casts doubt on the progress being made toward the protection of individual rights by the Canadian judiciary. Minimally,
this is consistent with the theme of our discussion—that histori-

cally Canada has adopted a significantly more modest role than
the United States in formally protecting and safeguarding individual "rights" in the criminal process.

One final indication that Canada historically has adopted
a different response to crime from that in the United States is
found in the area of penal reform. Jaffary (1963; see also Bellomo, 1972; Beattie, 1977) has compared the progress of penal
reform in Canada, the United States, and Britain, and concludes
again that Canada lags behind. One illustration of this fact is
that penal reform really did not get under way in Canada until
1946, and then only after years of activist support from the
first female Member of Parliament, Agnes Macphail. Like Clark
and Lipset, Jaffary argues that interest in penal reform was restrained by early and enduring problems of developing the
country's resources.

What remains unresolved is the issue of whether the restrictive historical pattern we have identified persists in contemporary Canadian, as contrasted with American, strategies of
dealing with crime. It will be recalled that Horowitz, Davis, and
Hiller have doubted such persistence, arguing that the two countries are becoming "homogenized." In the following sections,
this issue is posed in terms of two central areas of procedural
criminal law, the exclusionary rule of evidence and right to
counsel, both of which are focal concerns in discussions of the
crime-control versus due-process models of law enforcement.
This discussion will be followed with an updating of the crime
and police statistics originally presented by Lipset, with the goal
of relating statutory provisions and judicial statements to behavioral and organizational patterns in Canadian and American
responses to crime.

Right to Counsel

The critical role of legal counsel in representing a defendant in criminal proceedings is well recognized in both Canada
and the United States. As well, the courts, the legal profession,
and the public increasingly are coming to the realization that
proper functioning of the adversary process demands more than

the mere *presence* of counsel. Representation must be informed and vigorous; counsel must be competent and effective. Yet, a common awareness of the significance of effective legal representation has resulted in somewhat different judicial and legislative responses in the Canadian and American legal systems. Differing bases in law for the "right to counsel" and diverse judicial attitudes toward the denial of this right color considerations of incompetency and ineffectiveness in these two systems.

The "right to effective representation" is essentially an American notion that has developed from an expansion of the concept of a constitutional right to be provided with counsel under the Sixth and Fourteenth Amendments.[3] In general, Canadian courts have been slow to follow American jurisprudence in defining the right to be provided with counsel in Canadian criminal proceedings.[4] Thus, the Supreme Court of Canada has consistently dismissed the relevance of the American Bill of Rights for interpreting the Canadian Bill of Rights. For example, in *R.* v. *Miller and Cockriell* the majority reasoned that the two "differ so radically in their purpose and content that judgments rendered in interpretation of one are of little value in interpreting the other."[5] This position was preceded by an earlier opinion that "American cases . . . turn on an interpretation of a constitution basically different from our own and particularly on the effect to be given to the 'due process of law' provision of the Fourteenth Amendment of that Constitution for which I am unable to find any counterpart in the British North America Act, 1867 which is the source of legislative authority for the Parliament of Canada" (*Hogan* v. *the Queen*).[6] While these statements admittedly are no more than judicial interpretations of legal documents, the contrast with the trend toward Americanization predicted by Horowitz and Davis is apparent.

An absolute right to counsel has yet to be affirmed in Canada (see Grossman, 1967). A person who retains counsel is entitled to counsel's assistance, but a court is not deprived of jurisdiction, by statute or by common law, to try an accused person not represented by counsel. Rather, the primary concern is that the accused not be denied a "fair" trial. On the issue of "fairness," there are various views. For example, in *Re Gilberg and The Queen* the appellate division of one provincial supreme court advises that "counsel is not always a necessary concomitant to a fair trial."[7]

Nonetheless, (1) the absence of counsel is a factor that is assigned significant weight on appeal in determining whether there was a "substantial wrong" or "miscarriage of justice" at trial; (2) the Canadian Bill of Rights has been interpreted as providing the right to retain counsel in certain pretrial situations; (3) the Criminal Code of Canada entitles an accused "to make full answer and defense personally or by counsel" at trial; and (4) various provincial legal aid programs provide some of the necessary assistance to make these provisions meaningful. Thus, it might be argued that by alternative means the Canadian accused is placed in approximately the same position as the American accused. The limits of this argument depend on the significance attached to the difference between a constitutionally guaranteed right and a discretionary power available to judges and to the personnel of legal aid programs, as well as on the significance of the issue of effectiveness we consider next.

As we have indicated, the right to *effective* representation, as an element of the constitutional right to counsel, is an evolving concept in American law. The requirement of effectiveness was established in *Powell* v. *Alabama* and subsequently affirmed in later Supreme Court decisions.[8] Historically, for representation by counsel to be ineffective, the assistance rendered had to be sufficiently inadequate to amount to a "farce," "sham," or "mockery of justice." More recently, however, the U.S. Supreme Court has indicated that counsel's actions should come "within the range of competence demanded of attorney in criminal cases."[9]

In contrast, Canadian provincial appellate courts to date have professed reluctance to address issues related to the competency of counsel at trial or alternatively have ignored the issue altogether. Even where a specific instance of a failure by trial counsel to take appropriate action is documented, appellate judges are hesitant to recognize this as justification for finding a substantial wrong or miscarriage of justice and hence for ordering a new trial. In *R.* v. *Draskovic,* a reason for this position is advanced: "We think it would be a very dangerous practice to review in this court the tactical procedures adopted by defense counsel, and if we thought that he should obviously have adopted some other course, then to declare the trial unfair to the accused to a degree constituting a mistrial. Many difficult decisions have to be made by defense counsel in a trial such as this, sometimes on the spur of the moment."[10]

It may be consistent with the "crime-control" emphasis of the Canadian criminal justice system "to accept incompetency in the practice of criminal law if it secures the long-range goal of bringing more alleged offenders to justice" (Cohen, 1977, p. 68). Yet, the distinction between *no* counsel and *ineffective* counsel is one of degree, and to create merely an *appearance* of representation may be misleading. In any event, we have noted that there are significant differences in "rights" to counsel in Canada and the United States. In Canada, access to counsel is more a matter of discretion rather than guarantee, and little attention is directed toward the disadvantages faced by an accused subjected to incompetent representation.[11] Mewett (1970, p. 18) effectively summarizes the Canadian view of the criminal process in suggesting that with "an adequate system of legal aid" and a "desire on the part of the courts not to prejudice unfairly an accused," concern in Canada is better conceptualized in terms of "prevention of abuses" rather than "the enforcement of 'rights.' " That is, "There must be rules to safeguard the individual but those rules cannot be formulated with a disregard for the interests of the community."

Illegally Obtained Evidence

The "exclusionary rule" renders much illegally obtained evidence inadmissible in American courts of law. Under this rule, material or testimonial evidence may be excluded when it is obtained directly by illegal methods or, with some notable exceptions, when such evidence is indirectly secured by illegal methods.

The development of the American exclusionary practice

can be traced through a series of cases that highlight judicial concern with constitutional guarantees of individual liberties and fundamental human rights. Briefly, in *Weeks* v. *United States*[12] the American Supreme Court held that evidence obtained contrary to the Fourth Amendment of the Constitution was inadmissible in that to admit such evidence would eliminate the protection intended by this amendment. Further to the point, in *Wolf* v. *Colorado*,[13] rights secured by the first eight amendments to the American Constitution were held to be protected by the Fourteenth Amendment. Thus individual states could not deprive a person of his life, liberty, and property without "due process of law." More specifically, in *Mapp* v. *Ohio*,[14] the exclusionary rule was held to extend to all American courts, removing earlier constitutional doubts about the application of this rule in the state courts.

Although there is continuing debate in the United States about the advisability of an exclusionary rule (for example, Spiotto, 1973a, 1973b), advocates typically cite two justifications: first, that application of the exclusionary rule should have the effect of deterring the police from using illegal tactics, and second, that the existence of this rule confirms the precedence given by the American Constitution to "due process" over "crime control." In short, the American position on illegally obtained evidence is an attempt, at least symbolically, to preserve and protect the constitutionally entrenched rights of individuals.

In contrast, the Canadian position and the English tradition from which it is derived are less concerned with the rights of individuals than with the *relevance* of the evidence. This English attitude toward evidence is expressed candidly in *R.* v. *Leatham*: "It matters not how you get it; if you steal it, it will still be admissible in evidence."[15]

The Canadian position on illegally obtained evidence is staked out most recently in the 1970 Supreme Court decision in *R.* v. *Wray.*[16] Contrary to the "American connection" postulated by Horowitz and Davis, "in this decision, the Supreme Court examined the English common law in some detail, particularly as expressed by the English courts in *Kuruma* v. *The*

Queen, Noor Mohamed v. *The King,* and *Callis* v. *Gunn,*[17] but almost completely ignored American cases that have dealt with this topic" (Law Reform Commission of Canada, 1974, p. 7). As a result, the Canadian position is now much like that asserted in England by the Privy Council (in upholding Kuruma): "In their Lordships' opinion, the test to be applied in considering whether the evidence is admissible is whether it is relevant to the matters in issue. If it is, it is admissible, and the court is not concerned with how the evidence was obtained."[18]

In Canada, the road to Wray can be traced to the 1886 case of *R.* v. *Doyle.*[19] In this case, the Ontario Court of Appeal established the admissibility of objects found during an illegal search. In 1949, a judge of the Ontario High Court, in *R.* v. *St. Lawrence,*[20] further indicated that evidence discovered as a result of an involuntary (and hence inadmissible) confession was admissible. The Kuruma principle was specifically adopted by the Supreme Court of Canada in the case of *Attorney General of Quebec* v. *Begin.*[21] Most significantly, however, in the 1970 case of *R.* v. *Wray,* the Supreme Court of Canada reaffirmed the St. Lawrence decision and then held that a trial judge does not have the authority to exclude evidence otherwise admissible, unless that evidence would operate "unfairly" for the accused. Furthermore, "It is only the allowance of evidence gravely prejudicial to the accused, the admissibility of which is tenuous and whose probative force in relation to the main issue before the court is trifling which can be said to operate unfairly."[22] Thus, in Canada the prime if not sole criterion of admissibility is relevance, with the Canadian judge's discretionary power to exclude evidence severely constrained. This principle applies notwithstanding clear violations of the Canadian Bill of Rights.[23]

In summary, the Canadian attitude toward illegal evidence derives from English precedents and places concern for social order ahead of individual rights. The common Canadian response to the American rule of exclusion is that "the price paid by society for such a rule is too high" (Law Reform Commission of Canada, 1974, p. 22). Thus, "The State has the right and the duty to protect and promote respect for the security of social life" (p. 26). To the extent that proposals for reform are seriously considered in Canada, they involve assigning judges increased discretion to decide the *degree* to which social concerns should override individual rights with regard to the exclusion of illegally obtained evidence.

The Statistics of Crime and Its Control
in Canada and the United States

We have reviewed a considerable amount of historical and contemporary evidence indicating that judicial responses to crime differ in Canada and the United States. Our final concern is to determine how these differences may be reflected in national statistics of crime. It will be recalled that Lipset has suggested an historical continuity in these statistical differences, while Horowitz has doubted their persistence. The tables presented in this section speak to this issue. Also, a comparison is presented of recent resource commitments of the two countries in responding to crime.

Table 1 focuses on the crimes (burglary, homicide, for-

Table 1. American and Canadian Adults Charged with Selected
Indictable Offenses, 1960 and 1970, per 100,000 Population.

	United States		Canada		United States and Canada	
	1960	1970	1960	1970	1960	1970
Burglary	124	200	46	57	2.7	3.5
Criminal Homicide	7	12	1.2	1.5	5.8	8.0
Forgery and Counterfeiting	21	32	6	9	3.5	3.6
Fraud and Embezzlement	35	59	14	22	2.5	2.7
Theft and Larceny	208	432	87	149	2.4	2.9

Sources: Lipset (1964, p. 177); U.S. Bureau of the Census (1972, p. 150); Statistics Canada (1970, pp. 38-40, recomputed). The American figures for 1960 are taken from U.S. Bureau of the Census (1972), rather than from Lipset; the differences are minor and relate to the population bases included. The population base used for the 1970 Canadian figures is the 1971 census estimate, excluding Quebec and Alberta so as to correspond to the absence of these provinces from the 1970 Canadian crime statistics. Included within Lipset's "burglary" category are a small number of extortions and robberies.

gery and counterfeiting, fraud and embezzlement, theft and larceny) originally selected by Lipset (1964) and compares their incidence per 100,000 population in 1960 (the year originally considered by Lipset) and 1970 in the United States and Canada. The results reveal conclusions opposite to those of Horowitz. During this period, the ratio of U.S. to Canadian arrests increased rather than declined in all five crime categories, with the American rates (per 100,000 population) ranging from 2.7 to 8 times the Canadian rates in 1970. In short, the national difference in reported crime in 1970 is substantial, and more so than in 1960.

Table 2 further examines homicide rates in the two countries in 1957, 1967, and 1968. It is often suggested that

Table 2. American White and Nonwhite Adults and Canadian White Adults, by Sex, Charged for Homicide, 1957, 1967, and 1968, per 100,000 Population.

	Males			Females		
	1957	1967	1968	1957	1967	1968
United States	7.6	11.3	13.4	2.4	3.4	3.4
White	3.5	5.4	6.6	1.4	2.0	2.0
Nonwhite	43.4	58.8	68.6	10.8	13.2	13.6
Canada	1.5	1.9	2.2	.9	1.2	1.3
United States and Canada	5.1	6.0	6.1	2.7	2.8	2.6
Nonwhite United States and Canada	28.9	30.9	31.2	12.0	11.0	10.5
White United States and Canada	2.3	2.8	3.0	1.6	1.7	1.5

Source: U.S. Bureau of the Census (1973, p. 149, recomputed).

the differing crime rates of the two countries result from the racial problems that characterize American history. Homicide is one of the crimes that is most strongly connected to race in the United States (Wolfgang, 1958). Table 2 illustrates this point but also reveals that the biggest increase in homicide rates over the decade occurred among *white American males* and that the white American male homicide rate was three times the Canadian rate in 1968. Again, contrary to the prediction of Horowitz, this national difference showed evidence of expansion rather than contraction during the preceding eleven years.

Furthermore, as Lipset originally indicated, these differing patterns of crime are paralleled by different levels of police strength. Thus, although both Canada and the United States have increased their per capita levels of police strength since Lipset's (1964, p. 176) analysis in the early 1960s, in 1972 the United States continues to be significantly more highly policed (with 279.3 officers per 100,000 population) than is Canada (202.6 officers per 100,000 population).[24] The implication of this finding is that the United States is assigning a larger share of its resources to police work.

The issue of resource commitment also can be pursued by comparing the official costs of police work, court work, and corrections in each country. As predicted by our previous findings, the United States spends more proportionately on its police than does Canada ($33.06 compared to $31.21 per 1,000 population), substantially more on its courts ($9.92 compared to $5.02 per 1,000 population), and more as well in the area of corrections ($11.60 compared to $8.73).[25] Overall, there is consistency: Canada assigns significantly less of its per capita resources in each area of crime control than does the United States. We are now in a position to draw some conclusions.

Conclusions

On the basis of our brief discussion, it is possible to describe for further consideration two quite different approaches used on this continent to establish and maintain legal order. We have conceptualized these two national strategies on a scale bounded at either end by the "crime-control" and "due-process" models of law enforcement. Canada comes closer to the former model, while the United States, at least formally, comes closer to the latter. We must emphasize that neither nation nor model, of course, openly encourages *or* eliminates abuses of the criminal process; rather, each symbolizes a different balance between individual and community interests. In this chapter, we have considered historical and contemporary correlates and consequences of the Canadian and American approaches. Historically, the southern part of this continent contained resources that could be exploited with less governmental involvement and consequently less government control. As well, the United States purportedly was conceived as a nation devoted to the rights and responsibilities of individuals. This "revolutionary" ideology came to be symbolized in part by constitutionally safeguarded rights to due process and to equality before the law. One result was an ideology of individualism that, combined with exploitable resources, allowed and encouraged more extensive variations from the norm than was the case in the northern part of the continent. Thus, the American frontier was also a criminal frontier, a model in some ways for the city life that followed. In Bell's (1953) apt phrase, "Crime is an American way of life."

However, as the United States developed as a nation the establishment of a viable legal order also became a priority. On a formal and symbolic level, the American commitment to a due-process model of law enforcement continued to be ideologically important. The antidote to this ideology was a similar national commitment and assignment of resources to policing and punishing deviant behavior. The United States was to have a legal order that combined higher levels of crime with a very active and coercive police response. Some of the historical irony of this situation is captured in Skolnick's (1975, p. 246) description of the police as America's "asphalt cowboys."

In contrast, the Canadian approach was one of initially more firm, but also necessarily more strategic, control. Historically, the Canadian attitude placed a stronger emphasis on social order in relation to individual rights. Thus, the Canadian frontier was a closed frontier, in the sense that its development was to be closely controlled. This historical emphasis on social order is today commonly noted in the greater "respect" given by Canadians to the ideal of "law and order" (Wrong, 1955, pp. 37-38). For our purposes, it makes little difference whether this respect is identified as evidence of "hegemony"—resulting from class domination—or "consensually shared values"—democratically conceived and supported. It probably is both. The point is that Canada has been able to limit its resource commitment to crime control by reemphasizing its ideological commitment to the Burkean ideal of social order first and individual rights second. Thus, in Canada, the police role is preeminently symbolic, a reminder that social order ideologically precedes individual freedoms. As the Canadian novelist Margaret Atwood (1972, p. 171) has noted, "Canada must be the only country in the world where a policeman is used as a national symbol." Here legal order is built on a broader base of consensus—albeit a consensus that legally and historically is situated in a demonstrated willingness to apply coercion in a systematic and concerted way.

The consequences of the Canadian and American strategies of dealing with crime are essentially the same for the socially advantaged of both countries. Both nations possess a legal order that allows the safe and stable conduct of social and economic affairs. However, the consequences for the socially disadvantaged in each country can be quite different. The American situation allows a freedom to deviate that is matched for those in subordinate statuses by a heightened likelihood of criminalization. The Canadian situation discourages deviation and at the same time decreases the proportionate likelihood of criminalization for subordinates. Which of these situations is "better," if either, is less an empirical than a moral issue. Alternatively, it is the consequences of such situations that we are best suited to study.

Canadian-American differences in the control of criminal behavior, and the potentially changing character of these societal differences, represent a unique opportunity for a type of comparative research that today is too seldom done in North American sociology of law. The purpose of the comparative framework outlined in this chapter is to counter the unjustified neglect, and to promote further exploration, of the differing means used to establish legal order on this continent.

Notes

1. One notable exception to this conclusion involves Canadian bail reform legislation (Criminal Code of Canada, ss. 457-462).

2. *Attorney General of Canada* v. *Lavell*, [1974] S.C.R. 1349; *Morgentaler* v. *The Queen*, [1976] 1 S.C.R. 616.

3. *Powell* v. *Alabama,* 287 U.S. 45 (1932); *Johnson* v. *Zerbst,* 304 U.S. 458 (1938); *Gideon* v. *Wainwright,* 372 U.S. 335 (1963); *Argersinger* v. *Hamlin,* 407 U.S. 25 (1972); *Miranda* v. *Arizona,* 384 U.S. 436 (1966).

4. *Re Ewing and Kearney and the Queen* (1974), 18 C.C.C. (2d) 356 (B.C.C.A.). It should be noted that the Canadian configuration of the right to counsel is dealt with both in the provisions of the Criminal Code of Canada and in the Canadian Bill of Rights.

5. (1976), 31 C.C.C. (2d) 177, 198. It should be noted that Chief Justice Laskin of the Supreme Court of Canada dissented from this decision, indicating that he "would not discount [recent American decisions] as being irrelevant" (184; see generally Laskin, 1969). This is consistent with the "quasi-constitutional" status assigned by the Chief Justice to the Canadian Bill of Rights. As indicated, this view has been rejected by the majority of the Court in *Hogan* v. *The Queen,* [1975] 2 S.C.R. 574, and again in *R.* v. *Miller and Cockriell.* The call for more Canadian attention to American legal developments in various areas of law has been heard recurrently (Laskin, 1969; Mowat, 1857; MacIntyre, 1966), and sometimes has been followed, but less in the area of criminal law and particularly with regard to individual rights in the criminal process.

6. [1975] 2 S.C.R. 574, 583-584.

7. (1974), 53 D.L.R. (3d) 441, 453 (Alta. S. Ct., A.D.). For a useful expression of contrasting Canadian judicial views on this issue, see *Barrette* v. *The Queen* (1976), 29 C.C.C. (2d) 189 (S.C.C.).

8. 287 U.S. 45 (1932); *Avery* v. *Alabama,* 308 U.S. 444 (1940); *Glasser* v. *U.S.,* 315 U.S. 60 (1941).

9. See *Diggs* v. *Welch,* 148 F. 2d 667, 669 (D.C. Cir., 1945), cert. denied 325 U.S. 880 (1945); *McMann* v. *Richardson,* 397 U.S. 759, 770 (1970); *Tollett* v. *Henderson,* 411 U.S. 258 (1973).

10. (1973), 5 C.C.C. (2d) 186, 192 (Ont. C.A.).

11. For further discussion of issues considered in this section, see Law Reform Commission of Canada (1974).

12. 232 U.S. 383 (1914).

13. 338 U.S. 25 (1949).

14. 367 U.S. 643 (1961).

15. (1861), 8 Cox. C.C. 498, 501.

16. [1971] S.C.R. 272.

17. [1955] 1 All E.R. 236; *Noor Mohamed* v. *The King,* [1949] A.C. 182; *Callis* v. *Gunn,* [1964] 1 Q.B. 495.
18. [1955] 1 All E.R. 236, 239.
19. 23 (1886), 12 O.R. 347.
20. [1949] O.R. 215.
21. [1953] S.C.R. 593.
22. [1971] S.C.R. 272, 292-293.
23. *Hogan* v. *The Queen,* [1975] 2 S.C.R. 574. This decision is described by one Canadian commentator as "Perhaps the most unfortunate decision of the Supreme Court on the effect of a clear contravention of one of the provisions of the Canadian Bill of Rights" (Tarnopolsky, 1975a, p. 660).
24. These data are drawn from the U.S. Bureau of the Census (1973, p. 433) and Statistics Canada (1972, p. 14), with the population base for Canada as per the 1971 census.
25. These statistics are taken from the U.S. Department of Justice (1974) and Solicitor General (1973, p. 7). The court figures exclude legal aid expenditures, which are not recorded for Canada.

References

Atwood, M. E. *Survival: A Thematic Guide to Canadian Literature.* Toronto: Anansi, 1972.
Beattie, J. M. *Attitudes Towards Crime and Punishment in Upper Canada, 1830-50: A Documentary Study.* University of Toronto: Centre of Criminology, 1977.
Bell, D. "Crime as an American Way of Life." *The Antioch Review,* 1953, *13,* 131-154.
Bellomo, J. J. "Upper Canadian Attitudes Towards Crime and Punishment (1832-1851)." *Ontario History,* 1972, *64,* 11-26.
Bruton, P. W. "The Canadian Bill of Rights: Some American Observations." *McGill Law Journal,* 1962, *8,* 106-120.
Clark, S. D. *The Social Development of Canada: An Introductory Study with Select Documents.* Toronto: University of Toronto Press, 1942.
Clark, S. D. *The Developing Canadian Community.* Toronto: University of Toronto Press, 1962.
Clark, S. D. "The Post-Second World War Canadian Society."

Canadian Review of Sociology and Anthropology, 1975, *12,* 25-32.

Clark, S. D. *Canadian Society in Historical Perspective.* Toronto: McGraw-Hill Ryerson, 1976.

Cohen, S. A. "Controlling the Trial Process: The Judge and the Conduct of Trial." *Criminal Reports* (new series) 1977, *36,* 15-84.

Davis, A. K. "Canadian Society and History as Hinterland Versus Metropolis." In R. J. Ossenberg (Ed.), *Canadian Society: Pluralism, Change and Conflict.* Scarborough, Ontario: Prentice-Hall, 1971.

Grossman, B. A. "The Right to Counsel in Canada." *Canadian Bar Journal,* 1967, *10,* 189-211.

Hiller, H. *Canadian Society: A Sociological Analysis.* Scarborough, Ontario: Prentice-Hall, 1976.

Horowitz, I. L. "The Birth and Meaning of America: A Discussion." *Sociological Quarterly,* 1966, *7,* 3-20.

Horowitz, I. L. (Ed.). *Masses in Latin America.* New York: Oxford University Press, 1970.

Horowitz, I. L. "The Hemispheric Connection: A Critique and Corrective to the Entrepreneurial Thesis of Development with Special Emphasis on the Canadian Case." *Queen's Quarterly,* 1973, *80,* 327-359.

Inciardi, J. A. *Careers in Crime.* Chicago: Rand McNally, 1975.

Innis, H. A. *The Fur Trade of Canada.* Toronto: University of Toronto Press, 1927.

Innis, H. A. *Problems of Staple Production in Canada.* Toronto: Ryerson Press, 1933.

Innis, H. A. *The Cod Fisheries: The History of an International Economy.* Toronto: University of Toronto Press, 1954.

Innis, H. A. *Essays in Canadian Economic History.* Toronto: University of Toronto Press, 1956.

Jaffary, S. K. *Sentencing of Adults in Canada.* Toronto: University of Toronto Press, 1963.

Laskin, B. *The British Tradition in Canadian Law.* London: Stevens, 1969.

Law Reform Commission of Canada. *The Exclusion of Illegally Obtained Evidence.* Ottawa: Information Canada, 1974.

Lipset, S. M. "The Value Patterns of Democracy: A Case Study in Comparative Analysis." *American Sociological Review,* 1963, *28,* 515-531.

Lipset, S. M. "Canada and the United States—A Comparative View." *Canadian Review of Sociology and Anthropology,* 1964, *1,* 173-185.

Lipset, S. M. *Revolution and Counterrevolution: Change and Persistence in Social Structure.* New York: Basic Books, 1968.

MacIntyre, J. M. "The Use of American Cases in Canadian Courts." *University of British Columbia Law Review,* 1966, *2,* 478-490.

McLeod, A. J., and Martin, J. C. "The Revision of the Criminal Code." *Canadian Bar Review,* 1955, *33,* 3-19.

MacLeod, R. C. *The North-West Mounted Police and Law Enforcement 1873-1905.* Toronto: University of Toronto Press, 1976.

McNaught, K. "Political Trials and the Canadian Political Tradition." In M. L. Friedland (Ed.), *Courts and Trials: A Multi-Disciplinary Approach.* Toronto: University of Toronto Press, 1975.

McWhinney, E. *Judicial Review in the English-Speaking World.* Toronto: University of Toronto Press, 1965.

Mewett, A. W. "The Criminal Law, 1867-1967." *The Canadian Bar Review,* 1967, *45,* 726-740.

Mewett, A. W. "Law Enforcement and the Conflict of Values." *McGill Law Journal,* 1970, *16,* 1-18.

Mowat, O. "Observations on the Use and Value of American Reports in Reference to Canadian Jurisprudence." *Upper Canadian Law Journal,* (old series) 1857, *3,* 3-7.

Naegle, K. D. "Canadian Society: Some Reflections." In B. R. Blishen, F. E. Jones, K. D. Naegle, and J. Porter (Eds.), *Canadian Society.* Toronto: MacMillan, 1964.

Packer, H. "Two Models of the Criminal Process." *University of Pennsylvania Law Review,* 1964, *113,* 1-68.

Porter, J. "Canadian Character in the Twentieth Century." *Annals of the American Academy of Political and Social Science,* 1967, *370,* 48-56.

Quinney, R. *The Social Reality of Crime.* Boston: Little, Brown, 1970.

Risk, R. C. B. "A Prospectus for Canadian Legal History." *Dalhousie Law Journal,* 1973, *1,* 227-245.

Russel, P. H. "The Political Role of the Supreme Court of Canada in Its First Century." *The Canadian Bar Review,* 1975a, *53,* 576-593.

Russel, P. H. "Judicial Power in Canada's Political Culture." In M. L. Friedland (Ed.), *Courts and Trials: A Multi-Disciplinary Approach.* Toronto: University of Toronto Press, 1975b.

Skolnick, J. H. *Justice Without Trial: Law Enforcement in Democratic Society.* New York: Wiley, 1975.

Smiley, D. "Courts, Legislatures, and the Protection of Human Rights." In M. L. Friedland (Ed.), *Courts and Trials: A Multi-Disciplinary Approach.* Toronto: University of Toronto Press, 1975.

Solicitor General. "Information Systems Report on Canadian Criminal Justice Systems Costs." Ottawa: Queen's Printer, 1973.

Spiotto, J. E. "Search and Seizure: An Empirical Study of the Exclusionary Rule and Its Alternatives." *Journal of Legal Studies,* 1973a, *2,* 36-49.

Spiotto, J. E. "The Search and Seizure Problem—Two Approaches: The Canadian Tort Remedy and the U.S. Exclusionary Rule." *Journal of Police Science and Administration,* 1973b, *1,* 36-59.

Statistics Canada. *Statistics of Criminal and Other Offenses.* Ottawa: Queen's Printer, 1970.

Statistics Canada. *Police Administration Statistics.* Ottawa: Queen's Printer, 1972.

Tarnopolsky, W. S. "The Supreme Court and the Canadian Bill of Rights." *Canadian Bar Review,* 1975a, *53,* 649-670.

Tarnopolsky, W. S. *The Canadian Bill of Rights.* (2nd rev. ed.) Toronto: McLelland and Stewart, 1975b.

Truman, T. "A Critique of Seymour M. Lipset's Article, 'Value Differences, Absolute or Relative: The English-Speaking Democracies.'" *Canadian Journal of Political Science,* 1971, *4,* 497-525.

Turk, A. T. *Criminality and the Legal Order*. Chicago: Rand-McNally, 1969.

Turk, A. T. "The Problem of Legal Order in the United States and South Africa: Substantive and Analytical Considerations." *Sociological Focus*, 1977, *10*, 31-41.

U.S. Bureau of the Census. *Statistical Abstracts of the United States*. Washington, D.C.: U.S. Government Printing Office, 1972.

U.S. Bureau of the Census. *Statistical Abstracts of the United States*. Washington, D.C.: U.S. Government Printing Office, 1973.

U.S. Department of Justice. *Expenditure and Employment Data for the Criminal Justice System, 1971-1972*. Washington, D.C.: U.S. Government Printing Office, 1974.

Vallee, F. G., and Whyte, D. R. "Canadian Society: Trends and Perspectives." In B. Blishen, F. E. Jones, K. D. Naegle, and J. Porter (Eds.), *Canadian Society: Sociological Perspectives*. Toronto: MacMillan, 1971.

Wolfgang, M. *Patterns of Criminal Homicide*. Philadelphia: University of Pennsylvania Press, 1958.

Wrong, D. *American and Canadian Viewpoints*. Washington, D.C.: American Council on Education, 1955.

7

Robert Sharlet

Soviet Legal Policy Making

A Preliminary Classification

This chapter is an attempt to explore a virgin territory of Soviet legal studies, namely the uncharted area of legal policy making or, quite specifically, the kinds of policies made by the Communist Party that bear on the social regulation process in Soviet society. By social regulation, I mean the process by which the norms of interpersonal relations and the relations between citizen and state are defined, sanctioned, and regulated through the legal system, the administrative control apparatus, and officially sponsored peer-group controls (Sharlet, 1971). While we have several pioneering studies of legal policy making in certain branches of Soviet law, we have yet to examine closely the broader legal policy-making context within which the narrower codification issues have been and are being resolved.[1]

Under Stalin, this problem was considerably easier to

Note: This chapter is a part of a larger study on Soviet legal reform since Stalin, for which the author has received support from the Ford Foundation.

address, especially after 1929. Stalin was given to announcing
policy changes in general, in a variety of forums, and on diverse
occasions. As Stalinism took shape, decision-making variables
became more clearly defined, more firmly sited, and, generally,
policy making (including legal policy making) became more
bureaucratized and hence more routinized. However, during his
regime Stalin never relied exclusively on the duly established
party and governmental forums in exercising his personal domination over Soviet policy making.

Certainly, some of Stalin's most important pronouncements bearing directly on legal policy were made in the orthodox policy making forums, including his call for intensifying the
class struggle and strengthening the dictatorship of the prole-
tariat at the Central Committee Plenum of April 1929; his revision of the "withering away" doctrine at the Sixteenth Party
Congress in 1930; and his demand for legal stabilization before
the Eighth Congress of Soviets of the USSR of 1936, among
others.[2] These might be taken as indications of Stalin's commitment to a formal policy-making process. However, in the course
of his long tenure Stalin also operated in a more informal, diffuse, and ad hoc policy-making style as well. Policy cues would
be explicitly dropped or implied in a wide range of sources, and
those officials charged with making or implementing legal policy would be quick to publicly acknowledge these cues by drawing the appropriate inferences (usually in print) and promptly
acting on them. Examples abound. Although he was frequently
addressing the full gamut of "official Russia" on these occasions, Stalin's letter-to-the-editor of the journal *Proletarian
Revolution* in 1931, his interview with the American journalist
Roy Howard in 1936, the first appearance of the *Short Course*
in 1938, as well as the publication of Stalin's *The Economic
Problems of Socialism in the USSR* in 1952 were all significant
if indirect sources for Soviet legal policy.[3]

Legal policy making under Stalin's successors has become
more consistently bureaucratized and routinized, largely for
two overriding reasons. No single personality has been able to
achieve hegemony over his associates, and hence there appears
to be a tacit understanding among Stalin's successors to confine

their leadership struggles and policy conflicts to closed or at least heavily veiled policy-making arenas. Even without these circumstances, the imperatives of governing an increasingly complex post-Stalin society would still have required the leadership to more formally institutionalize the policy-making process in general and, for our purposes, the legal policy-making process in particular.[4] However, now because of the greater number of relevant participants and the greater diversity of policy inputs, as well as the fact that legal policy has sometimes become a factional issue of leadership politics, the problem of charting the contemporary Soviet legal policy-making process is, if anything, difficult. What is within reach, however, is the output of the process or the spectrum of legal policies announced since 1953.

The post-Stalin leadership began making new legal policies in the wake of the dictator's death as a matter of urgent necessity as much as of choice. As Robert C. Tucker pointed out, destalinization began immediately with Stalin's death since without him it was impossible to maintain the Stalinist system unchanged (Tucker, 1971, pp. 173-202). In the area of legal policy, changes were quickly forthcoming in aborting the fabrication of the "doctors' plot," in reestablishing party control over the secret police, and through the first of a series of amnesties bringing relief to some of Stalin's victims.[5] Other legal policy changes followed, including deconcentration and reorganization of the secret police, repeal of its "special boards," destalinization and reform of the prosecutor general's office, and the beginning of the process for legal rehabilitation of many of the victims of the purges.[6]

These initial legal policies, being reactions to Stalinism, were basically corrective or restorative. Although the content of legal policy might have been changing, the style of legal policy making was not. Most of the early post-Stalin legal policies were decided and, in some instances because of their politically charged nature, even implemented, in camera. Witness the secret trials of Beria and his leading collaborators in 1953 (Medvedev and Medvedev, 1976, pp. 7-12). Nevertheless, the collective leadership's first ventures in legal policy making (motivated in part by fear for their own personal safety) provided the essen-

tial impetus for the major reformist legal policies that came
steadily forth, beginning in 1956.

It is for the period running from 1956 through 1976,
from the Twentieth through the Twenty-Fifth Party Congresses,
that I will try to map out the contours and main features of
Soviet legal policy under Khrushchev and Brezhnev, using selective examples. Basically, I will argue that the Communist Party
is ultimately the source of four types of legal policy that, in the
order that I will discuss them, become progressively more specific: (1) metalegal policy, (2) structural legal policy, (3) substantive legal policy, and (4) ad hoc legal policy.

Metalegal Policy

Metalegal policy has a significant impact on the social
regulation process, although it is not intended to apply exclusively to that process. A metalegal policy may be either a general political policy with system-wide application within which
the social regulation process is subsumed or a policy more limited in scope that is primarily directed toward another systemic
process but that has a "spillover" effect on the social regulation
process or one of its component parts.

The domestic sources of metalegal policy include indi-
vidually or in combination, leadership conflict or change, ideological reinterpretation or emendation, major reorganization or
reconstruction of another systemic process tightly interrelated
to the social regulation process.[7] Obviously, in a system as
highly integrated as the USSR, it could reasonably be argued
that almost any general domestic policy, personnel, or institutional change has a ripple effect throughout the entire system.
However, metalegal policy can be distinguished from other
sources of "domino" effects by the criterion that a metalegal
policy must have a systemic rather than just an incremental
impact on the social regulation process. Thus, Khrushchev's destalinization policy was a metalegal policy whereas his pro-
consumerist policy was not, for the former made "waves,"
while the latter, at best, made only "ripples" in the social regulation process.[8] A similar distinction can be made between

Brezhnev's policy of decelerating destalinization (which heavily affected the social regulation process, but less visibly than Khrushchev's metalegal policy) and his policy of scientific-technical revolution, which, to date, has been little more than rhetorical.[9]

To illustrate this first type of legal policy, Khrushchev's destalinization policy has been the paramount metalegal policy of the post-Stalin period. As indicated, destalinization began in 1953 and a number of structural, substantive, and ad hoc legal policies ensued that were primarily of a corrective or restorative character. The great watershed of destalinization as a metalegal policy, however, was the Twentieth Party Congress of 1956; Khrushchev's "secret speech" crystallized as metalegal policy in one of the congress' resolutions, which called for "putting an end—severely and decisively—to any manifestations of lawlessness, arbitrariness, or violation of the socialist legal order."[10] Beginning in 1956, then, Soviet legal policy took on a predominantly reformist, reconstructive, and occasionally innovative character, despite certain retrograde tendencies that subsequently developed. In short, destalinization as a metalegal policy had a profound impact on the received Stalinist social regulation process, systematically restructuring it and fundamentally revising the interrelationship of its major components, the legal system and the administrative control apparatus.

This impact can be most clearly understood with reference to Ernst Fraenkel's conception of the "dual state" as adapted to a communist system.[11] In essence, the party controls and manipulates the Soviet "dual state," which comprises a normative and a prerogative sector, separated by a flexible analytical boundary. In the normative sector of the social regulation process (the legal system), the party regulates social behavior indirectly through a system of legal rules that define and sanction permissible social conduct. The party governs directly through the prerogative sector of the social regulation process (the administrative control apparatus), by such means as unrestricted political action, administrative fiat, and the ad hoc exercise of public power vis-à-vis the individual citizen. In the context of Fraenkel's dual state, destalinization as a metalegal policy has had the powerful effect of expanding the normative sector while contracting the prerogative sector or, in other words, enlarging legal "space" by decreasing the extralegal "space" in the society. This major realignment within the social regulation process is more concretely reflected in the following discussions of structural and substantive types of legal policy.[12]

Structural Legal Policy

Structural legal policy is the policy type through which the party as the hegemonic policy maker addresses itself primarily and directly to problems of social regulation at a macroscopic level. Through structural legal policy, the party effects major structural changes in several different ways, including institutional, or processual innovation; deinstitutionalization, or processual revision; reinforcement or refinement of existing institutions or procedures. These various routes of structural change are intended to enhance efficiency and effectiveness in attaining the goals and purposes posited by the party, for example, Khrushchev's twin objectives of building the economic base for communism and creating the "new man" and Brezhnev's design for strengthening the "developed socialist society" through scientific-technical revolution.[13]

Flowing from destalinization as a metalegal policy, the most significant structural legal policies since 1953 have been the de-Vyshinskyization of legal education and scholarship; the extensive legal reform program; and the introduction of a peer-justice process.[14] Since Vyshinsky was the principal legal Stalinist, destalinization of the Soviet system led quite naturally to de-Vyshinskyization of its social regulation process. The posthumous legal rehabilitation in late 1956 of Pashukanis and Krylenko, purged by Stalin and Vyshinsky in the late 1930s, was the first highly visible public signal that Vyshinskyism was under critical attack within the social regulation process.[15] Vyshinskyism had become synonymous with a "jurisprudence of terror," the co-optation and subversion of legal process or normative regulation by the prerogative authorities for political ends (Sharlet, 1977c, pp. 163-168). Legal discourse had been frozen within this mold. Therefore, de-Vyshinskyization of the legal profession meant, first, reopening theoretical discourse on the nature and functions of Soviet law, then the reorientation of legal education and the revitalization of legal scholarship. This process was already underway after Vyshinsky's death in 1954, but the events of 1956 culminated in public criticism of Vyshinsky at the Twenty-Second Party Congress of 1961, and de-Vyshinskyization continued under both Khrushchev and Brezhnev.[16]

Without de-Vyshinskyization, the structural policy of legal reform through codification and recodification probably could not have been successfully undertaken.[17] The legal reform program through a combination of revision, restatement, and clarification has had a most visible and enduring effect on the social regulation process. This continues as an ongoing structural legal policy, as indicated by Brezhnev's references to the forthcoming *svod zakonov* (collection of laws) of economic legislation and the need for administrative law codification in his report to the Twenty-Fifth Party Congress of 1976 (Brezhnev, 1976, pp. 97-98). Taken cumulatively, the now more than two decades of post-Stalin legal reforms have had a fundamental impact on the social regulation process through the modernization, rationalization, and systemization of Soviet legal norms, institutions, roles, and processes (see, for example, Hazard, Maggs, and Shapiro, 1969, pp. 48-71, 92-134).

Finally and briefly, I want to discuss the most innovative structural legal policy of the post-Stalin period, namely the introduction of a peer-justice process. Beginning in 1957 and culminating with the Extraordinary Twenty-First Party Congress of 1959, this institutional and processual innovation came to include the antiparasite legislation, the comrades' courts, and the *druzhinny*, or People's Voluntary Patrols (see Armstrong, 1967, pp. 163-182; Berman and Spindler, 1963; O'Connor, 1964). Collectively, these institutions and procedures were neither purely normative nor exclusively prerogative regulatory instruments. Instead, the peer-justice process was a dramatic departure from Stalin's and Vyshinsky's primary reliance on regulation of society from above, by in part reviving and in part

creating a supplementary process of "horizontal" social regulation.[18]

A product of Khrushchev's legal populism, peer justice
continues under Brezhnev but has lost much of its intended
effect as a relatively spontaneous source of peer pressure on
social conduct.[19] Essentially, Brezhnev has altered this structural legal policy in the direction of subtle deinstitutionalization
and processual revision of Khrushchev's horizontal peer justice,
the net result being that the process has now been largely ab-
sorbed by or subordinated to the normative and prerogative sectors of the social regulation process. Similarly, Khrushchev's
structural legal policy of decentralizing the control and supervision of the police and the courts were deinstitutionalized under
Brezhnev, who recentralized the two functions, respectively,
through reinstitutionalization of the Ministry of Internal Affairs
in 1968 and the Ministry of Justice in 1970 (Juviler, 1976, pp.
99-104).

Substantive Legal Policy

Substantive legal policy is a policy intended to affect
Soviet society as a whole through a major component or sub-
component of the social regulation process. As such, it is relatively more specific, focused, and content laden than structural
legal policy, the context within which it is formulated. However, the degree of specificity of substantive legal policies can
vary considerably, ranging from a sharply focused and narrowly
applicable body of all-union *osnovy* to a more diffuse but widely applicable "campaign."

The sweeping structural policy of legal reform has
yielded under Khrushchev and Brezhnev a harvest of substantive
legal policies in the form of *osnovy* or "fundamental principles
of legislation of the USSR and the union republics" for nearly
every branch of Soviet law from criminal and civil to health and
education law.[20] Each set of all-union principles is a substantive
legal policy, which in turn is implemented through relatively
more precise codes of law in each union republic. In contrast,
implementation of a campaign as a substantive legal policy

usually begins with publicity, after which most often follows (in the ideal scenario) the application of and/or obedience to a body of code and statutory law frequently encompassing the spheres of regulation of two or more branches of law.

Notable among such campaigns have been Khrushchev's campaign to restore "socialist legality" (repeatedly emphasized from the Twentieth through the Twenty-Second Party Congresses), which under Brezhnev has been transformed into a campaign for the maintenance of "socialist law and order" (a theme reiterated from the Twenty-Third through the Twenty-Fifth Party Congresses).[21] The two campaigns are not necessarily dissimilar, but each subtly reflects the different priorities of its author. Khrushchev's strong commitment to destalinization was imbedded in such phrases as "liquidating the cult of personality," "returning to the Leninist norms of Party life," and "restoring and strengthening socialist legality." As a (legal) campaign theme, the last phrase became a public code word for the party's shift of emphasis from prerogative to normative regulation of Soviet society. Simultaneously, Khrushchev tended to give his socialist legality campaign a discernible anti-arbitrariness tone as he sought to rebuild public confidence in the criminal justice system, which was then undergoing basic reform in the late 1950s and early 1960s.[22] Under Brezhnev, destalinization has been toned down, and his law-and-order campaign reflects his more pragmatic priority of dealing with the burgeoning crime problem in Soviet society. The orientation of Brezhnev's campaign, which operates through a more stabilized normative sector and a reconstructed criminal justice system, is therefore primarily merely antideviance.[23]

More specialized campaigns have also been launched as expressions of substantive legal policy, including Khrushchev's campaign against economic crime in the early 1960s,[24] and Brezhnev's hard line on political nonconformity, which he seems to have elevated to the status of a formal campaign against political deviance in his remarks to the Twenty-Fifth Party Congress in February 1976—a move foreshadowed by his praise of the KGB (secret police), which evolved from an anti-foreign-espionage organization at the Twenty-Third Party Con-

gress of 1966 to an antidomestic-subversion agency as well in
Brezhnev's reports to the Twenty-Fourth and Twenty-Fifth
Party Congresses of 1971 and 1976.[25] Currently, a "legal culture" campaign seems to be emerging, with the emphasis on
raising public legal consciousness through a mass legal socialization program.[26] As substantive legal policy, this should be an
interesting development to watch, since its scope is unusually
broad, cutting across numerous branches of law in its effort to
instill greater respect for the law. This still-elusive campaign
with its preventive orientation towards both white- and blue-
collar crime may eventually replace or at least subsume the present law-and-order campaign, with its essentially short- and
middle-run curative approach to lawbreaking.

Finally, it should be noted that substantive legal policy
probably offers the best opportunity for some kind of regular-
ized participation by the legal profession in the legal policy-
making process, especially in connection with drafting the various *osnovy*. Metalegal policy seems to be beyond the present
reach of the legal profession. There is some indication that the
party is co-opting or at least consulting the jurists in the making
of structural legal policy, but the evidence is quite strong that
the party is willing to delegate at least coresponsibility to the
legal specialists in the making of the more concrete substantive
legal policies.[27]

Ad Hoc Legal Policy

Ad hoc legal policy, the last and most specific type, is
frequently intended as a short-term problem-solving or crisis
management remedy. Ad hoc policies are usually addressed to
an individual or a group and as such resemble private bills in the
American policy-making process, with the crucial difference
that the former is normally designed to impose a penalty, while
the latter customarily grants special relief. In this sense, most ad
hoc legal policies (both the published and the unpublished ones)
tend to be regressive in terms of the overall positive direction of
post-Stalin legal development in the USSR.[28] Examples of policies directed against individuals include the regime's action in

depriving Chalidze and Zhores Medvedev of citizenship, expelling Solzhenitsyn from the Soviet Union, and apparently predetermining the outcome of major political trials, such as Kuznetsov's, at the highest level of the party.[29] Instances of ad hoc legal policies directed against groups would include, among others, the so-called "Sinyavsky-Daniel law" (Art. 190-1, RSFSR Criminal Code), intended to facilitate the suppression and prosecution of politically nonconforming behavior, and the now suspended "emigration tax" originally designed to impede Jewish emigration from the USSR. Although relatively few people are affected by it, ad hoc legal policy is probably the most pernicious type of legal policy used in the post-Stalin period.[30]

The New Soviet Constitution and Legal Policy

On October 7, 1977, the USSR ratified the long-awaited new constitution, a document that tends to reflect both the accomplishments and the limits of destalinization as a metalegal policy and functionally represents the culmination of the structural policy of legal reform by basically subsuming the main principles of the substantive legal policies embodied in the post-Stalin fundamental principles, statutes, and codes.

Last but not least, the new document incorporates most of the traditional caveats from the USSR constitution of 1936 (and even adds a few) that will continue to legitimate formally the regime's resort to ad hoc legal policy in selected cases. Constitutionally, the Soviet leadership seems to want the stability of a *Rechtsstaat* combined with the flexibility to bypass it when necessary, a reminder that the Communist Party is the ultimate source of legal policy in the Soviet dual state.[31]

Conclusion

This brings me to a final observation about this preliminary attempt to classify the different types of Soviet legal policy. Obviously, the posited distinctions are not impenetrable analytical boundaries; social reality in general tends to be composed more often of mixed than of pure types. Hence, the proposed framework is mainly intended as a first conceptual map to guide further explorations of the terrain of Soviet legal policy making. Hopefully, in the future, Soviet law specialists may be able to map out in greater detail other features, such as who makes Soviet legal policies and how the various types of legal policy are made; the modes and networks of political communication through which legal policies are disseminated; how implementation of the different types of legal policy is effected; the "feedback" channels and how they work and relate to legal policy revision; and comparisons of the style and outcomes of legal policy making under Khrushchev and Brezhnev.[32]

Ultimately, we should keep before us the long-term objective of developing some intellectual means of determining the impact of legal policies and of assessing the general efficacy of Soviet law as one of the party's most important political instruments for governing Soviet society and attaining its ideological goals.

Notes

1. On the Soviet legal profession as an interest group, see Barry and Berman (1971). For the legal policy-making case studies, see Barry (1964) on civil law; Juviler (1967); Solomon (1974); Van den Berg (1975); Gorgone (1976).

2. For Stalin's 1929-1930 policy statements, see Hazard (1951, pp. 227-235). On Stalin's 1936 position, see Sharlet (1977c, pp. 169-178).

3. For the influence on legal policy of Stalin's *History of the CPSU (Bolshevik): Short Course,* see Sharlet (1977c, pp. 169-170). For his 1952 book as a source for legal policy, see Bratus (1952).

4. On the post-Stalin policy-making process generally, see Linden (1966, pp. 1-9). For recent developments, see Hoffmann (1973).

5. Fainsod (1964, pp. 447-449). On the amnesties and Soviet amnesty policy in general, see Zile (1976, pp. 37-49).

6. Berman (1963, pp. 70-72); Conquest (1968, pp. 23-24); Morgan (1962, pp. 126-130); and on the rehabilitation policy, see Medvedev and Medvedev (1976, pp. 12-23).

7. Linden (1966, pp. 10-21). For a complementary analysis of the Brezhnev period, see Hough (1976).

8. On the impact of destalinization, see Berman (1963, pp. 66-96). Khrushchev failed to gain a strong consensus for his consumerism, but even if he had succeeded, its impact on the social regulation process would have been secondary and incremental at most. See Linden (1966, pp. 69-71, 187-201).

9. On the Soviet efforts to develop a theory of "scientific-technical revolution," see Hoffmann (1977). On its minimal impact on the social regulation process, see, for example, Rinz (1972, pp. 230-248).

10. Quoted from Hodnett (1974, p. 42). For the relevant excerpts from the "secret speech," see Zile (1970, pp. 303-312).

11. See Fraenkel (1941, pp. 3-75). For its adaptation, see Sharlet (1977c, pp. 155-158).

12. While the differences between Khrushchev (1953-1964) and Brezhnev (1964-   ) over the politics of destalinization have been matters of scope and tempo, there has been much greater discontinuity between Khrushchev's general "populism" and Brezhnev's more pragmatic "realism" as metalegal policies.

13. For Khrushchev's goals, see the 1961 program of the CPSU in Triska (1962, pp. 68-72, 110-124). For an analysis of Brezhnev's goal, see Laird (1975, pp. 8-17).

14. Berman (1963, pp. 72-84, 88-96). Specifically on legal education and research, see also the collective position of the USSR Academy of Sciences' Institute of the State and Law (1956, pp. 3-14).

15. For a translation of the relevant parts of the unsigned lead article in the principal law journal on the rehabilitations, see Zile (1970, pp. 312-314).

16. For a very sharp attack on Vyshinskyism inspired by the 22nd Party Congress, see Karev (1962). Karev is a leading criminal law specialist and has served as Dean of the Moscow University Juridical Faculty. See also I. S. Samoshchenko's critique in Aleksandrov and Bratus (1963, pp. 91-95).

17. See, for example, A. K. R. Kiralfy's study of labor law reform in Barry, Butler, and Ginsburgs (1974, pp. 158-174); and generally Barry, Feldbrugge, and Lasok (1975).

18. For two comrades' court cases, see Sharlet (1965). For an antiparasite proceeding, see Feifer (1964, pp. 188-199).

19. The antiparasite proceedings have been transferred from the courts in "administrative session" to the Ministry of Internal Affairs, losing their remaining public participatory aspects in the process. The comrades' courts that once flourished throughout the society from factories to universities now seem to be used mainly in large apartment houses for settling minor disputes among neighbors. The voluntary auxiliary police who used to be so visible with their red armbands are now largely used for late night patrols and are rarely seen by the average citizen.

20. The twelve "fundamentals" enacted from 1958 through 1973 have been translated in *Fundamentals of Legislation of the USSR and the Union Republics* (1974). See also Butler (1975) for a comprehensive list of the all-union fundamentals, the special federal codes and statutes, and the Russian Republic codes, which have been translated into English.

21. Compare Strogovich (1958, pp. 7-16), written under the influence of Khrushchev's Twentieth Party Congress, and Kerimov (1973, pp. 169-193) written after a "Brezhnev" congress. Peter H. Solomon, Jr., of the University of Toronto has called to my attention the useful distinction that Soviet legal "campaigning" tends to be split-level, simultaneously being addressed to legal personnel in an attempt to reshape their priorities, and to the mass public to gain its compliance with the subject of the campaign.

22. See Samoshchenko (1960, pp. 23-24), and Berman's "Introduction " (1972, pp. 20-70). Given the different audiences to which it was concurrently addressed, Khrushchev's campaign was a hybrid—at the level of legal cadres, it was a structural legal policy; while at the mass level it was a substantive legal policy.

23. Juviler (1976, pp. 84-92). Antideviance was by no means ignored under Khrushchev as can be seen in Walter D. Connor's *Deviance in Soviet Society* (1972), but as Juviler points out, the emphasis has been considerably greater under Brezhnev.

24. The most complete account of this campaign is the International Commission of Jurists' staff study, "Economic Crimes in the Soviet Union" (1964). Stanislaw Pomorski of Rutgers Law School at Camden, New Jersey, has been kind enough to share his forthcoming research with me on this point. He persuasively demonstrates that the tensions between the re-

quirements of legality and the demands of political expediency in Soviet legal campaigning in general, and Khrushchev's economic crime campaign in particular, "invariably involve substantial abandonment of the rules for the sake of expediency" (forthcoming, p. 10).

25. Compare Brezhnev's remark on the KGB in *The Twenty-Third Congress of the CPSU* (1966, p. 131) with Brezhnev (1976, p. 98). For his campaign against dissidence, see Sharlet (1977a).

26. See, for example, Chkhikvadze (1970) and Terebilov (1973). The former is a prominent jurist who previously headed the prestigious Institute of the State and Law of the Soviet Academy of Sciences, while the latter author is currently USSR Minister of Justice.

27. In addition to the legal policy-making case studies cited in Note 1, my own interviews with Soviet jurists indicate that they have been consulted in both the drafting and revision of legislation with increasing frequency and regularity as implementation of the structural legal policy of law reform has progressed since the mid 1950s. As my colleague Erik P. Hoffmann of State University of New York, Albany, so felicitously observed (personal communication), the party permits the jurists to participate in the "politics of legal details" while reserving to itself the "politics of legal principles" and, of course, metapolicy.

28. On legal rules not made public, see Loeber (1970). I have emphasized the predominantly repressive character of ad hoc legal policy, but as Peter H. Juviler of Barnard College, Columbia, has helpfully pointed out (personal communication), it has a secondary function of sometimes being "facilitative" by helping individuals bypass cumbersome bureaucracy in civil matters, such as family law. Either way, repressive or facilitative, ad hoc-ism is not practiced exclusively by the central authorities, but is visible in one form or another throughout the Soviet system. The party has tried to maintain its monopoly by building certain checks and balances into the system for the purpose of holding official arbitrariness to a tolerable level, but the countless cases that rise through the court system over official abuses are probably just the tip of the iceberg.

29. See Sharlet (1977a) for the developing "pattern" of ad hoc legal policies against Soviet dissidents.

30. See Berman (1972, pp. 81-83, 180-181) and "Special

Issue" (1974, pp. 181-196) for several cases of ad hoc-ism or "legal" discrimination against dissidents.

31. For more on the new Soviet constitution, see Sharlet (1977b).

32. I have made a first attempt to address the last topic in a paper entitled "Legal Policy Under Khrushchev and Brezhnev: Continuity and Change" (1976).

References

Aleksandrov, N. G., and Bratus , S. N. (Eds.). *Razvitie Mark-sistsko-Leninskoi teorii gosudarstva i prava XXII s"ezdom KPSS [The Development of the Marxist-Leninist Theory of the State and Law by the Twenty-Second Congress of the CPSU]*. Moscow: Gosudarstvennoe Izdatel'stvo Juridiches-koi Literatury, 1963.

Armstrong, M. "The Campaign Against Parasites." In P. H. Juvi-ler and H. W. Morton (Eds.), *Soviet Policy-Making*. New York: Praeger, 1967.

Barry, D. D. "The Specialist in Soviet Policy Making: The Adoption of a Law." *Soviet Studies*, 1964, *16*, 152-165.

Barry, D. D., and Berman, H. J. "The Jurists." In H. G. Skilling and F. Griffiths (Eds.), *Interest Groups in Soviet Politics*. Princeton, N.J.: Princeton University Press, 1971.

Barry, D. D., Butler, W. E., and Ginsburgs, G. (Eds.). *Contemporary Soviet Law: Essays in Honor of John N. Hazard*. The Hague: Nijhoff, 1974.

Barry, D. D., Feldbrugge, F. J. M., and Lasok, D. (Eds.). *Codification in the Communist World: Symposium in Memory of Zsolt Szirmai (1903-1973). Law in Eastern Europe Series*, No. 19. Leiden: Sijthoff, 1975.

Berman, H. J. *Justice in the USSR: An Interpretation of Soviet Law.* (rev. ed.) Cambridge, Mass.: Harvard University Press, 1963.

Berman, H. J. (Ed. and Trans.). *Soviet Criminal Law and Procedure: The RSFSR Codes.* (2nd ed.) Cambridge, Mass.: Harvard University Press, 1972.

Berman, H. J., and Spindler, J. W. "Soviet Comrades' Courts." *Washington Law Review*, 1963, *38*, 842-910.

Bratus, S. N. "O sootnoshenii zakonov ekonomicheskikh i zakonov iuridicheskikh pri sotsialisme" ["On the Interrelationship of the Laws of Economics and the Laws of Jurisprudence Under Socialism"]. *Sovetskoe gosudarstvo i pravo,* 1952, (2), 13-22.

Brezhnev, L. I. *Report of the CPSU Central Committee to the 25th Congress of the CPSU.* Moscow: Novosti, 1976.

Butler, W. E. "Checklist of Soviet Normative Acts Available in English Translation." *American Journal of Comparative Law,* 1975, *23,* 530-549.

Chkhikvadze, V. M. "Zakonnost' i pravovaia kul'tura na sovremennom etape kommunisticheskogo stroitel'stva" ["Legality and Legal Culture in the Contemporary Stage of Communist Construction"]. *Kommunist,* 1970, (14), 42-53.

Chkhikvadze, V. M. (Ed.). *XXIV s"ezd KPSS i voprosy teorii gosudarstra i prava [The Twenty-Fourth Congress of the CPSU and Questions of the Theory of the State and Law].* Moscow: Juridicheskaia Literatura, 1972.

Connor, W. D. *Deviance in Soviet Society.* New York: Columbia University Press, 1972.

Conquest, R. (Ed.). *The Soviet Police System.* New York: Praeger, 1968.

"Economic Crimes in the Soviet Union." *Journal of the International Commission of Jurists* (Geneva), 1964, *5,* 3-47.

Fainsod, M. *How Russia Is Ruled.* (rev. ed.) Cambridge, Mass.: Harvard University Press, 1964.

Feifer, G. *Justice in Moscow.* New York: Simon & Schuster, 1964.

Fraenkel, E. *The Dual State: A Contribution to the Theory of Dictatorship.* (E. A. Shils and others, Trans.) New York: Oxford University Press, 1941.

Fundamentals of Legislation of the USSR and the Union Republics. Moscow: Progress, 1974.

Gorgone, J. "Soviet Jurists in the Legislative Arena: The Reform of Criminal Procedure, 1956-1958." *Soviet Union,* 1976, *3,* 1-35.

Hazard, J. N. (Ed.). *Soviet Legal Philosophy.* Cambridge, Mass.: Harvard University Press, 1951.

Hazard, J. N., Maggs, P. B., and Shapiro, I. (Eds.). *The Soviet*

Legal System: Contemporary Documentation and Historical Commentary. (rev. ed.) Dobbs Ferry, N.Y.: Oceana, 1969.

Hazard, J. N., Maggs, P. B., and Butler, W. E. *The Soviet Legal System: Contemporary Documentation and Historical Commentary.* (3rd ed.; 2 vols.) Dobbs Ferry, N.Y.: Oceana, 1977.

Hodnett, G. (Ed.). *The Khrushchev Years: 1953-1964.* R. H. McNeal (Ed.), *Resolutions and Decisions of the Communist Party of the Soviet Union.* Vol. 4. Toronto: University of Toronto Press, 1974.

Hoffmann, E. P. "Soviet Metapolicy: Information Processing in the Communist Party of the Soviet Union." *Journal of Comparative Administration,* Special Issue on Bureaucracy and Administration in Socialist States, F. J. Fleron, Jr. (Ed.), 1973, 5, 200-232.

Hoffmann, E. P. "The 'Scientific Management' of Soviet Society." *Problems of Communism,* 1977, 26 (3), 59-67.

Hough, J. F. "The Brezhnev Era: The Man and the System." *Problems of Communism,* 1976, 25 (2), 1-17.

Juviler, P. H. "Family Reforms on the Road to Communism." In P. H. Juviler and H. W. Morton (Eds.), *Soviet Policy-Making.* New York: Praeger, 1967.

Juviler, P. H. *Revolutionary Law and Order.* New York: Free Press, 1976.

Juviler, P. H., and Morton, H. W. (Eds.). *Soviet Policy-Making.* New York: Praeger, 1967.

Karev, D. "Likvidirovat' posledstviia kul'ta lichnosti v Sovetskoi pravovoi nauke" ["Eliminate the Vestiges of the Cult of Personality in Soviet Legal Science"]. *Sotsialisticheskaia zakonnost',* 1962, (2), 56-62.

Kerimov, D. A. (Ed.). *XXIV s"ezd KPSS ob ukreplenie Sovetskogo gosudarstva i razvitii sotsialisticheskoi demokratii [The 24th Congress of the CPSU on the Strengthening of the Soviet State and the Development of Socialist Democracy].* Moscow: Mysl', 1973.

Laird, R. "Post-Industrial Society: East and West." *Survey,* 1975, (4), 1-17.

Linden, C. A. *Khrushchev and the Soviet Leadership, 1957-1964.* Baltimore, Md.: Johns Hopkins University Press, 1966.

Loeber, D. A. "Legal Rules 'for Internal Use Only': A Comparative Analysis of the Practice of Withholding Government Decrees from Publication in Eastern Europe and in Western Countries." *International and Comparative Law Quarterly,* 1970, *19,* 70-98.

Medvedev, R. A., and Medvedev, Z. A. *Khrushchev: The Years in Power.* New York: Columbia University Press, 1976.

Morgan, G. G. *Soviet Administrative Legality: The Role of the Attorney General's Office.* Stanford, Calif.: Stanford University Press, 1962.

O'Connor, D. M. "Soviet People's Guards: An Experiment with Civic Police." *New York University Law Review,* 1964, *39,* 579-614.

Pomorski, S. "Communists and Their Law." In a special issue of the *University of Puerto Rico Law Review* honoring H. Silving, forthcoming.

Rinz, M. P. "Pravo i nauchno-tekhnicheskii progress" ["Law and Scientific Technical Progress"]. In V. M. Chkhikvadze (Ed.), *XXIV s"ezd KPSS i voprosy teorii gosudarstra i prava [The Twenty-Fourth Congress of the CPSU and Questions of the Theory of the State and Law].* Moscow: Juridicheskaia Literatura, 1972.

Samoshchenko, I. S. *Okhrana rezhima zakonnosti Sovetskim gosudarstvom [The Protection of the Policy of Legality by the Soviet State].* Moscow: Gosiurizdat, 1960.

Sharlet, R. "Russia's Courts of Public Pressure." *The Nation,* 1965, *200,* 55-57, 68.

Sharlet, R. "Law in the Political Development of a Communist System: Conceptualizing from the Soviet Experience." In R. E. Kanet (Ed.), *The Behavioral Revolution and Communist Studies.* New York: Free Press, 1971.

Sharlet, R. "Legal Policy Under Khrushchev and Brezhnev: Continuity and Change." Paper presented at the Ford Foundation Conference on the Individual and the State in Soviet Law, New York, October 29-31, 1976.

Sharlet, R. "Dissent and Repression in the Soviet Union." *Current History,* 1977a, *72,* 112-117, 30.

Sharlet, R. "The New Soviet Constitution." *Problems of Communism,* 1977b, *26* (5), 1-24.

Sharlet, R. "Stalinism and Soviet Legal Culture." In R. C. Tucker (Ed.), *Stalinism: Essays in Historical Interpretation.* New York: Norton, 1977c.

Skilling, H. G., and Griffiths, F. (Eds.). *Interest Groups in Soviet Politics.* Princeton, N.J.: Princeton University Press, 1971.

Solomon, P. H., Jr. "Soviet Criminology: Its Demise and Rebirth, 1928-1963." *Soviet Union,* 1974, *1,* 122-140.

Special Issue on Soviet Law in Honor of John N. Hazard, R. Sharlet (Ed.), *Soviet Union,* 1974, *1,* 103-206.

Special Section on Soviet Criminal Policy and Law, R. Sharlet (Ed.), *Soviet Union,* 1976, *3,* 1-62.

Strogovich, M. S. *Kurs Sovetskogo ugolovnogo protsessa [A Course on Soviet Criminal Procedure].* Moscow: Akademiia nauk SSSR, 1958.

Terebilov, V. "Pravovoe vospitanie trudiashchikhsia" ["The Legal Education of the Working People"]. *Kommunist,* 1973, (16), 113-124.

Triska, J. F. (Ed.). *Soviet Communism: Programs and Rules— Official Texts of 1919, 1952 (1956), 1961.* San Francisco: Chandler, 1962.

Tucker, R. C. *The Soviet Political Mind: Stalinism and Post-Stalin Change.* (rev. ed.) New York: Norton, 1971.

The Twenty-Third Congress of the CPSU. Moscow: Novosti, 1966.

USSR Academy of Sciences, Institute of the State and Law. "XX s"ezd KPSS i zadachi Sovetskoi pravovoi nauki" ["The Twentieth Congress of the CPSU and the Tasks of Soviet Legal Science"]. *Sovetskoe gosudarstvo i pravo,* 1956, (2), 3-14.

Van den Berg, G. P. "Codification of Soviet Labour Law—A Case Study on the Influence of Expert Opinion." In D. D. Barry, F. J. M. Feldbrugge, and D. Lasok (Eds.), *Codification in the Communist World: Symposium in Memory of Zsolt Szirmai (1903-1973). Law in Eastern Europe Series,* No. 19. Leiden: Sijthoff, 1975.

Zile, Z. L. (Trans.). *Ideas and Forces in Soviet Legal History: Statutes, Decisions and Other Materials on the Development and Processes of Soviet Law.* (2nd ed.) Madison, Wis.: College Printing & Publishing, 1970.

Zile, Z. L. "Amnesty and Pardon in the Soviet Union." *Soviet Union,* 1976, *3,* 37-49.

Part 3

Special Studies: USA

New legislation is an important part of the goal attainment functioning of law. (As Parsons points out, once new legislation becomes relatively routinized, it also becomes part of the integrative subsystem, in that adjudication becomes central.) Susan Schwarz neatly summarizes existing studies (including some of her own) and shows (1) that even full-time representatives cannot have informed opinions on all political issues, (2) that when ordinary citizens are consciously concerned about an issue their representatives are extremely sensitive to this concern, and (3) that on less conspicuous (but not necessarily less important) issues representatives rely on the informed opinions of colleagues whose general orientation they trust. How these summary facts are evaluated depends on one's theory of government. Representative government is in one aspect a compromise with extreme participatory democracy, and as a compromise it is sometimes regarded as relatively "bad." However, from another point of view representative democracy is an improvement over pure democracy in that it is an important instance of functional specialization: If full-time representatives cannot be experts on everything, ordinary citizens, who are typically occu-

231

pied "full-time" in "business" other than the "business" of government, are even less capable of being all-around experts. With this in mind, Joseph A. Schumpeter (1947) went so far as to believe that elected representatives should ignore the pressure of constituents on particular issues. According to this philosophy, representatives would act not as simple reflectors of popular wisdom but as more independent trustees of the public interest, subject only to the periodic control of elections. In effect, Schwarz shows that representatives actually tend to adopt what might be regarded as a fairly reasonable, certainly understandable, compromise between these two normative definitions of their role.

I have already commented on Simon's chapter on the functioning of juries in certain politically sensitive cases. Here I should like to emphasize two points. First, the performance of the juries studied is perhaps even more impressive if we pay attention to their implicit attitudes (and therefore their values) than it is if we focus exclusively on the decisions they reached. Secondly, and closely connected with this first point, even with regard to the decisions or outcomes, we must bear in mind that the two standards of fairness that we apply, namely, the independent opinions of judges and the consensus reached by careful study by scholars, are not necessarily altogether fair to the juries. In the first place, judges are far from infallible. In the second place, juries must decide in the heat of battle, whereas scholars have the benefit of the perspective of time. Much more could be said about the jury system, of course, but I think that with respect to the focus of her study Simon's positive evaluation seems justified.

In Part One of this book, Parsons deals with ideological "dedifferentiation" and shows that it is rather common. In this part, Charles Lidz and Andrew Walker provide an example of social-structural dedifferentiation due to fairly specific pressures. Their chapter also points up a dilemma that arises in a relatively sophisticated society, namely, the dilemma of concern for the individual versus concern for others' welfare. Another way of stating this dilemma is in terms of the decision to emphasize individual "responsibility" versus the decision to emphasize "therapy."

In a genuine sense, Travis Hirschi's chapter on juvenile delinquency is last "but not least." It is an unpretentious combination of theory and empirical confirmation. Statistical evidence tends to confirm the importance, for effective law, of both commitment to values and negative situational sanctions. Another aspect of Hirschi's article that I find commendable is his recognition that in a field of interdependent variables there may well be more than one causal path to the same result.

Reference

Schumpeter, J. A. *Capitalism, Socialism, and Democracy.* (2nd ed.) New York: Harper & Row, 1947.

8   *Susan Bowker Schwarz*

Legislation
and Legislatures

In a democratic society, we must have some mechanism for deciding what is to be a "law." As Weber pointed out (1947), laws that are believed to be legitimate may be based on rational grounds, traditional grounds, or charismatic grounds. In the United States, we attempt to base laws on rational grounds. By this, Weber means that we establish laws by agreement on grounds of expediency or rational values and that the body of law consists essentially in a consistent system of abstract rules that have normally been intentionally established.[1] In order to accomplish this, we have established the institution of the elected legislature. With the election process, we hope to assure that laws are established with our consensus. By designating a particular group of people who meet together and evaluate and discuss issues, we hope to ensure that we will get a consistent system of rules based on rationality or expediency. Like other institutions, legislatures can be suspected of failing to perform their intended functions or of performing other functions that were not intended. Social scientists have studied legislatures and legislators from many perspectives, but the goals are almost always to gain an understanding of how the social structure of the legislative institution affects legislative output.

The differing perspectives in the literature are the result of different fundamental questions one can ask about legislatures and the wealth of information that is available for investigating these questions. Legislatures are unusual organizations to study, because so much information is either publicly available or easily obtainable. For the U.S. Congress, for example, biographies of all members are available; there is information on the demographic characteristics of the member's constituency; there are records of a member's roll call votes in Congress and all speeches the member made in Congress (plus many that were not made but that the member inserts in the *Congressional Record* anyway). There are records of other public statements of members, such as publicity releases or newspaper columns; there are some types of financial data on members, and there is information on a member's work and social interaction record (committee memberships, party memberships, and memberships in other formal or informal groups in Congress). In addition to all of this, one can go to the organization and observe the actions of members at certain times, and, given the large number of interview studies, it appears that members are reasonably accessible for questioning. The bills that are voted on, committee reports, and the positions of outsiders such as various interest groups on these proposed laws are available. Most rules, traditions, and changes in the formal rules of the organization are public information. There are some parts of the decision process that cannot be observed or are not recorded in publicly available written form, but we can certainly use the information we have to learn something about the decision process. The way this information is used to answer questions about legislatures and legislators may be illustrated by looking in detail at some well-known studies of the U.S. Congress.[2] The House and the Senate are two somewhat different organizations, but the same questions may be asked, and the same information is usually available about each organization.

One of the common perspectives in the literature is the study of the "role" of the legislator. The primary sources in such studies are interviews with legislators and direct observation. Other information may be used to explain or defend statements made by legislators. Other factors, such as constituency demands and pressure from the executive branch and interest groups, are discussed in connection with the legislator's role. The main purpose of such studies is to give the reader an understanding of the situation as the legislator sees it. As one author (Clapp, 1963) says of his book: "Its purpose is to help inform the public about the responsibilities and difficulties of members of the House and the ways in which representatives meet them." The book (*The Congressman: His Work as He Sees It*) from which this quote is taken is a good illustration of this perspective. The research is based on interviews and discussions, although information from other sources (particularly facts and figures on various topics) is used to illustrate some points. The book is organized into topic areas that are clearly important issues in the lives of legislators. There are chapters on relationships with constituents, on legislative work, pressure groups, committee assignments, the committee system, the leadership, reelection problems, the impact of the job on family, and the satisfactions of the job. It is interesting to note that in this list of topics only one chapter deals directly with the process of creating legislation. The other chapters deal with descriptions of legislators' dealings with various formal and informal groups (constituency, committees, family). The legislator is presented as a member of a complex social network constantly involved with conflicting demands on time and energy as well as conflicting political demands. The image that emerges is that of a group of well-meaning and hard-working individuals doing their best to labor at contradictory and/or impossible tasks and of their attempts to set up formal and informal rules to deal with these tasks. On the subject of legislation, it is conceded that legislators have little time to discuss and consider legislation, due to the large volume of legislation (thousands of bills are introduced in each session of Congress) and due to the technical knowledge required to understand the background of each piece of legislation. The legislator attempts to "represent" a constituency but is impeded by a lack of knowledge of constituency attitudes on many issues. A representative must face reelection every two years, and a good relationship with the constituency is important; however, this is usually reflected in ways that are not directly concerned with creating legislation. The direct demands from constituents often include helping constituents deal with bureaucratic problems and directly answering communications (this includes answering mail, seeing constituents who come to Washington, and seeing constituents in the district). In addition to responding to direct constituent demands, legislators feel it is necessary for them to initiate communications with constituents. They maintain mailing lists of "interested" constituents, they send out newsletters and questionnaires, they appear on speaker programs and talk shows. Constituents seem to expect that their representatives will be available in their districts and will always respond to requests for information or help. Some of the time and energy spent on serving constituents does inform a representative about constituency attitudes on legislation, but most of the time and energy is either irrelevant to legislation or is more concerned with maintaining good relationships with constituents than anything else. Most legislation is of little interest to constituents, and a strong and unified district interest in an issue is rare. It is one of the contradictory conditions of the representative's job that constituents expect their representative always to be available, to spend much time communicating with them, and yet to have ample time and energy to consider complex legislative matters.

Except for specialized legislation relating to his or her committee, there is little incentive for the legislator to spend much time on legislative issues. The average constituent is not concerned and/or has no way of knowing how much time a legislator spends contemplating legislation. The legislator has many other ways to occupy time and most of them are psychologically more rewarding than reading about legislation. Most bills are so complex and/or specialized that the amount of effort required to really understand them is very great. Thus there is little opportunity for "gaining understanding" as a psychological payoff on most legislation. The alternatives of spending time on helping a constituent solve a problem with the federal bureaucracy or working in a specialized area, where one can have both an understanding of the issues and a large influence on the resulting law, are likely to lead to more psychologi-

cal satisfaction, if psychological satisfaction comes from a feeling of achievement.[3] There is some incentive to participate in
legislative work, and that incentive comes from colleagues and is
mainly concerned with encouraging specialization.[4]

Clearly, legislation must be written, and legislators must
have some ways of making decisions about it. Formal rules and
informal norms make this possible. It would be impossible for
435 people to sit in a room and discuss 10,000 or more bills
over a period of two years. The structure that has been devised
to handle this problem is the committee system. Every representative is assigned to at least one committee. The committees
report on legislation in their specialized areas, and the House
amends (sometimes) and votes on this legislation. The extensive
debate on legislation almost always occurs at the committee
level. The formal rules of committee assignments make it possible to remain on a committee for many terms, and the informal norms of the House make it desirable to do so. Specialized
knowledge and committee work are rewarded with prestige
among colleagues and with large amounts of influence in certain
specific areas of legislation. This means that very few of the 435
members have any detailed knowledge of any given issue. All
members may vote on an issue, but the issue has been discussed
and summarized by only a few. While this system enables the
House to deal with a large workload, it does introduce some
biases into the legislative results. Committees, because they are
small, can be dominated by members with certain points of
view or certain interests. This would be true even if committee
assignments were randomly distributed, and, of course, the
assignments are not randomly distributed. Committee actions
can work as a tollgate. If committees do not report bills, the
House cannot vote on them.[5]

The committee system and the social and deference recognition that other members give to specialized knowledge are a
very rational way to deal with legislative work, although it may
result in certain biases. Those issues that are highly publicized
are dealt with in another way. A few issues each year command
enough public attention that each legislator is required to consider the legislation. Much of this consideration may be in the

form of summarized opinions presented by various interest groups or interested individuals. The legislator may receive these opinions from constituents, interest groups (both constituency groups and national groups), party leaders, the executive branch, or newspaper columns and opinion polls. Strong outside pressures may make these issues more difficult to deal with as rational legislation, even though legislators may have the advantage of increased information on the issues.[6]

Books such as that by Clapp cannot provide entirely adequate information. Legislators can tell us how they attempt to represent us, but they cannot tell us to what degree they actually do so. It appears likely that they represent on some issues more than on others, but on these issues it is not clear if they represent full consensus, majority opinion, or the opinions of organized and vocal minorities. Legislators may be aware that specialization is a way to deal rationally with legislation, but they may be unaware of the implications of specialization on their own voting decisions. They may mention a number of factors involved in voting decisions, but these may be rationalizations about the process rather than descriptions of it. They may fail to see patterns in their own behavior.

Other kinds of studies are necessary to provide us with information on actual behavior and to discuss the implications of that behavior on the representative and legislative functions of legislatures. The two functions are related to one another, and those social scientists who begin by investigating the representative function will ultimately tell us something about the legislative function, and vice versa. We will begin with studies on representation and then proceed to studies of legislative behavior.

Representation Studies

We have deliberately chosen to have an elected legislature to provide for "accountability" and "representation." No legislator is going to admit a complete disregard for constituency interests, but an objective observer might question what some legislators mean by "representing" their district interests, particularly since the constituents do not express an interest in most issues, and only a small number of constituents are likely to express interest on any legislation. There have been three general approaches to the "representation" question:

1. One approach is to attempt to match representatives' opinions on issues and their perceptions of constituents' opinions with opinions of a random sample of constituents.
2. A second approach is to compare demographic characteristics of districts (percent urban, median income, and so on) with votes of representatives. A variant of this approach is to compare demographic characteristics of legislators (education, former occupation, and so on) with those of constituents.
3. The third approach is theoretical. It deals with the theoretically logical consequences of the election system.

The first approach seems to ask a straightforward question but turns out to be quite complex. A classic study on this topic was by Miller and Stokes (1963), in which they tried to compare constituency attitudes, representatives' attitudes, and representatives' perceptions of constituency attitudes in several issue areas. They found accurate perceptions and agreement on some domestic issues. These were issues that were highly publicized or of long standing and tended to be associated with traditional party rhetoric.[7] One suspects that more disagreement might be found if one went into specific detail on how to deal with issues in legislation. These issues may change with time, and there is no sure way to predict which issues will produce agreement at another point in time. Legislators' prediction of district attitudes may be quite correct on one issue and at one point in time and incorrect on another issue or another point in time. In any case, we expect more of our legislators than that they reflect a random sample of district opinion at the exact moment that they cast a vote. If we did not, we would abandon legislatures in favor of referendum. This would probably lead to control of legislation by a few strong interest groups or by those who could advertise best. It would to some extent abandon the idea that legislation should be consistent and should be debated rationally. Legislators may have an inaccurate perception of district opinion as a whole, but they may have an accurate perception of the opinions of certain groups within the district (usually those groups that have a strong opinion on an issue). Furthermore, there is no way for a legislator who tries to follow district opinion to decide issues that are of no current interest in the district or to decide on strategies and details in legislation.

The second approach tries to deal with some problems by assuming a connection between demographic characteristics and interests on the part of both legislators and constituents. Studies of social backgrounds of legislators show that they are not "typical" Americans. They tend to be well educated (many are lawyers) and successful. (Would you vote for a legislator who had been a failure at all other endeavors?) Their biographies indicate a high level of formal social activity. It is hard to find a representative who does not belong to at least ten organizations. Even if legislators had "typical" backgrounds, they would cease to be "typical" once they moved to Washington and became legislators. Nevertheless, legislators have varying opinions, related to the nature of the district they come from. There is no doubt that districts where certain issues are important will usually elect representatives with the "right" opinions on these issues. Those authors who concentrate on highly salient issues are likely to find constituent influence, and those that concentrate on the vast majority of legislation are likely to notice the importance of colleagues rather than constituents.

The third approach considers the theoretical implications of our current election system. This type of model is derived from the economic literature. Probably the most famous of these theories is by Downs (1957). His theory states that political parties are most interested in election and will alter their stands on issues (over time) to attempt to capture a majority of the votes in a two-party system. Where most of the public have attitudes toward the middle of a continuum on an issue, the party will attempt to capture votes from the other party by moving close to the center on this issue. Their reasoning would be that they would not lose votes from people with an extreme position on the issue unless they moved so far that the other candidate or party was closer to this extreme position than they themselves were. There are many votes to gain by moving toward the center and attracting voters from the other candidate or party.[8] Of course, parties cannot usually alter issue positions in a very short time period. Over the long run, however, the result of this reasoning on the part of both parties will be two parties that differ very little from each other on major issues. The relationship of this theory to U.S. legislators is not simple. The parties may have stands on issues, but legislators often do not vote with their party. Each district may have a different distribution of opinions on an issue, and the result could be a large diversity of opinion in Congress.

A recent book by Mayhew (1974) has extended the Downs model and elaborated a theory about legislative behavior that starts with the premise that the major goal of representatives is to get reelected.[9] Representatives are usually successful in this goal. (Senators have a little more trouble, but they do not have to face reelection as often.) Since all representatives face the same problem, they design the rules of the organization to help each other.[10] They vote themselves staffs to handle district mail and problems, they get office supplies and free postage (for certain kinds of material), and they arrange legislative work so that members can devote time to constituency activities. Members use the resources of their position to make themselves known to their constituents (sending out questionnaires, making commencement speeches), generating particular benefits in the form of legislation or casework for particular constituents, and taking public stands on popular issues. Mayhew goes on to derive from this a series of consequences on policy matters. Members will spend a good deal of time being ombudsmen. They will voice a lot of opinions about government policy in order to obtain publicity and recognition. Members may be more interested in stating a position than in winning. Constituents cannot blame a representative for not being on the winning side. They can only blame representatives for taking the "wrong" position. They have no way of knowing how hard a representative tried to push legislation. All this results in delays in legislative work. Such delays are useful, because they allow time for public reaction. When legislation is passed, there is a tendency toward particularized benefits that legislators can take credit for, and there is deference toward organized groups that can influence elections. Also when legislation is passed, more attention is paid to the policy side of legislation or its symbolic effect than to implementation details. Implementation details are not seen by the public as the representative's job except for his or her role of ombudsman. If one does not think that Congress functions efficiently in passing legislation and designing implementation, it is no solution to remove old members and elect new ones. The new members will have the same set of constraints to deal with. Mayhew seems to conclude that rational reelection behavior leads to nonrational legislation. He does not deal with legislation in those areas where reelection pressures are unimportant.

The representation studies have pointed out that there really are some salient issues on which there is agreement between legislator and constituency and that reelection pressures do provide legislators with an incentive to follow constituency opinion on these issues. There is, however, a tendency for legislators to use their positions on these for reelection purposes and to be more concerned with the symbolic nature of the legislation than with rational implementation plans or with rational discussion of the issues. The evidence supports the legislators' perceptions of their relationships with constituencies, although it does not assure us that legislators will be able to predict constituency opinion on many issues.

Legislative Behavior

It is a convenient feature of attempting to study Congress that one does not have to be satisfied with legislators' accounts of their own behavior. Many of their actions are publicly recorded, and one can study the actual behavior. It was mentioned in the previous section that researchers have tried to explain constituency influence by comparing votes by representatives with constituency characteristics. Votes have also been used to study other parts of the decision process.[11] Votes can be used in a number of ways to tell us something about voting rationality.

1. They can be used to analyze the decision process for a particular issue.
2. They can be used to determine how issues are related to one another.
3. They can be used to say something about the relationships between legislators.

The first use of votes is likely to focus on a highly salient issue, and the other approaches usually focus on the pattern of voting on all issues. It is, therefore, not unexpected that these approaches tell us different things about decision making on legislative matters. The first use of votes is similar to studies that discuss the representation issue. The difference is that the emphasis here is on the decision process rather than on the issue of representation. The other approaches suggest different kinds of reasons for voting behavior, reasons that are not based on political pressures.

An example of the first type of vote analysis is an article by Cummings and Peabody on a decision in 1961 to enlarge the Rules Committee (Peabody and Polsby, 1963). In the years before 1961, the Rules Committee had been dominated by conservatives who had used the power of the Rules Committee (on the scheduling of legislation and terms of debate) to stop or alter liberal legislation on social welfare. The conservative nature of the members of this committee is documented by voting indices.[12] The new Kennedy administration, the Democratic House leadership, and many "liberal" Democrats saw the Rules Committee as a serious impediment to proposed legislation. A resolution was introduced to add three members to the Rules Committee in order to alter the majority opinion on the Committee. There is an analysis of events leading up to the vote based on newspaper reports and interviews with participants. An analysis of the vote follows, separated by party and region. The focus is on those Republicans who voted for the resolution and those southern Democrats who voted against it. Constituency characteristics (urban or rural and percent black) and organization characteristics (position in the House and relationships with the Speaker) are used to explain some of the Democratic votes. Region and urbanism and presidential vote in the congressional district in 1960 are used to explain the Republican votes. Previous scores on a liberalism index are also used for both parties. The attempt is to explain the vote mostly by finding district characteristics or ideological characteristics (based on past votes) that are associated with a certain position on the issue. If representatives had been asked to explain their votes, they may or may not have chosen to mention these particular characteristics.

In studies of this type, the emphasis is often on political pressures from various interested sources and on explicit political bargaining. This emphasis reflects salient issues that fit into a political pattern (such as a liberal-conservative dimension on social welfare issues). These issues are chosen for their strategic importance and high salience. It is not really possible to study a minor issue, because there is no extensive background history or explicit political bargaining, but such minor issues constitute the great majority of roll calls. How can one study decisions on these types of issues? The solution in the literature is to show that there are patterns to voting behaviors. The patterns are a result of legislators' efforts to make sense out of an excess of information, a lack of time to process the information, and a demand for "rational" decisions. They respond by classifying issues and sources of information. Once a piece of legislation has been classified as being in a certain category, one can use past relations and behavior to establish an opinion or find a further source of information (such as a colleague who is knowledgeable in this area). Analysis of votes shows that this reasoning is probably correct. Votes on one piece of legislation are frequently related to votes on others in the same topic area, and there are groups of members with similar voting patterns.

One of the early studies that used votes to find patterns and relationships is by Truman (1959). The study covers both the House and Senate for a two-year period (1949-1950). Roll

calls were divided into groups on the basis of the degree of
unity within each party on the roll calls, and legislators are divided into blocs depending upon the number of times they
voted the same way. In a later book by MacRae (1970), on various methodologies for studying issues and parties using voting
data, the mathematics has become more complicated, but the
principle remains the same. Votes in Congress form scales[13] that
appear to be composed of items with similar substantive content. Legislators can be given scores on these scales, or, in a
more complex method, they can be assigned factor scores,
which are a summary measure of their positions relative to one
another on all votes. In the voting studies, the most important
variable for predicting voting behavior turns out to be party
membership. This is surprising, in light of the fact that a vote on
which all Democrats vote against all Republicans is very rare. It
is also surprising in light of the fact that legislators do not see
party as a strong source of influence. The party leadership rarely makes an effort to encourage members to vote in a certain
direction. The importance of party must then be related to the
informal information network and social ties.[14] Other bases for
clusters of legislators are region, ideological similarities, and
district similarities. (These are sometimes hard to separate from
one another, and it is difficult to say which comes first, since
ideology is based on voting records that are influenced by
sources of information, and sources of information may be
groups of friends chosen for their ideological compatibility.)
One of the more interesting descriptions of groupings of legislators comes from a study (Young, 1966) of the House in the
early 1800s. At that time, members came to Washington only
for the winter and resided in boardinghouses. These boardinghouses were the basis for voting blocs. The members lived together, ate together, and voted together. It is true that the
boardinghouse groups were not random to start with; they
tended to have members from the same region. At this time,
turnover from term to term was about 40 percent, and boardinghouse groups were constructed on arrival in Washington, so
the original ideological match of members in a boardinghouse
was not perfect. This example illustrates very nicely the impor-

tance of social structure and information exchange on voting behavior. It was clear in the early 1800s when the issues voted on were fewer and less complex than today. Information based on social networks is undoubtedly still important in voting behavior.

An interesting study that attempts to test the notion of information networks is described in a book by Matthews and Stimson (1975). The assumption is that members look to other members (called *cue givers*) for information on how to vote. Cue givers may be experts in the subject area or intermediaries (such as party leaders) who interpret the experts but add a partisan viewpoint. Information goes from the experts to the intermediaries to the cue takers.[15] A test of the theory is made by defining nine possible cues: the president, the state party delegation (if there is a three fourths majority agreement), the floor leader and whip if they vote together, the chair of the relevant committee, the ranking minority member of the relevant committee, the conservative coalition (a majority of southern Democrats voting with a majority of midwestern Republicans), the seven leaders of the Democratic Study Group (a group of liberal Democrats), a two thirds majority of the member's party, and a two thirds majority of the House. It should be noted that the voting system in the House allows members to see how others vote before they vote themselves. Matthews and Stimson take each legislator and use the first fifty votes in a session (the study used the years from 1958 to 1969) to determine the proportion of agreement with each of the mentioned cue givers. For each vote, they then use the *best* cue giver for that legislator (if available) to predict a vote on the roll call. If no cue is available from that cue giver, they go to the next-best cue-giver. Votes, then, are predicted on the basis of one cue giver, but that cue giver will differ from one vote to another and from one legislator to another. Using this system, they predict correctly 88 percent of the time. This figure varies somewhat, depending on the size of the majority, the year, the member's party, and other factors. This is an impressive figure when one considers that it includes all members and all roll call votes.[16] The policy implications of these results depend on the nature of the cue givers. The initial cue givers are experts in a particular policy area. They have probably chosen this area and may not be unbiased. The intermediate cue givers may give a political interpretation to the experts, but they are also somewhat at the mercy of the experts. This once again points out the importance of specialization and division of labor in the legislative process.

Because specialization and division of labor are so important, researchers have studied some of these specialized groups in some detail. The obvious groups for such research are the committees. The committees are the source of most expertise on legislative issues. The committees do differ from each other in terms of their social norms and their reputation in the entire legislature. The most prestigious committees have fairly stable memberships, and over time they have each developed a set of norms and expectations and a reputation concerning the reliability of their expertise. The committees can be studied in many of the same ways as Congress. In addition, one can study how the committee relates to the larger institution. Different committees arrive at decisions in different ways. For each policy area, one would have to study the relevant committee to understand how legislation is written and debated and reported.

As was mentioned previously, committees are not chosen randomly, and the area of expertise is often a matter of choice. In theory, the advice of the specialists must be debated by the whole House, but in practice it appears that the specialists occupy key positions in the information network and are usually not challenged. This leads to questions about the representative nature of most legislation. The studies on the role of the legislator from the legislator's perspective usually underestimate the importance of voting patterns that are based on specialization, although they do recognize the importance of specialization for writing legislation.

Conclusion

We began this chapter by asking if it is true that laws are established with our consensus and that laws are likely to be a consistent system based on rationality or expediency, given our legislative system The evidence suggests that our legislative system is somewhat representational and somewhat rational but that those elements in the system that make it representational make it less rational and those elements that lead to rationality make it less representational.

One consequence of an election system is to make legislators somewhat accountable. They listen to constituent opinion on some issues, and they communicate with constituents in a regular manner because they are concerned about reelection. They also act as negotiators between constituents and the federal bureaucracy, and this makes them sensitive to some implementation problems. In doing this, however, they decrease the chances that they can deal rationally with legislation. Obviously, if they vote only in accordance with district opinion, they may not make a rational decision on the merits of the legislation (although it will be a rational decision for reelection purposes). In addition to this, the time and effort that they spend with constituents is taken away from the time and effort they can spend learning about legislation. Given the large numbers of complex bills in specialized areas and the large amount of information that is available, this is a serious problem. The pressures of reelection may cause legislators to focus on certain aspects of legislation. They may be more interested in taking a certain position on legislation rather than on getting legislation passed or creating rational implementation plans.

Some aspects of the legislative process are very rational. Specialization and division of labor are what enables Congress to cope with the volume and complexity of legislative work. However, specialization and division of labor must lead to some loss of the representation function of Congress. Legislation is not really considered by all members of Congress. It is considered mostly by small subgroups, who are frequently self-selected. The necessity for specialization usually also means that Congress essentially defers to its experts for most legislative decisions. The conflict between the legislator as a representative and the legislator as a rational decision maker is not new. This debate over the proper role of the legislator was of great interest when parliamentary democracies were established in western

Europe. What is recent in this debate is the element of increasing size and complexity of the legislative workload due to the increased governmental function in the twentieth century. The increased workload has resulted in a new way to deal "rationally" with legislation and makes representation more difficult.

The empirical evidence suggests that conclusions about this conflict will be influenced by the methodology of the study. Studies that focus on highly salient issues are likely to find that legislators take constituency opinion into account. Highly salient issues are those on which there is ample publicity and opportunity for interested parties to make their views known. These same issues are the ones likely to be remembered at election time, so a legislator will usually attempt to assess district opinion. They are also the issues that reflect political bargaining and explicit pressures to vote in one direction or another. Because of this, the analysis of such issues has a political tone (political reasons are given for decisions). Those studies that focus on patterns of actual behavior on all issues are likely to find a system of decisions that are not based on explicitly political considerations but that can be explained by using theories about the social structure of the legislature as an organization. Key aspects of this social system are an information network and deference toward rational expertise. Such studies minimize outside influence, such as constituency pressures or interest groups, for most legislation. Any conclusions about decision making rest on the choice of salient versus nonsalient issues. Salient issues are those with at least short-run importance in the electorate. Nonsalient issues involve the vast majority of legislation and may have great impact on our lives in the long run.

None of the methods of studying Congress suggest that it is possible to greatly alter the type of legislative results without altering some of the electoral or organizational rules. The organizational rules have changed slowly over time in response to demands to alter legislative output. The 1961 decision to enlarge the Rules Committee is one example of such a change. Because of that change, some additional legislation was probably passed, but the change did not alter the basic problem that

keeps a legislature from functioning as a perfect model of representation and rationality. Electing new members will not
produce large changes, either, since they must cope with the
same conflicts. As in most organizations, reforms come when
the organization is under pressure from members (possibly new
members) or from external sources. One of the external forces
that has produced some change in Congress in this century is
the increase in government functions and responsibilities that
has increased the amount and complexity of legislation. Other
forces for change have been an increased technical ability for
legislators to communicate with constituents and an increased
need for am ombudsman role with the growth of the federal
bureaucracy. These are just some examples of external forces
that were not explicitly intended to produce change in Congress
but that have done so anyway. Congress is not a perfectly rigid
organization, but large changes in type or quality of legislation
are not likely to happen except over a long period of time and
changing circumstances.

Notes

1. This differs from traditional law, based on the sanctity
of tradition, and from charismatic laws, based on devotion to
the exemplary character of one person and revealed or ordained
by that person.

2. There are many studies of state legislatures and legislatures in other countries, but it is easiest to provide a sense of
typical perspectives by keeping to one institution.

3. Biographies of legislators show that they are people
much concerned with achievement.

4. Some legislation is written by the executive branch,
but it can be changed by Congress, so there must be a procedure
for this.

5. Bills must be scheduled for a vote by the rules committee. Only a small percentage of bills that are introduced actually
make it through the committee process.

6. The Senate is different from the House in a few ways.
Senators are elected from much larger districts and have different reelection problems. They need to concentrate more on

publicity than representatives, they need the cooperation of the state party organization, and they deal with a wider range of interest groups. In many cases, representatives need to build their own party organizations, since their districts are geographically unique, and they concentrate more on casework and local publicity. Senators are less specialized than representatives, because there are fewer of them and they are on more committees.

7. On social welfare issues, the correlation between district and representative opinion was .3, on civil rights the correlation was .6, but on foreign affairs there was no correlation between district and representative opinions.

8. This assumes that individuals vote on the basis of issue preference and that parties respond in a rational manner by changing preferences.

9. At one time (in the previous century) being in Congress was a temporary part-time job. Members came to Washington for a short time each year and left after legislative business was completed. Now, with a much larger workload, a full-time job, and the emphasis on specialization that requires years of socialization and learning, being in Congress has become a career.

10. As Mayhew (1974, p. 85) puts it, "Office resources are given to all members regardless of party, seniority, or any other qualification. They come with the job."

11. There are other records of behavior beside votes, but votes are the most commonly used source of information on actual behavior.

12. These are indices on a series of issues chosen for their liberal or conservative ideological content. The indices are constructed by organizations who wish to classify members of Congress as liberal or conservative.

13. These scales differ from previously mentioned indices, where an organization picks several important votes and gives each legislator a score. The scales mentioned here are defined by the actual votes. They consist of a group of roll calls where the votes have a particular pattern.

14. Social friendships usually do not cross party lines in the House.

15. This theory is related to previous sociological theories on information-seeking behavior in the public and to decision theories about executives in organizations.

16. There are a few members whose votes cannot be accurately predicted from this model. Presumably they operate with a different information system The 88 percent should not be compared to a figure of 0 percent. If you predicted "yes" on all votes, you would be correct more than half the time.

References

Clapp, C. *The Congressman: His Work as He Sees It*. Washington, D.C.: The Brookings Institution, 1963.

Clausen, A. *How Congressmen Decide*. New York: St. Martin's, 1973.

Downs, A. *An Economic Theory of Democracy*. New York: Harper & Row, 1957.

MacRae, D., Jr. *Issues and Parties in Legislative Voting: Methods of Statistical Analysis*. New York: Harper & Row, 1970.

Matthews, D. *U.S. Senators and Their World*. New York: Random House, 1960.

Matthews, D., and Stimson, J. *Yeas and Nays: Normal Decision-Making in the U.S. House of Representatives*. New York: Wiley, 1975.

Mayhew, D. *Congress: The Electoral Connection*. New Haven, Conn.: Yale University Press, 1974.

Miller, W., and Stokes, D. "Constituency Influence in Congress." *American Political Science Review*, 1963, 57, 45-56.

Peabody, R., and Polsby, N. (Eds.) *New Perspectives on the House of Representatives*. Chicago: Rand McNally, 1963.

Truman, D. *The Congressional Party*. New York: Wiley, 1959.

Weber, M. *The Theory of Social and Economic Organization*. New York: Oxford University Press, 1947.

Young, J. *The Washington Community 1800-1828*. New York: Columbia University Press, 1966.

9

Rita James Simon

The American Jury

Instrument of Justice or of Prejudice and Conformity?

~~~~~~

The American jury system dates back to 1606 when James I granted a charter to the Virginia Colony. At the time of the American Revolution, the right to trial by jury was common in all the British North American colonies. After independence, trial by jury was guaranteed by the Sixth Amendment to the Constitution for federal prosecutions, and, in respect to state prosecutions, by way of the due-process clause of the Fourteenth Amendment.

   Prentice Marshall described the purpose of the jury, historically and in contemporary times, as follows: "The primary purpose of the jury is to provide the accused with a safeguard against governmental oppression: the corrupt or overzealous prosecutor; the compliant, biased, or eccentric judge. It is an interposition between the accused and his accuser of the commonsense judgment of a group of fair-minded laymen, representative of a cross section of the district in which the defendant allegedly committed the offense with which he stands accused" (in Nagel, 1972, p. 214).

Even critics of the modern jury grant the historical importance of the jury in strengthening democratic institutions in the early days of the American republic. Jerome Frank, a severe critic of the modern jury, characterized the jury in its earliest days on American soil, especially prior to independence, as the champion of the popular cause. "The jury was considered . . . a bulwark against oppressive government, acclaimed as essential to individual liberty and democracy" (Simon, 1967, p. 5).

The verdict of a New York jury in the case of John Peter Zenger (1735) is referred to some 240 years later as a demonstration of the jury's effectiveness as a check on government oppression. In effect, the New York jury overrode the judge and the royal governor, and declared Zenger not guilty of publishing defamatory statements against the Crown's representative, because, the jury said, the editorials were true.

In the period preceding the Civil War, northern juries regularly and frequently refused to convict persons who aided escaping slaves through the underground railroad. In the period following reconstruction after the Civil War, juries in the South were composed only of white men. It is during this period that the jury gained a reputation for relinquishing its role as a champion of justice and a bulwark against oppressive government. Indeed, it is during this period that many of the current attacks on the integrity of the jury originated.

But as recently as 1956, Lord Justice Devlin, in delivering the eight Hamlyn Lectures, said of the jury: "Each jury is a little parliament. The jury sense is the parliamentary sense. I cannot see the one dying and the other surviving. The first object of any tyrant in Whitehall would be to make Parliament utterly subservient to his will; and the next to overthrow or diminish trial by jury, for no tyrant could afford to leave a subject's freedom in the hands of twelve of his countrymen. So that trial by jury is more than an instrument of justice and more than one wheel of the constitution: it is the lamp that shows that freedom lives" (in Kalven and Zeisel, 1966, p. 6).

In recent years, major criticisms of the jury have centered around three issues. The first is that "The jury is expensive; [it] contributes to delay in civil litigation; and [it] imposes an unfair tax and social cost on those forced to serve" (Kalven and Zeisel, 1966, p. 8).

The second criticism centers on the issue of the jury's competency. Critics of the jury are most skeptical about whether jurors are capable of and in fact understand and follow the questions of law and facts that may be involved in any given trial. Carl Becker, a noted historian and student of American institutions, commented, "Trial by jury as a method of determining facts is antiquated and inherently absurd—so much so that no lawyer, judge, scholar, prescription-clerk, cook, or mechanic in a garage would ever think for a moment of employing that method for determining the facts in any situation that concerned him" (Simon, 1967, p. 6).

The third issue also concerns the jury's competency but in addition questions its motivation. Critics claim that jurors do not follow the law, in part because they do not understand it and in part because they do not like or agree with the rule of law applicable in the case they are considering (see, for example, Kalven and Zeisel, 1966, p. 18). In addition, critics claim that exposure to jury duty disenchants the citizen and causes him to lose confidence in the administration of justice.

Much of the recent empirical research on the jury, beginning with the work done at the law school of the University of Chicago in the 1950s, has shed light on each of these issues. The first of the monographs to emerge from the Chicago studies, *Delay in the Court* (Zeisel, Kalven, Buchholz, 1959), countered the charge that juries are mainly responsible for delay and backlog in civil litigation. Surveys of citizens who have served on the jury consistently find that juries are almost unanimous in feeling that their service was interesting and worthwhile and that they would like to serve again.

The competency issue has been examined in various ways. Kalven and Zeisel's comparison of the verdicts reported by juries against those that judges claimed they would have reached in the same cases shows that judges and juries agreed about 80 percent of the time. In the largest group of cases about which juries and judges disagreed, moreover, the judges felt that the evidence was about even for plaintiff and defendant or for prosecution and defense. In their opinion, the decision could have gone either way without causing a miscarriage of justice.

After observing the performance of ninety-eight juries in two recorded criminal trials involving a defense of insanity and listening to the recording of their deliberations, I wrote, "By the time the jurors have finished deliberating they have usually considered every bit of testimony, expert as well as lay, and every point offered in evidence.... The most consistent theme that emerged from listening to the deliberations is the seriousness with which the jurors do their job and the extent to which they are concerned that the verdict they reach be consistent with the spirit of the law and with the facts of the case" (Simon and Marshall, 1972, p. 221).

My purpose in this chapter is not to review once again the strengths and weaknesses of the jury system. Instead, it is to focus on one aspect of the jury's performance and to examine how well it performs that function for which the founders of this country had the highest expectations. In brief, my purpose is to assess whether the jury's initial function as a bulwark against oppressive government and, in the words of Lord Delvin, "as an instrument of justice," is still being performed or whether the jury in the contemporary period primarily reflects the collective prejudice and ignorance of the national citizenry. I shall go about this task by reviewing the performance of the jury in many of the major trials that have involved issues of individual liberty, the right of dissent, and other questions surrounding First Amendment civil liberties that have been heard in federal and state courts throughout the United States in the past three decades, beginning roughly with the end of World War II.

It will not be practical to review all the jury trials heard during this period in which such issues were considered. I would defend my selection of particular trials by the criteria of their importance (as attested to by experts in the law), by the attention they have received in the media, and by the objective consequences of the verdicts. It is only fair, however, for me to confess at the outset, that I am biased. My own empirical study

of the jury system and my reading of other studies have led me
to believe that the jury system works well, that the participants
perform their task with intelligence and interest, and that juries'
verdicts are consistent with those of experts, that is, verdicts
that judges claim they would have reached.

Before proceeding, I will say a few more words about how
to interpret juries' verdicts in the trials to be discussed. Are verdicts of acquittal, for example, always to be regarded as a sign
of the jury's integrity and of its effectiveness as a check against
governmental oppression? Likewise, are verdicts of guilty likely
to be viewed as instances of prejudice, corruption, and compliance with governmental power? Such simplistic interpretations would distort the usefulness and the meaningfulness of
this analysis. Rather, what I intend to do is examine the jury's
verdicts within the context of the nature of the acts the defendants are accused of having committed; the social, economic,
and political characteristics of the defendants; the extent and
tone of the media coverage; the prevailing political mood of the
country; the decisions reached by judges in bench trials of a
comparable type heard during the same period; and whether the
juries' verdicts were upheld on appeal.

Listed below are the names, not the formal names by
which the cases may be identified in judicial records, but the
names by which they are known in the press and by common
usage. For example, the trial in New York City of the thirteen
Black Panthers on grounds of conspiracy will be referred to as
the Panther 13 Trial and not as *The People of the State of New
York* v. *Lumumba Shakur and others.*

Trial	Verdict	Decision on Appeal
Period: Late 1940s, Early 1950s		
Smith Act Trials: Eugene Dennis and others	Guilty	Upheld
Alger Hiss	First—Hung jury 8 convicted 4 acquitted	
	Second—Guilty	Upheld
Julius and Ethel Rosenberg	Guilty	Upheld

Trial	Verdict	Decision on Appeal
Period: Late 1960s, Early 1970s		
Angela Davis	Not guilty	
Huey Newton	Guilty of lesser charge	Reversed
New York Panther 13	Not guilty	
Chicago 8	Guilty of lesser charge	Reversed
Harrisburg 7	Hung jury 2 convicted 10 acquitted No retrial	
Spock, Coffin	Guilty	Reversed
Period: Mid 1970s		
Mitchell, Stans	Not guilty	
Watergate Cover-Up Trial: Haldeman, Ehrlichman, Mitchell	Guilty	Upheld

Political Trials in the Late 1940s and Early 1950s

Like the period following the end of World War I, the era of the late 1940s and early 1950s that followed the end of World War II was marked by zealousness on the part of the government in seeking out those individuals and political organizations whose loyalty to the United States they doubted. As in the earlier period, concern focused primarily on the political left, on the Communist Party, and on "communist front" groups, including civil rights organizations, cultural and social movements, labor unions, and parties (for example, the American Labor Party in New York State) that had been identified as supporting the Soviet Union or leftist causes generally. Loyalty programs and oaths were introduced at the national and state levels, at universities, among trade unions, in the mass media and entertainment fields, in the state and federal bureaucracies. The Justice Department organized and published lists of organizations believed to be disloyal and subversive; passports of prominent persons in academia, entertainment, the professions, and other fields (the case of Paul Robeson stands out as one of the most notorious) were revoked; blacklists were drawn up in the movie and television industries that effectively prevented directors, actors, and writers from finding employment.

Bills such as the Mundt-Nixon bill and the McCarran Internal Security Act were passed by the Congress, requiring members of the Communist Party to register with the Justice Department. Failure to do so made them liable to criminal action. Both the House and the Senate activated committees on internal subversion (the subcommittee headed by Joseph McCarthy, junior senator from Wisconsin, became the most famous of these) that examined the personal and political histories of thousands of American citizens.

Public opinion polls conducted during this period indicated that the activities of Senator McCarthy, the passage of the Mundt-Nixon bill, and loyalty oaths as a qualification for employment received a good deal of popular support. For example, when the public was asked during debate over the Mundt-Nixon bill whether the Congress ought to pass it, 63 percent answered yes. A year or two later when asked whether they favored registration of Communist Party members, 80 percent said yes in 1949 and 67 percent said yes in 1950 (Simon, 1975, p. 109).

On the matter of loyalty oaths, 70 percent of the public agreed with the actions of the board of regents of the University of California when it required all of its teachers to take an oath that they were not communist. Concerning the activities of Senator Joseph McCarthy, in the summer of 1950 the public was asked whether it thought that Senator McCarthy's charges (that there were communists in the state department) were doing the country more good than harm. Among those who had an opinion (16 percent did not) or were familiar with the senator's charges (16 percent were not), 57 percent compared to 43 percent believed that Senator McCarthy's charges were doing the country more good than harm (Simon, 1975, p. 109-110).

It is within the context of this political environment that we examine the jury's action in the major political trials of this era: the Dennis case (or the Smith Act Trial), the trial of Julius and Ethel Rosenberg, and the Alger Hiss case. All three involved trial by jury: In each, the defendants were eventually found guilty (the first Hiss trial resulted in a hung jury: Four jurors voted for acquittal, eight for conviction). The trial court judge in the first Hiss trial and in the Rosenberg case was Samuel Kaufman: in the Dennis case, Harold Medina; and, in the second Hiss trial, Henry Goddard. All three cases were upheld on appeal. The defendants in the Rosenberg case were sentenced to death and were executed on June 19, 1953. Alger Hiss was sentenced to five years in prison. The eleven defendants in the Dennis case were sentenced to five years in prison. Their lawyers were also sentenced for contempt of court.

We turn first to the Dennis case. In January 1949, the U.S. government brought eleven top leaders of the Communist Party to trial.[1] Each of them was charged with conspiracy to teach and advocate the violent overthrow of the U.S. government. The trial lasted twenty weeks. The first six weeks were devoted to pretrial motions that included a challenge by the defense attorneys to the federal jury system. In essence, the defense challenged the system of picking "blue-ribbon juries." They charged that blue-ribbon juries were "superior" citizens chosen from such lists as college directories and the *Social Register*. They claimed that Jews and blacks were systematically excluded.

When the jury was finally selected, it consisted of eleven women and one man. Three of the jurors were black, and nine were white. The foreman of the jury was a black woman who earned her living as a dressmaker.

In retrospect, the behavior of the defense attorneys in the Dennis Trial was similar to the behavior of the attorneys in the Chicago 8 Trial. Like Kunstler and others in the Chicago 8 Trial, at the end of the Dennis Trial the attorneys for the defense were also charged with contempt and sentenced by the trial judge to several months in prison. During the course of the long trial, Judge Medina also declared three of the defendants, John Gates (editor of *The Daily Worker*), Henry Winston, and Gus Hall guilty of contempt, which meant that they spent in jail the time that they were not in the courtroom, rather than being free on bail. Throughout the twenty weeks that the trial lasted, supporters of the defendants picketed the courtroom, held testimonial fund-raising dinners and organized streetcorner rallies.

Unlike reporters covering Judge Hoffman's behavior during the Chicago 8 Trial, reporters wrote admiringly of Judge Medina's demeanor on the bench. *Time* magazine described one scenario as follows:

> The judge, not the U.S. Attorney, had become their main adversary. Sometimes sallies flew so fast between judge and lawyers that the jurors swiveled their heads like a gallery at a tennis match. After only two weeks of such exchanges, the jury began to fidget wearily—but Judge Medina had been at it for nine weeks before the jury entered the box. He was growing a little tired and a little testy. . . .
>
> So it went as the lawyers collecting $2,275 a week from the C.P. [Communist Party] in fees worked to goad the judge into making a prejudicial error: It would be handy on appeal. Medina occasionally reddened with wrath as they darted in at him. Isserman with his soft way, Gladstein with his air of righteous plausibility turning to outraged innocence when the judge caught him laying a legal trap. Harry Sacher, the little man with the bull voice chivying the Court, then smiling impishly, eyes cast down, while the judge mildly upbraided him. Dennis rushing in occasionally to make a choked, impassioned speech. (Dennis was acting as his own attorney.)
>
> Toward the end of the week, Judge Medina handed down a patient man's exasperated opinion: "This is the doggonedest trial I ever saw. . . . You'll probably make a motion for a mistrial, but I'm not going to take it back" ["Doggonedest Trial," 1949, p. 23].

At the end of twenty weeks, both sides rested. When the judge instructed the members of the jury, he told them in essence that they had one question to decide. Did the eleven communist leaders violate the Smith Act by conspiring to "teach the duty or necessity of overthrowing or destroying the government of the United States?" The jury began its deliberations late in the afternoon of October 13. After about six hours of deliberating, the jurors were taken to a hotel for the night. They continued to deliberate the next morning for about two more hours before announcing that they had reached a verdict. The jury found each of the defendants guilty.

The Dennis Trial had lasted 169 days—it was the longest, and in the words of *Newsweek,* "the dreariest and most controversial criminal trial in American legal history" ("His Honor, Judge Patience," 1949, p. 22). Each of the defendants except Thompson was sentenced to five years in prison and $10,000 in fines.[2] Medina refused the defendants' request for bail pending their appeal. The verdict was appealed both to the U.S. Court of Appeals and to the Supreme Court and was upheld at each level.

The first of the two Alger Hiss trials was held in the same building and at the same time as the Dennis trial. It began on May 31, 1949. The specific charge against Alger Hiss was that he had committed perjury when he testified before the federal grand jury in 1948. If Hiss had perjured himself, then he was in fact guilty of espionage, consisting of delivering secret and restricted documents of state to a foreign power while he held an important position in the State Department.[3]

Unlike the Dennis and Rosenberg trials and most of the subsequent political trials of the 1960s, in the Hiss trial the business of selecting a jury was completed quickly and without any questioning of the principles of the jury system. Within two and a half hours, forty veniremen had been called and examined. All claimed they had read about and/or heard of the case, but the ten men and two women who were chosen claimed that they were without prejudice in the matter.

The trial lasted twenty-seven days. Although some seventy-five witnesses testified, one witness stood out above all others, and at the beginning and end the major question posed by the two sides was "Who will the jury believe—Whittaker Chambers, the accuser, or Alger Hiss, the accused?" Chambers, an admitted former member of the communist underground, accused Hiss of providing him with secret and restricted documents that Hiss had access to because of his position in the State Department. According to Chambers, Hiss acted in this fashion from 1934 to 1938, when Chambers broke with the party. Chambers testified that he had urged Hiss to do the same, but Hiss had refused. Hiss, according to Chambers, might still, up to the time of the trial, be a member of a Communist Party cell. At first, Alger Hiss denied knowing or having ever met Whittaker Chambers. On the witness stand, Hiss, a graduate of a prep school at Duxbury, Johns Hopkins University, and Harvard Law School, and secretary to Supreme Court Justice Oliver Wendell Holmes, testified that he was not and never had been a member of the Communist Party, a fellow traveler, or a communist sympathizer. He denied that he had ever "furnished, transmitted, or delivered" any "restricted, secret, or confidential documents of the State Department of any kind, character or description whatever" to Whittaker Chambers or any other unauthorized person.

Twenty-seven days later, the Court told the members of the jury that if they believed Hiss, their verdict should be not guilty. If they believed Chambers, their verdict might be guilty.

The jury deliberated nineteen hours. During that time it asked the Court for a copy of the indictment, the bill of particulars, and the exhibits. Twice it asked to have the judge's charge reread to it, and four times it informed the court that it could not agree. In the end, it was deadlocked, eight for conviction, four for acquittal.

The second trial commenced on November 17, 1949. It lasted three weeks. The two main characters performed the same roles, Chambers the accuser, Hiss the accused; but the presiding judge had been changed, and some of the attorneys were new. Again, a jury was selected quickly, without any basic challenge to the system. Of the eight women selected seven were housewives: of the four men, one worked in an office, one was an optician, one a plant manager, and one a retired manufacturer.

The prosecution met directly the issue of the unsavoriness of their chief witness. Chambers, they said, had had an "unguided and unfortunate boyhood." After joining the Communist Party, he lied, cheated, and stole for the party. But he broke with the party and repented. He testified before the House Un-American Activities Committee out of a sense of duty. Hiss' testimony in the second trial was substantially the same as it had been in the first. The major new event in the second trial was the appearance for the defense of two "expert psychiatric witnesses" who, without having examined Chambers, declared him to be suffering from a psychopathic personality. This opinion they reached from having observed him in the courtroom and from having studied his writing.

The judges instructed the jury on the matter of expert testimony essentially as follows: "This testimony, like all expert testimony, was purely advisory and the jury might reject the doctors' opinions entirely if it found either that 'the hypothetical situation presented to it in the question was incomplete or incorrect' or 'the reasons [given in support of the opinions] unsound or not convincing'; that 'the jurors had seen and heard Mr. Chambers for several days while he was on the witness stand,' and it was for them to say 'how much weight, if any,' they would give to the testimony of the experts" (Morris, 1967, p. 476).

The jury deliberated for almost twenty-four hours before it announced that it had reached a verdict. It found the defendant, Alger Hiss, guilty of perjury. The Court sentenced him to five years in the penitentiary. Hiss' appeal to the Federal Court of Appeals (2nd Circuit) was rejected. The Court (Justices Chase, Augustus Hand, and Swan) unanimously affirmed the judgment of the district court. The U.S. Supreme Court denied Hiss' petition for further review.

The trial of Ethel and Julius Rosenberg has to be the most important case that we consider in this article because the defendants in this case were sentenced and put to death. The trial began on March 6, 1951, before Judge Irving R. Kaufman (the judge who presided over the first of the Hiss trials). The defendants were charged with conspiracy to commit espionage by transmitting atomic secrets to agents of the Soviet Union.

The trial lasted approximately one month. The jury found the defendants guilty. Judge Kaufman sentenced Ethel and Julius Rosenberg to death in the electric chair. Morton Sobell, a coconspirator, was sentenced to thirty years, and David Greenglass, another coconspirator who collaborated with the prosecution, was sentenced to fifteen years.[4]

On February 25, 1952, the case was appealed to the U.S. Circuit Court of Appeals, and the convictions were affirmed. On October 13, 1952, the Supreme Court declined to review the case, with Justice Black dissenting. Between then and June 19, 1953, the date Ethel and Julius Rosenberg were executed, protest rallies were held in most countries of western Europe; and pleas for clemency were sent to the president from Pope Pius, from the president of France, from clergy, statesmen, scientists (such as Albert Einstein and Harold Urey), and writers all over the world. The attorneys for the Rosenbergs introduced appeals for a new trial on grounds that evidence had been discovered and that the Atomic Energy Act of 1946 should have applied to the case. The day of the execution, protest rallies attended by thousands of persons were held in New York City and in capital cities all over the world.

How important a role did the jury play in determining the fate of Julius and Ethel Rosenberg? Had the jury not found them guilty or had the jury found them guilty of lesser acts than those for which they were charged, the trial judge would not have sentenced them to death. In the hundreds of commentaries that have been written about their trial (the Rosenberg case now ranks with Sacco and Vanzetti as being among the most controversial political trials in American history), the jury is almost forgotten. Attention is focused on the trial judge and to a lesser extent on the team of prosecutors and defense attorneys. In passing the sentence that he did, Judge Kaufman became the first judge ever to sentence an American citizen to death for treason during peacetime. In explaining his reason for the death sentence, Judge Kaufman said, "I consider your crime worse than murder. . . . I believe your conduct in putting into the hands of the Russians the A-bomb . . . has already caused, in my opinion, the communist aggression in Korea, with the resultant casualties exceeding 50,000 and who knows but that millions more of innocent people may pay the price of your treason. Indeed, by your betrayal you undoubtedly have altered the course of history ... we have evidence of your treachery all around us every day—for the civilian defense activities throughout the nation are aimed at preparing us for an atom bomb attack" (Transcript of Record, 1952, p. 1614).

But what of the jury? First of all, who were the members of the jury? The jury was composed of eleven men and one woman; of eleven whites and one black. Although the trial took place in New York City, where about one out of every three persons is Jewish, there were no Jews on the jury. Neither were there any laborers. Almost all the jurors were managers, entrepreneurs, accountants, or auditors (five). Some had business or other ties with government agencies.

Before the jury was selected, the court permitted the reading aloud to the prospective jurors the names of the 105 organizations that the U.S. Attorney General had deemed subversive (the so-called Attorney General's List). After the list was read, Judge Kaufman asked, "Well, now, the question is whether any juror has been a member of, contributed to or been associated with, or any member of his family, or close friend, with any of those organizations that have been just read to you" (Transcript of Record, 1952, p. 69). In addition to the Attorney General's List, the prosecution submitted to the jury a list of 140 publications, and the defense submitted a list of fourteen, all of which the judge read to the prospective jurors and asked, "As a result of having read anything in any of these papers, would you be so prejudiced that you could not render a verdict in this case based on the evidence and the evidence alone" (1952, p. 71).[5]

It is impossible to know specifically how exposure to the judge's announcement homogenized the characteristics of the remaining potential jurors, to know exactly which types of jurors excluded themselves from the voir dire. But the fact that there were no Jews and no laborers among those finally selected suggests that there had been extensive self-selection and that the twelve persons who finally qualified to determine the guilt or

innocence of Julius and Ethel Rosenberg were neither representative of the community from which they were called nor
"peers" of the defendants.

The trial was over one month after it began. The jury deliberated for about seven hours before it announced that it had
reached a verdict. The jury found the defendants guilty as
charged. The judge thanked the jury (a not unusual procedure),
but then announced, "Again I say a great tribute is due to the
FBI and Mr. Hoover for the splendid job that they have done in
this case." The jury had no say in the sentence handed down by
Judge Kaufman.

The Dennis, Hiss, and Rosenberg trials were the three
major political trials of that era. The jury found all the defendants guilty. All the verdicts were upheld on appeal.

Political Trials in the Late 1960s and Early 1970s

Looking back on American society only a few years, to
the latter part of the 1960s, we recall an era in which the divi-
siveness and bitterness between generations and between racial
groups was comparable only to the class bitterness of the 1930s
or the regional bitterness of the Civil War era. It was a period of
the worst urban race riots in the country's history and the most
severe acts of civil disorder. The United States had been involved in unpopular wars prior to Vietnam, but no other had
evoked a more violent response on the part of the young people
in this country than that war did.

The law-making and law-enforcing agencies of the government did not respond to the disorder and violence of the late
1960s as they did to the existence of communist-led and "infiltrated" movements of the post-World War II era. Loyalty oaths,
registration of political parties, subversive lists, blacklists, all of
the apparatus used by the government twenty years ago was not
reinstituted, perhaps because the enemy in this period was too
diffuse. The loyalty issue could not be characterized as a choice
between the Soviets and the United States. No "foreign ideologies" were involved. The leaders of the New Left emphasized
the adjective *new* as much as or more than they did the noun

left in describing the objectives and goals of their movement. The blacks who organized sit-ins, who set fire to urban ghettos, and who threw rocks at the police were 100 percent Americans.

Between 1965 and 1970, a few items concerning the right to dissent appeared on national public opinion polls. In that five-year period, there was a noticeable increase in the proportion who opposed dissent. For example, when asked in 1967, "Do you think people have the right to conduct peaceful demonstrations against the war in Vietnam?" 68 percent said yes. In 1970, 25 percent said yes (Simon, 1975, p. 117).

While the government was not as active in passing laws that stigmatized dissidents and restricted their activities, it did pursue them from the streets into the courtroom. The era of the late 1960s will be remembered as the era in which the political trial and the "movement attorney" came into their own.

There were too many political trials in the late 1960s and early 1970s for me to describe and analyze all of them in this paper. I think I have included the major and most representative ones.[6] The defendants in the trials selected came from every stratum in American society. Some were upper-middle-class, well-educated professionals, who had, until their involvement in radical politics, enjoyed the respect and admiration of their colleagues and a broad stratum of the American public. Some were young, long-haired, pot-smoking, college-educated persons whose vocabularies consisted primarily of four-letter words. Some were militant, tough, ghetto blacks who declared with raised, clenched fist that their goal was political power. There were men and women who belonged to Catholic orders and declared they were still loyal to their vows but who were charged with conspiracy to blow up federal buildings and kidnap Henry Kissinger. One was a black university instructor who admitted membership in the Communist Party and friendship with an inmate of San Quentin.

Each of the trials lasted many weeks, and each involved a jury selected with the aid of social scientists who delved deeply into the prospective jurors' social, economic, and political status as well as their psyches. In each case, the jury was sequestered for the entire length of the trial. Each of the defendants was represented by lawyers who "designed not only to refute the charges but also to introduce political and moral issues" (Barkan, 1977, p. 326).

All the trials received extensive publicity from the mass media, and most of the media during this period (as in previous eras of political trials, such as the late 1940s or the 1920s, which witnessed the Debs and Sacco-Vanzetti trials) believed the defendants were dangerous and guilty of the acts for which they were charged. Most of the media were also critical of the defendants' attire, demeanor, and behavior during the trials. The defendants' failure in many instances to exhibit proper respect for the judge and for the symbols of the state, was reported in a critical vein. Barkan (1977, p. 334) claims that "the Chicago 8 defense achieved worldwide publicity at the expense of antagonizing the jury."

Before commenting on each of the trials separately, I think it important to emphasize that most of the defendants were acquitted or found guilty of a lesser charge. Benjamin Spock, William Sloan Coffin, and others are the conspicuous exceptions. The juries in the Angela Davis Trial, the Panther 13 Trial, and the Chicago Conspiracy Trial all decided that the defendants either were innocent of all of the acts for which they were charged or were guilty of less serious acts. The defendants' color, social status, the seriousness of the acts for which they were charged, or the style and reputation of their attorneys would not have been useful predictors of the juries' verdicts. William Kunstler received about as bad a press as any of the lawyers involved in the political trials of that period, yet his clients were acquitted or found guilty of lesser charges. The lawyers in the Spock and Others Trial were more sedate, respectful, and traditional, but four of the five defendants were found guilty as charged. I turn now to an examination of the characteristics of the jurors in each of the trials to see whether a useful explanation may be derived from that source.

In the Huey Newton Trial, the defendant was one of the leading figures in the Black Panther Party in Oakland, California. Newton was accused of shooting and killing a policeman. Prior to the examination and selection of the jury, social scientists testified for two days claiming essentially that the selection system violated the due-process section of the Fourteenth Amendment. They argued that the selection procedure (a random sample of registered voters) systematically excluded low-income groups, young people, and blacks. The judge ruled that a black defendant could receive a fair trial under the prevailing system of jury selection. The attorneys then spent two weeks selecting a jury that consisted of seven women and five men. One of the men was black. By occupation, the jury included a laboratory technician, a housewife, an engineer, a secretary, a junior executive secretary, a bookkeeper, a bologna slicer, a drugstore clerk, a machinist, a bank lending official, a bank trust official, and a landlady. Juror 10, the bank lending official and the only black on the jury, was elected foreman. After four days of deliberating, the jury found Huey Newton guilty of voluntary manslaughter, not murder. They found him not guilty of assault with a deadly weapon. The judge sentenced Huey Newton to two to fifteen years. On May 30, 1970, the California Appeals Court reversed the decision, and the federal government opted not to appeal higher.

In the Panther 13 Trial, which took place in New York City, the jury deliberated for two and a half hours and found all the defendants not guilty of all fifteen of the charges, which included conspiracy, attempt to commit murder, arson, and possession of dangerous instruments and weapons. The jury profile of eleven men and one woman looked like this: a composer, a history teacher, a graduate student in political science at Columbia University, two editors from leading publishing firms, a film editor from ABC, a housing authority supervisor, a supervisor of welfare workers, a post office employee, a senior clerk of a state insurance fund, a shop teacher, and a retired longshoreman. Five of the jurors were black; one was Puerto Rican.

It is interesting to compare the composition of this New York City jury with that of the jury who heard the Rosenberg case some twenty years earlier. The Rosenbergs were Jewish and of ghetto, working-class background. There were no Jews on their jury, and only one person who was employed as a laborer. In the same city, today, a trial involving thirteen members of the Black Panthers was heard by a jury that included five blacks and one Puerto Rican. After the trial, one of the lawyers, Afeni, said, "All we wanted was a jury with a conscience." A friend's wife remarked, "And you got one with soul" (Kennebeck, 1973, p. 238).

One of the defendants in the political trials of this era was a member of the Communist Party of the United States. In addition, Angela Davis was black and a supporter of the Black Panthers. The charges against her included murder and kidnapping. In his closing argument, Leo Branton, Angela Davis's attorney, addressed the jury in these words: "Ladies and gentlemen, before I came here, my friends told me that I could not get a fair trial for Angela Davis in this country; I could not find twelve white people who would be willing to be fair to a black woman charged with the serious crimes with which she is charged in this case. . . . Whether you want to or not, you are going to be a part of history. We on the defense are a part of history. We have labored hard and long to try to get over to you the gigantic hoax that has been committed, not only against this defendant but against the name of American justice in this country" (Major, 1973, p. 283).

The jury in the Angela Davis Trial did indeed consist of twelve white people: seven women and five men. As was the procedure in all of the political trials of this era, the defense attorneys challenged the practice of selecting jurors from the voter registration lists. They introduced testimony that included a comparison of five high-income election precincts with five low-income precincts and showed that 56 prospective jurors were drawn from the high-income precincts as opposed to sixteen prospective jurors from the low-income precincts, even though there were 2,000 more people living in the low-income precincts. Judge Arnason overruled the defense's objections and directed the attorneys to proceed with the voir dire. With the help of five black psychologists, Moore and Branton selected twelve jurors from among a panel of 116. The task of selecting the jury took nine days and then an additional four days to pick four alternates. The jury that tried Angela Davis consisted of a maintenance electrician who had once been a school teacher; an accountant; a sales supervisor; two housewives, one of whom had a brother who had been an inmate of San Quentin; an air traffic controller; an employee of IBM; a student; an unemployed, recently divorced woman; a medical research assistant; a retired librarian; and a collection agent.

The trial began on March 27 and ended on June 2, 1972. The jury began their deliberation on a Friday afternoon. On Sunday morning, they announced that they had reached a verdict. When their verdict of not guilty was announced, it seemed to stun the courtroom. After a couple of seconds of silence, some of the spectators burst into tears, some into song, some into cheers of "Right on." The District Attorney said, "I'm shocked beyond belief by the not guilty verdicts. Apparently the jury fell for the purely emotional pitch offered by the defense. Despite what happened I'm still firmly convinced Angela Davis is as responsible for the killing of Judge Harold J. Haley and the crippling of my assistant, Gary Thomas, as Jonathan Jackson and undoubtedly more so because of her age and intelligence" (Major, 1973, p. 295).

Eight of the jurors showed up at a party that was taking place two hours after they had announced their verdict, and at the party several of them talked about what had transpired during their deliberations. According to Major (1973, p. 300), "The elimination of the only black on the panel, a person whom several of the jurors had come to know and respect might have left them with a feeling that somehow they had been complicit in a racist act. They remembered Mrs. Hemphill's, 'there's been a lot of things I've had to put out of my mind,' knowing that she probably would never forget the experience of having been eliminated from a jury solely because of race." Major's assessment about why the jury acquitted Angela Davis is as follows: "The combination of pretrial publicity describing Angela as a black militant communist gun provider, coupled with the security around the trial, predisposed the jury to be apprehensive of Angela Davis. The jury had a collective sense of unease, one which was helped along by the prosecution's constant reminder of the fate of three women hostages on August 7. As the trial proceeded much of this feeling of dread was abated as the panel had an opportunity to see Angela Davis in action. Many of them were present when Angela conducted the voir dire of one prospective juror which resulted in his disqualification for being prejudiced against Angela for being a communist. They were impressed by her opening statement, but more important, they observed her day after day, taking notes, conferring with her attorneys, and acting like any defendant concerned with the problem of confronting a number of serious charges" (Major, 1973, pp. 300-301).

The biggest and the most sensational of the political trials of this period was the Chicago Conspiracy Trial. Eight defendants were charged with conspiracy to cross state lines with intent to cause a riot, to interfere with law enforcement officers and firemen in the performance of their duties, and to teach and demonstrate the use of incendiary devices. Twelve alleged coconspirators were also named but not indicted. Weiner and Froines were charged with teaching and demonstrating the use of incendiary devices, and the remaining defendants were charged with violating the H. Rap Brown law—crossing state lines with intent to cause a riot. Except for Weiner and Froines, the defendants were well known (Danelski, 1971, p. 145).[7] The defendants included leaders of the Hippies (Abbie Mann and Jerry Rubin), a former head of Students for a Democratic Society (Tom Hayden), one of the founders and leaders of the Black Panthers (Bobby Seale), a founder of the National Mobilization Committee to End the War in Vietnam and disciple of the late A. J. Muste (David Dellinger). Judge Julius Hoffman presided. William Kunstler headed a team of defense attorneys, and Thomas Foran was the chief prosecutor. The trial lasted five months. During it, one of the defendants (Bobby Seale) sat in the courtroom bound and gagged. All of the defendants engaged in catcalls and heckling. They refused to stand when the judge entered the courtroom, and they addressed him as "Mr. Hoffman."

For a trial that had aroused so much interest and publicity and promised to be long and spectacular, the jury was selected in record time—less than a day. The reason for this according to Danelski is that "Judge Hoffman had ruled earlier that there would be no voir dire examination of prospective jurors, but that the defense and the government could submit questions which he would consider. He accepted a few of the government's questions but virtually none of the defendants.' Among those excluded were 'Do you believe that young men who refuse to participate in the armed forces because of their opposition to the war are cowards, slackers, or unpatriotic?' 'Do you have any hostile feelings toward persons whose life-styles differ from your own?' 'Would you let your son or daughter marry a Hippie?' The one defense question accepted in substance was whether the prospective jurors had any close relatives and friends who were law enforcement officers or employees of the city, state, or federal governments" (Danelski, 1971, p. 151).

From the original panel of 300 prospective jurors, 70 excluded themselves. Of those remaining, the defense had seventeen peremptory challenges and the government six. The jury chosen consisted of ten women and two men. One of the men was an elderly car cleaner for the Chicago Transit Authority, and the other was an unemployed house painter who lived on Skid Row. Both of the men were white, two of the ten women were black. Six of the women were housewives, one was a retired cook. The others worked as a customer's representative, a nurse's aide, a cashier.

According to Danelski, during the first witness's testimony something happened that affected the composition of the jury and perhaps the outcome of the case:

> The families of two of the jurors—Kristi King and Ruth Peterson—had received notes saying "You are being watched. The Black Panthers." The notes were reported to the FBI, and Judge Hoffman met with counsel in chambers to decide what should be done about the matter. Neither judge nor government counsel wanted the existence or contents of the notes made public, because the other jurors might learn of them. Kunstler informed Seale of the notes and told him that Foran and Schultz did not want the notes publicized.

"Don't want publicity about it?" Seale retorted.
"We's not going to send any stupid notes like that,
man. Somebody's railroading us." Seale wrote a
statement for the press that was given to Hayden.
Later, at a press conference, Hayden told reporters
of the notes and said, "What we are facing here is a
frame-up on trumped-up charges." He then read
from Seale's statement, "There is a plot by the FBI
and other lackey pig agents to tamper with the jury
and then try to blame it on the Black Panther
Party." When the judge heard of the press conference, he immediately ordered the jury sequestered.

Judge Hoffman questioned jurors King and
Peterson about the notes. Miss King was given the
note and asked if she had seen it. She said she had
not. He asked if any member of her family had
brought it to her attention, and she again said no.
He then said: "All right. Read it, Miss King. Read
it, please." After she read it aloud, he asked whether, having read the note, she could continue to be
fair and impartial in this case. She stared at Bobby
Seale and, on the verge of tears, said, "No, sir."
Kunstler objected to the revealing of the contents
of the note to Miss King, but it was too late. She
was excused as a juror, and Kay Richards, a twen-
ty-three-old computer operator, took her place.
Mrs. Peterson said she had seen the note but it did
not affect her impartiality. She also said she had
mentioned the note to her roommate, Mrs. Burns.
The latter said the note would not affect her impartiality, and both women remained as jurors. The
jury was complete and underwent no further
changes.

Far more was involved in this incident than
the replacement of a juror. For the next four and a
half months, the jury was to be sequestered—shut
up with each other and federal marshals in hotel
rooms, away from their families and loved ones.
Perhaps such measures were inevitable, but they
were a blow to the defense, because jurors often
blame the defendants for their plight. Indeed, the

jurors envied the defendants' freedom—all but
Seale were out on bail during most of the trial—and
at least one of them appreciated the sentiment of a
sign Lee Weiner held up one day outside the courtroom as the jury boarded the bus for its hotel. It
said, "Free the jury" (Danelski, 1971, p. 153).

The jury deliberated for four days. While the jury was
out, Judge Hoffman adjudged the defendants and their lawyers
guilty of 159 contempt citations and sentenced them to jail
terms ranging from two months and eight days (Weiner) to four
years and thirteen days (Kunstler).

According to post-deliberation interviews, initially eight
jurors were for conviction on all counts, and four were for acquittal. At one point, the vote was nine to three for conviction
on all counts. Then one of the jurors suggested a compromise: a
verdict of not guilty on the conspiracy charge and complete
acquittal for Weiner and Froines. Danelski claims "that was the
turning point; on the fourth day of deliberations all of the
jurors had agreed to the compromise" (Danelski, 1971, p.
176).[8] "After the verdict was announced and the jury dis-
charged, some of the jurors expressed their views on the case
and the defendants. Edward Kratzke, the jury foreman, said: 'I
was a streetcar conductor. I've seen guys, real bums with no
soul, just a body—but when they went in front of a judge, they
had their hats off. These defendants wouldn't even stand up
when the judge walked in. When there's no respect, we might as
well give up the United States.' During a television interview,
Mrs. Ruth Peterson said the defendants 'needed a good bath and
to have their hair cut. . . . They had no respect for nobody, not
even the marshals. When they told them to get their feet off
their chairs, they just put them right back again. I don't think
that's nice' " (Danelski, 1971, p. 176). Each defendant received
the same sentence—five years in prison and a $5,000 fine.

On May 11, 1972, a three-judge panel overturned the
contempt of court conviction of Bobby Seale and defense attorneys Kunstler and Weinglass and remanded the case to the U.S.
District Court for a new trial before a new judge. The judges

also said that Judge Hoffman provided a caricature of judicial authority and that the penalties he handed down constituted a judicial disaster. Judge Gignoux of the Federal District Court heard the trial without a jury and acquitted the defendants of eighteen of the thirty-eight contempt of court charges. Defendants Davis and Hayden and attorney Weinglass were acquitted of all the contempt charges. The convicted defendants appealed, and on November 21, 1972, the U.S. Court of Appeals for the 7th Circuit reversed the trial court. Judge Hoffman was sharply rebuked by the Appellate Court. The court also stated that one of its reasons for reversing the trial court decision was that there had been inadequate questioning of prospective jurors about attitudes that were possibly prejudicial to the defense.

Part of the notoriety that surrounded the Harrisburg 7 Trial was due to the fact that six of the defendants who were charged with conspiracy to raid federal offices, to bomb government property, and to kidnap the then presidential adviser, Henry Kissinger, were members of the Roman Catholic clergy.[9] The trial was viewed by sympathizers of the defendants as an organized attack on the leadership of the Catholic Left in the United States. Lay and clerical leaders of the Catholic Left movement, liberal intellectuals, clergy of Jewish and Protestant denominations, and antiwar supporters of all denominations rallied around the Harrisburg 7. Many of them came and remained in Harrisburg (Pennsylvania) for the entire length of the trial, which began in January 1972 and lasted three months. They held prayer meetings and protest meetings. They called press conferences and they raised funds for the defendants' attorneys. They kept the Harrisburg 7 Trial in the public eye throughout the length of the trial.

The attorneys for the defendants (which included such famous names as Ramsey Clark and Paul O'Dwyer) worked closely with a group of social scientists who aided them in selecting the jury. Throughout the voir dire, Jay Schulman advised the defense attorneys about the prospective jurors and helped interpret and evaluate their responses. Prior to the trial, the city of Harrisburg had been surveyed, and the social scientists advised the defense attorney:

On statistical grounds alone, it's imperative that we fight to see as many jurors as possible. Thus if Lynch is going to reject young people, the more frames [blocks of people randomly chosen from a population] of people we go through the more likely we are to land a young person on the jury. It is also to our advantage in other ways to extend the jury selection process. The more people we see, the better feel we will get for how our estimates fit the actual individuals coming through the array. A frame of one hundred people: fifty-seven will be male; forty-three will be female; eight will be under 30, fourteen will be 30-39, twenty-three will be 40-49, twenty-six will be 50-59, twenty-one will be 60-69, seven will be 70 and over. Thirty-three will have less than a high school education, forty-six will be high school graduates, twenty-one will have some college or more. . . .

In order to get twelve, close to four hundred were summoned. The panel of forty-six resulted in seventeen males, twenty-nine females. Three blacks: two female, one male. Thirty-two Protestants, five Catholics, three no-church, and six unknown. Fifteen were urban, four suburban, and twenty-seven rural and small-town. Four single women are among them and one bachelor [O'Rourke, 1972, pp. 45, 71].

From this selection came twelve jurors, nine women and three men. One of the women was black, one was Catholic. One of the men was married to a Catholic. One of the women belonged to the Brethren in Christ Church and had four sons, all of whom had sought and received conscientious objector status. She, along with one other juror, a white Lutheran male in his forties who owned a local store, were the two holdouts for conviction. In thinking aloud about the jurors, Boudin, one of the defense attorneys, is quoted by O'Rourke as having said about that juror, " 'How did he get on the jury?' Boudin mused. The defense had learned he was a 'staunch reform Democrat.' The government had counted on getting twelve just like him. 'In that crowd of forty-six [from which the twelve were picked],' I said, 'someone was bound to slip right past everyone; he was your Jack Ruby.' Then I remembered why he did get on; he had made everyone in the courtroom laugh with his joke about golfing. The laughter bespoke a humanity that could be trusted" (O'Rourke, 1972, p. 261). On Holy Thursday, the day of the Last Supper, the jury took the case, and a week later, on Good Friday, the day of the Crucifixion, the jury sent the judge a note, "After a long, serious, and conscientious deliberation . . . we are unable to arrive at a unanimous verdict on nine counts of the indictment." The judge urged the jury to keep trying, citing the length of the trial and the expense involved. In the end, the jury hung ten to two for acquittal on the conspiracy and threatening letter counts. They voted to convict Philip Berrigan and Sister Elizabeth McAlister on seven contraband counts.

Following the trial, two of the defendants, Fathers Wenderoth and McLaughlin, returned to their duties as diocesan priests in Baltimore. Sisters McAlister and Egan returned to New York City to continue their work with the order of the Religious of the Sacred Heart of Mary. Eqbal Ahmad went off on a vacation. Philip Berrigan was returned to Dauphin County Prison. Eventually he was transferred back to Danbury Federal Correctional Institute.[10]

Of all the political trials of this era, none had a more illustrious roster of defendants than did the trial of the *United States of America* v. *William Sloane Coffin, Michael Ferber, Mitchell Goodman, Marcus Raskin, and Benjamin Spock*. Spock is a household word in millions of American families as the author of *The Common Sense Book of Baby and Child Care*, Marcus Raskin is the codirector of the Institute for Policy Studies in Washington, D.C., William Coffin is the Chaplain at Yale University, Mitchell Goodman is a writer, and Michael Ferber was a graduate student at Harvard University. All of them were charged with carrying on a continuing conspiracy to aid, abet, and counsel violations of the Selective Service Act. Their case was tried in the Federal District Court before Judge Francis J. Ford, who at the time of trial in 1968 was eighty-five years old.

Judge Ford's conduct during the trial bore many similarities to that of Judge Julius Hoffman in the Chicago 8 Conspiracy Trial. Ford, like Hoffman, restricted the process of selecting the jury. Boudin, one of the lawyers for the defense, challenged the list of potential jurors on the ground that it was not representative of the community (for example, of the eighty-eight names there were only five women). Ford interrupted: " 'My understanding is that women don't have to serve unless they wish. No further colloquy from you, please.' (It turned out the judge was wrong about this, he was confusing Massachusetts state courts, where women are not obliged to serve, with federal courts, in which there is no such rule.) Boudin stood his ground, announced that he intended to challenge the venire and wished to question Russell Peck, chief clerk of the court charged with assembling the jury, about his methods of selection" (Mitford, 1969, p. 97).

This was finally allowed. Peck then testified that he sent out summonses to appear for jury duty to names on the police list, "which is a street list of residents." When Boudin asked Peck to demonstrate how he went about selecting the names to which he sent notices, Peck explained that "He just looked up in the air and put his finger down on the list—wherever his finger landed, he put a mark next to the name and that was the name to receive the notice. 'Is there a reason why you don't use the method of taking every third, fourth, or ninth name instead of sort of looking in the air and putting your finger on the book?' asked Boudin. 'I would suppose there isn't enough time and help to make the mathematical computations necessary' " (Mitford, 1969, p. 98). According to Mitford, a Harvard mathematics major sitting in the audience, after a few minutes of writing in his notebook, passed a note to the press that explained in essence that if the selection had been truly random the probability of this proportion of women to men (five out of eighty-eight) would be about one in a trillion.

James St. Clair, another of the defense attorneys, elicited from the chief clerk the opinion that women who show up for jury duty, particularly housewives, are more likely to be excused than men and that this makes for more paperwork. But Judge Ford had had enough. He denied Boudin's motion and

insisted that the attorneys go about their business of selecting a
jury. The defense was allowed fifteen peremptory challenges
and the government ten. The task was completed in a day. The
jury consisted of twelve white males. The two women and one
black male whose names had been called were challenged by the
government. Of the men, two were self-employed, six were
white-collar employees, three were blue-collar workers, and one
was a professional. They were meat cutters, printers, hardware
clerks, loan supervisors, technicians, engineers, and customer
service representatives. According to Mitford, James St. Clair
groaned when he saw the list and said, "I wanted mothers,
beards, and eggheads" (Mitford, 1969, p. 218).

The trial lasted four weeks. At the end of it, the judge
charged the jury: "Members of the jury, our duty is joint. There
are two domains in which we serve. It is your duty to receive
the applicable law from me, and it is my duty to explain it to
you as correctly as I can. You must apply the law that I lay
down. If I fell into error in laying down the principles of law,
my error or errors can be reviewed in a higher court. If you
apply your own law and make an error, it cannot be reviewed
and corrected. Your domain is the determination of the facts"
(in Mitford, 1969, pp. 198-199). The defense attorneys had submitted instructions bearing on the motives of the accused. For
example, Boudin, on criminal intent, had written, "It is for the
jury to determine the fact as to whether the defendants acted in
good or bad faith, or with an evil or innocent intent. You may
take into consideration the sincerity or insincerity of the defendants' belief that the war in Vietnam was illegal and that the
draft was unconstitutional. If you find that the defendants sin-
cerely and in good faith entertained such a belief, it is your
duty to acquit" (in Mitford, p. 199).

Judge Ford, however, used none of the instructions proposed by any of the defendants' attorneys. He did, however,
adopt the language that the prosecuting attorney, John Wall,
had used in his closing argument and instructed the jury as
follows:

> Motive, no matter how laudable or praise-
> worthy that motive may be, cannot negate a spe-

cific intent to commit a crime. Good or innocent personal motive alone is never a defense where the act committed is an intentional violation of law—a crime. . . . When a statute has been knowingly violated, to show that a defendant had a good motive —such as dissemination of religious beliefs or the fulfilling, as he saw it, of a mission imposed upon him by the Deity, or his conscience—is no excuse whatsoever.

There is no freedom to knowingly conspire to violate a law of the United States with impunity merely because one believes or doubts that the law is immoral or illegal or unconstitutional . . . a bona fide, sincere belief on the defendants' part that the Vietnam conflict and the conscription of young men to serve in it was illegal, immoral, or unconstitutional, or a belief that the Selective Service Act was unconstitutional, or a belief that they were protected by a constitutional right of free speech would be no defense or excuse whatsoever to an intentional and wilful violation of that law by the defendants, and such beliefs, members of the jury, must not be considered by you in determining the guilt or nonguilt of the defendants.

Further, I charge you that if you should find from the evidence that the defendants, or any of them purposed to test the law by conspiring to counsel, aid, or abet someone to violate the law, then the fact that their purpose was to make a test case is no defense to the charge here presented against them . . . the reason for such violation is immaterial to you in your consideration of the question of their guilt or innocence [Mitford, 1969, pp. 199-200].

The jury deliberated for almost eight hours. They found all the defendants, save Raskin, guilty of all of the charges but conspiracy to turn in their draft cards.

Before sentencing the defendants, Judge Ford's remarks were reminiscent of those made by Judge Kaufman in the trial of Julius and Ethel Rosenberg. Kaufman held the Rosenbergs responsible for the Korean War and the death of 50,000 American soldiers. Ford said to Spock, Coffin, and the others: "The government has charged in this case what amounts to rebellion against the law. . . . The defendants have been found guilty of intentional and wilful violation of the law. . . . Rebellion against the law is in the nature of treason. The law deserves our obedience" (Mitford, 1969, p. 208). He then sentenced the four of them to two years in prison and fined Spock, Coffin, and Goodman $5,000 each. Ferber, probably because he was a student, received a $1,000 fine.

In post-deliberation interviews with three of the jurors, Mitford reports (1969, p. 219): "All three were strongly opposed to the Vietnam War, all expressed the highest regard for the defendants as individuals and for what they were trying to accomplish—and all said they felt, after hearing the judge's charge, that they had no alternative but to find them guilty. . . . After talking with the jurors, we were left with the impression that Raskin's acquittal stemmed not from any special merit that would distinguish his case from the others, but rather from a tacit desire of the jury to assert its independence, to vote, in some token way, its conscience" (Mitford, 1969, p. 219).

The defendants appealed their verdict to the Court of Appeals for the 1st Circuit, and the Court of Appeals reversed the decision. On August 8, 1969, the Justice Department said it would drop the matter. All the defendants were released.

The Political Trials of the Mid 1970s

The last group of trials concern the Watergate Cover-Up. For this period, I review the Mitchell-Stans Trial and the Cover-Up Trial involving Ehrlichman, Haldeman, Mitchell, Mardian, and Parkinson. The defendants in these trials differ in important ways from any of the defendants considered hitherto (with the possible exception of Alger Hiss). They were all prominent members of the government. Until their indictment, they represented the "establishment" at least of the executive branch of the federal government. Several of them (for example, Mitchell and Mardian) were directly responsible for the indictments of defendants in the political trials of the previous period. They exuded authority, connections, prestige, and wealth. How did such defendants fare at the hands of the jury?

On January 6, 1975, a jury in Washington, D.C., composed of nine women and three men, of eight blacks and four whites, deliberated for fifteen hours and found the defendants in the Watergate Cover-Up Trial (John Mitchell, former attorney general, H. R. Haldeman, chief of staff to the president, John Ehrlichman, the president's chief of the domestic council, Robert Mardian, chief of the internal security division of the Justice Department under Mitchell) guilty of conspiracy, perjury, and obstruction of justice. Kenneth Parkinson, a Washington attorney who worked for the 1972 Committee to Reelect the President, was acquitted.

Unlike the jury in the Rosenberg case, which was composed of eleven whites, one black, no Jews, and no laborers, the jurors selected to hear the Watergate trial seemed to represent a cross section of Washington, D.C., society: a doorman, a clerk in a dimestore, a retired maid, a clerical worker at George Washington University, a loan specialist for the Department of Agriculture. The foreman was a retired U.S. Parks police sergeant.

Judge Sirica sentenced the four guilty defendants to from thirty months to eight years in prison. Their convictions were upheld by the Appellate Court, and the defendants are now awaiting a decision by the U.S. Supreme Court as to whether the Court will hear their case.

Less than a year prior to the Watergate Cover-Up Trial, another trial, involving one of the defendants in the Watergate Trial, John Mitchell, and another former member of the Nixon Cabinet, Maurice Stans (Secretary of Commerce), took place in the U.S. District Court for the Southern District of New York. The major charge against the two defendants was conspiracy to impede a Securities and Exchange Commission (SEC) investigation of Robert L. Vesco, a financier and a fugitive at the time of the trial, in return for a $200,000 cash contribution to President Nixon's reelection campaign.

Before the jury of nine men and three women was finally selected, 196 prospective jurors had been examined. The twelve

selected included a bank teller, a steel cutter, a telephone in-
staller, a Western Union messenger, a mail room supervisor, a
Post Office supervisor, a city highway department employee, a
shipping clerk foreman, a subway conductor, an insurance company clerk, an elderly retired lady (who became ill and was replaced by a vice-president of the First National City Bank).

The trial lasted ten weeks. The jury found the defendants
not guilty. Zeisel and Diamond (1976) report that the jury on
their first ballot was divided eight for conviction, four for acquittal.[11] Much of the Zeisel-Diamond piece concerns the role
played by one of the jurors.

> This jury came as close to the film story in
> *Twelve Angry Men* as one is likely to see in real
> life. In the film, Henry Fonda, one of the jurors,
> succeeded in reversing a first ballot that stood
> eleven to one for conviction. It seems the Mitchell-
> Stans jury gained its Henry Fonda when, some
> weeks into the trial, juror Violet Humbert fell sick,
> and alternate Andrew Choa, a vice-president of the
> First National City Bank, took her place. . . .
>
> Choa's role in this trial fell into two parts:
> what he did while the trial was in progress and
> what he did during the deliberation. The one role,
> it will be seen, is connected to the others.
>
> During the many and long evenings, Choa
> had helped to break the monotony. Occasionally,
> he took his fellow jurors to the movies in the pri-
> vate auditorium of the bank. When the jurors asked
> to see the St. Patrick's day parade and were told
> they could not go since this meant mingling with
> the street crowds, he arranged for them to watch it
> from one of the bank's branch offices. On one or
> more occasions when money was not readily avail-
> able for minor jury expenses such as for entertain-
> ment, 'Andrew paid them, then the government
> paid him back.' Choa's bank also loaned baseball
> bats to the jury. He became, as the *New York
> Times* reporter put it, the jury's 'social director.'
> His fellow jurors could hardly help being obliged to

the man who had used his high social position to make their sequestration more bearable. . . .

We know that Choa was one of the four jurors who from the outset voted for acquittal and, one must presume, began the arduous task of converting the majority to his view. We know no details but are told that he persuaded the jury at several points to have testimony as well as the judge's instructions reread. We do not know what testimony but are told that these requests were drafted by Choa for the forelady's signature.

When it came to the jury's appraisal of the memorandum written by Vesco (or an associate) to Nixon's brother, in which Vesco threatened to disclose his secret $200,000 cash contribution unless the SEC dropped his case, Choa said he considered it "trash"—and the jury seemed to have agreed. The end is known. The unlikely event did happen; the eight jurors, who at one point thought the defendants guilty, changed their minds. Both defendants were acquitted on all counts [Zeisel and Diamond, 1976, p. 162].

It is perhaps because Zeisel is such a strong champion of the jury system and perhaps because he believes that Mitchell and Stans in fact committed the acts for which they were charged that he and Diamond place such emphasis on Choa's role. They show that juries split initially eight for guilty and four for not guilty will end up finding the defendant not guilty in only 5 percent of the cases. The twenty to one shot happened in the Mitchell-Stans Trial. Zeisel and Diamond attribute that unusual result to an unusual juror—Andrew Choa. Their faith in the system is not shaken. Their belief, however, that protectors of the jury must always be vigilant is strengthened by the events in the Mitchell-Stans Trial.

Concluding Remarks

In looking back on the jury's performance in the political trials of the 1950s, 1960s, and 1970s, we should note first that the defendants, the acts for which they were charged, and the ideology and political symbolism surrounding the trials differed considerably across the three time periods.

In the late 1940s and early 1950s, international communism with the Soviet Union as its home base, was perceived as the major threat to democracy in America. Public opinion and government officials were afraid that the United States would be subverted by its internal enemy—the Communist Party and its multitudes of front groups and secret agents. The defendants on trial during that era were persons who were publicly associated with positions of leadership in the American Communist Party (Dennis, Foster, and others), or persons whose membership in the party made them suspect, or persons who occupied responsible positions in government and were accused of belonging to communist cells and of being disloyal to the United States (Alger Hiss, Owen Latimore, and William Remington all fall into this category). In almost all the political trials that were heard during this era, the charges focused on the defendant's alleged disloyalty to the United States, his or her deception, and his or her identification with the Soviet Union. The socioeconomic and personal characteristics of the defendants varied considerably. Hiss, with his upper-middle-class WASP background and mannerisms, was charged with the same type of traitorous acts as were Julius and Ethel Rosenberg, who were part of the poor, Jewish, intellectual, working-class enclaves of the lower east side of Manhattan.

The defendants, the issues, the charges, the political ideology, and symbolism of the late 1960s differed markedly from the previous era of political trials. In the late 1960s, the defendants were young, many were well educated, some were black, practically all (Angela Davis was the major exception) disavowed any loyalty to the Soviet Union or to any. "foreign ideology." Their political activism grew out of their participation in student protests and demonstrations on college and university campuses or in the ghettos of Oakland, Detroit, or Newark, where blacks experienced at first hand the humiliation and discrimination that their skin color evoked.

The charges against the defendants in the late 1940s and

early 1950s were those of disloyalty, spying, passing of secrets to enemy agents. But in the next era political loyalty at least in the traditional sense of allegiance to one country as opposed to another was not an issue. Tom Hayden, Jerry Rubin, and Philip Berrigan were not accused of acting in the interests of a foreign government—their actions, which included protests that erupted into violence, civil disobedience, burning of draft cards, and inciting to rioting, had no foreign direction, support, or symbolism. So, too, the motivations and identities of the Black Panthers originated wholly out of their American experience and had no official foreign financial or moral endorsement.

Perhaps this absence of foreign interference and involvement is the single most important explanation for why the defendants in this era fared so much better at the hands of the jury than did the Rosenbergs, Dennis, Hiss, and others some twenty years earlier. All the defendants in the major political trials of the late 1940s and early 1950s were found guilty. All the convictions were upheld on appeal. Julius and Ethel Rosenberg were the first American citizens ever to be executed in peacetime for treason. None of the defendants who participated in the major political trials of the late 1960s were found guilty of the acts for which they were charged. Angela Davis and the defendants in the Panther 13 Trial in New York City were acquitted of all charges. The jury in the Harrisburg 7 Trial hung (ten in favor of acquittal, two for conviction), and the government chose not to try them again. None of the defendants in the Chicago 8 Trial were convicted of conspiracy to incite riot (the major charge), some were acquitted of all charges, the others were found guilty of the lesser charge of crossing state lines with intent to incite riot. Huey Newton was convicted of manslaughter, not first-degree murder, the act with which he was charged originally. In the Newton and Chicago 8 trials, the decisions were reversed on appeal.

A few years later, in the mid 1970s, the jury found itself confronted with still another type of defendant and another set of charges. In the case of Maurice Stans and John Mitchell, the jury was asked to determine the guilt or innocence of two men who only a short while before had been among the most respected and powerful people in the government. As members of the Cabinet, as close personal friends and advisors to the president, as leaders of the Republican Party, they had few peers to share the power and influence they exerted. The jury acquitted Stans and Mitchell.

H. R. Haldeman and John Ehrlichman had been portrayed in the press as assistant presidents, as men who themselves had no independent power, but who in their proximity to the president had access to the primary source of political power in the United States. For their participation in the planning, expediting, and cover-up of Watergate, Mitchell, Haldeman, and Ehrlichman were found guilty and sentenced to from thirty months to eight years in prison.

During none of these periods is there any evidence, or indeed any suggestion, of the jury's lack of independence, or of the jury's failure to understand the issues or complexities of the problems involved, or of the jury's failure to do its duty. The lack of consistency speaks well for the jury—different issues, different defendants, different contexts, and different evidence should and did make for different verdicts. In almost every trial, the jury deliberated for a long time. On the basis of posttrial interviews, we gather they worked hard during the deliberations, reviewing the evidence, the instructions, and the arguments put forth by the defense and prosecuting attorneys. When the jury voted to acquit, in no instance did the government attack the integrity of its decision.

If one compares the consistent string of guilty verdicts reached by juries in the late 1940s and early 1950s and argues that the jury was reflecting popular support for political conformity and fear of deviant ideas, that the jury's verdict represented public concerns about loyalty rather than serving the rule of law—one would have to explain the string of not-guilty verdicts reached by the same institution a decade and a half later, when popular opinion was just as favorable to political conformity and just as opposed and frightened by political dissent. The jury voted acquittal for blacks who threatened to blow the country up, for blacks and whites who openly ridiculed our society's most sacred symbols—its flag, its courts, its president.

The purpose of this chapter has not been to contend that the jury is beyond reproach or incapable of error. My aim has simply been to show how an institution run by amateurs, directed and organized by ordinary people, using their common sense and following formal rules, can perform its duty in a consistently responsible manner, how it can stand above popular prejudice and deliver verdicts that are respected by experts steeped and trained in the law.

Notes

1. Eugene Dennis (Party Secretary), Robert Thompson, Henry Winston, Gus Hall, John Williamson, Jack Stachel, Irving Potash, Carl Winter, Benjamin Davis, John Gates, and Gilbert Green were the eleven defendants. The trial of party chairman William Foster was postponed because of a serious heart condition.

2. Thompson, in recognition of his record during the war, was given a three-year sentence and a $10,000 fine.

3. The bar of the statute of limitations prevented indicting Hiss on the more serious offense.

4. David Greenglass was Ethel Rosenberg's brother.

5. The organizations that appeared on the attorney general's list included such ones as the School of Jewish Studies, the American Jewish Labor Council, and the Jewish Peoples' Committee. The publications included the *National Guardian,* the *Daily Mirror,* and the *Journal American.*

6. The Pentagon Papers Trial of Daniel Ellsberg and Anthony Russo, the Gainesville 8 trial, the Milwaukee 12 trial are not included but are representative of the same genre. They are not discussed because of the exigencies of time and space.

7. Weiner was a native of Chicago who had received a B.A. from the University of Illinois and an M.S.W. from Loyola University. Froines was born in Oakland, California, on June 13, 1939. After graduating from Berkeley in 1962, he spent a summer working in a black voter registration project in Louisiana and then went to Yale, where he received a Ph.D. in chemistry. While at Yale, he joined SDS and worked in a black community project in New Haven. His SDS affiliation led to friendships with Davis and Hayden.

8. At first three of the jurors who had favored acquittal

would not accept the compromise. They said the antiriot law was unconstitutional. But that was not, a juror explained, for them to determine. They had only to decide if the defendants had violated the law.

9. The seventh was a Muslim from Pakistan.

10. At the end of the trial, Boyd Douglas, the man who shared a cell with Berrigan and who testified against him, was awaiting a decision by the FBI about how they would repay him for his services on the stand.

11. Zeisel and Diamond (1976) report that *The New York Times* had published an article by Martin Arnold based on interviews with some of the jurors. In that article, he reported the eight to four initial split.

References

Barkan, S. E. "Political Trials and the *Pro Se* Defendant in the Adversary System." *Social Problems,* 1977, *24,* 324-336.

Danelski, D. "The Chicago Conspiracy Trial." In T. L. Becker (Ed.), *Political Trials.* Indianapolis: Bobbs-Merrill, 1971.

"Doggonedest Trial." *Time,* April 11, 1949, *53,* 23-24.

"His Honor, Judge Patience." *Newsweek,* May 23, 1949, *33,* 21-23.

Kalven, H., and Zeisel, H. *The American Jury.* Boston: Little, Brown, 1966.

Kennebeck, E. *Juror Number Four: The Trial of Thirteen Black Panthers as Seen from the Jury Box.* New York: Norton, 1973.

Major, R. *Justice in the Round.* New York: The Third Press, 1973.

Mitford, J. *The Trial of Dr. Spock.* New York: Knopf, 1969.

Morris, R. B. *Fair Trial.* New York: Harper & Row, 1967.

Nagel, S. S. (Ed.). *The Rights of the Accused: In Law and Action.* Beverly Hills, Calif.: Sage, 1972.

O'Rourke, W. *The Harrisburg 7 and the New Catholic Left.* New York: Crowell, 1972.

Simon, R. J. *The Jury and the Defense of Insanity.* Boston: Little, Brown, 1967.

Simon, R. J. *Public Opinion in America: 1936-1970.* Chicago: Rand McNally, 1975.

Simon, R. J., and Marshall, P. 'The Rights of the Accused." In
S. S. Nagel (Ed.), *The Rights of the Accused: In Law and
Action.* Beverly Hills, Calif.: Sage, 1972.

U.S. Supreme Court. Transcript of the Rosenberg Trial Record.
Vol. 2, Book 4. Washington, D.C.: U.S. Government Printing
Office, 1952.

Zeisel, H., and Diamond, S. "The Jury Selection in the Mitchell-
Stans Conspiracy Trial." *American Bar Foundation Research
Journal,* 1976, *1,* 151-174.

Zeisel, H., Kalven, H., Jr., Buchholz, B. *Delay in the Court.* Boston: Little, Brown, 1959.

10

Charles W. Lidz
Andrew L. Walker

Therapeutic Control of Heroin

Dedifferentiating Legal and Psychiatric Controls

A central theme of sociological theory in the last two decades has been the revival of interest in societal development. This had led to a revival of interest in and an elaboration of earlier evolutionary theories. Particularly important in these theories is the concept of functional differentiation. Parsons (1964) has noted that differentiation involves a process whereby multiple structures replace a single structure with each of the new structures specializing in different functions that were previously combined in one structure. The differentiation of the household

We wish to express our thanks to Rainer Baum, Victor Lidz, and Eviatar Zerubavel for reading an earlier draft, and especially Leroy Gould and Lansing Crane, whose work in collecting and analyzing data helped immensely. Work on this paper was partially supported by National Institute of Mental Health (NIMH) Narcotic Treatment Program Grant No. 1H 17 MH16356.

from the place of work during the Industrial Revolution is a frequently given example.

During an observational study of heroin use and control from 1969 to 1974, we watched the development of a new type of structure of social control of heroin. However, the emergence of this system did not entail its differentiation out of some other structure but rather involved a *dedifferentiation* of two systems of social control, psychiatry and criminal law, which have otherwise become increasingly differentiated over the past half century.

Mayhew (1968) has suggested that some relatively undifferentiated elements persist in modern society in spite of the increasing differentiation of the society as a whole. Durkheim (1933) insisted that modern societies maintain elements of mechanical integration. Other observers similarly noted that ascriptive and particularistic elements survive even in the economic subsystem (Cohen, 1969; Gellner, 1973). Eisenstadt, in his works on the collapse of political empires (1969), has described at some length the processes whereby social systems may dedifferentiate as a whole. However, there has been little description of how and under what circumstances particular structures in advanced and successful societies may dedifferentiate without a decline of the society in which they exist. In order to analyze some of the conditions under which such a dedifferentiation can take place without a general decline of the whole society or even major subsystems, we must begin by describing the nature of the general separation between these two systems and how it evolved.

Psychiatry and Criminal Law

In order to clarify the distinction between psychiatry and criminal law as systems of social control, let us briefly look at the historical origins of the two views of people and their deviance that mandate these two systems. While the criminal law has understood deviance as a willed *act* and the sanction of the criminal justice system, punishment, has been legitimated usually only as a response to deviant acts, psychiatry formulated its conceptions of deviance around the actor and its sanction, treatment, was the appropriate response to deviant properties of the *actor,* not the act. This may seem a spurious distinction, since one generally knows the nature of the actor through his or her acts, but much of the nature of these two systems of social control hangs on this distinction.

A concept of punishment for deviants' acts may well be as old as social organization. Such, at least, is the assumption of such theorists as Durkheim (1933) and Maine (1861). Durkheim clearly believed that it was impossible to have mechanical solidarity without punishment. Pollack and Maitland's history of English law traces the notion of punishment back to state sanctioning of personal revenge taking against the criminal and the expulsion of the outlaw from social protection and finds that, as far back as King Alfred, punishment came only as a response to the act (Pollock and Maitland, 1952, pp. 450-451).

Notions of madness and treatment for it are ancient and perhaps universal. But the origins of modern Western psychiatry are much more recent. Plato listed four types of madness: prophetic, ritual, poetic, and erotic (that is, being "madly" in love), but his concepts clearly do not refer to the generally deviant character with which modern psychiatry deals. Likewise, the notion of possession through witchcraft, while accounting for deviance more in terms of the character of the actor, is different from the modern notion that the character is fundamentally deviant. The individual is "possessed" by an outside source. His character remains fundamentally intact and by appropriate magic is restored untouched.

The psychiatric notion of sanctions responding to the *character* of the individual seems to have its modern origins in Protestant theology. The Protestant Reformation created a new image of human salvation. Although in Catholic theology salvation depended on God's grace, it was attained through the sacraments of the Church and thus depended on one's overt acts. For Calvin, and to a lesser extent Luther and Zwingli, salvation was predestined. One's activities had nothing to do with *determining* one's salvation. However, one's acts did *reflect* the state of one's soul. Saved individuals would act as if they were saved, although ultimately whether one was saved or damned was unknowable. Membership in the church was reserved for those who seemed likely to be among the elect.

Calvinist communities had both legal and medical systems of social control. However, their fundamental thinking about a person's potentialities and behavior was more deeply pervaded by the doctrine of election than can easily be understood today (Weber, 1958; Erikson, 1966, chap. 2). The reprobates were seen as failing to live up to their full human potential. The church kept them, at least in theory, under supervision to assure that they did not corrupt the rest of the community. They were, in a sense, less than full members of the moral community (Haskins, 1960; Miller, 1933). For our purposes, the critical aspect of reprobates was that their actions reflected their God-given status, that is, their true character. In theory, once it was clear that they had such a character, their actions could not reverse their status. Although the practical matter of who actually was damned could never be finally determined in this world, it was absolutely determined in the ultimate reality. This concept of the individual became the pattern on which the intellectual apparatus of psychiatry was built.

The Calvinist notion of action as reflective of but not affecting the soul was a useful basis for building a conceptual system for social control in a society that was becoming increasingly differentiated and in which proper behavior was becoming increasingly difficult to specify in detail as criminal law had traditionally done.[1] In America, the Protestant church functioned as the instrument of social control supplementing and to some degree overlapping with the law, until the beginning of the nineteenth century. At that point, increasingly secular concepts of man; the increasing separation of church and state as institutionalized in the First Amendment; and the growth of large cities, which made control by one or a series of churches difficult, rapidly broke down this pattern (Lubove, 1965, chap. 1). Rothman's (1971) data show quite clearly that psychiatry's initial development in America corresponded with the breakdown of tight religious control (see also Lipset, 1967, chap. 4).[2]

It is hardly surprising that psychiatry and social work

would borrow these basic cultural patterns for thinking about
the inner human being. The medical model of disorders of the
body was easily assimilated by the Calvinist notions and thus
became an important part of the secularization of the Protestant concept of the individual. By treating acts as "symptoms"
and mind as parallel to the organism, the same pattern was
achieved.[3] Although many of the clinicians we observed
thought that a medical model of addiction as a disease was silly
and would have shuddered at the formulation that addiction
was a sign of nonelection, the basic pattern remained throughout all of their formulations. Although compromises were made
with both the addicts and law enforcement agents, clinical accounts for colleagues and for professional audiences continued
to treat addiction as a *sign* of something wrong in the addict
rather than as the cause of the problem, as the addicts believed
it was.

Thus we see that the core distinction between criminal
law and psychiatry is what invokes the sanction. Normatively,
psychiatry responds to deviant internal states as reflected in behavior and criminal law mandates response only to deviant
behavior.[4] However, this does not produce a clear differentiation in practice, because all acts are performed by actors and
actors can only be known through their actions. A jurisdictional
boundary line has developed as a rule of thumb. The criminal
law has taken jurisdiction over behavior that is commonsensi-
cally formulated as being rationally motivated by the pursuit of
pleasure, profit, or other acceptable values but that violates
societal norms. Psychiatry and social work have gained jurisdiction where rationality is not reflected in the agent's actions. For
various classes of behavior, including the uses of illegal drugs,
plausible cases can be made both ways. Heroin may be thought
to be so pleasurable that all the disadvantages of use are rationally justifiable to the addict. In this view, stiffer punishments
are needed to prevent further use. Treatment ideologies, on the
other hand, have argued that the pains and disadvantages of
heroin use are so great that no rational person would use it. The
conflicts between these two macrosocial control systems occur
mostly at these vague boundaries, of which heroin use and control is only one.[5]

Although the focus of control on act or agent is the key point of differentiation between the two systems of social control, it is not the only one. The issue of human freedom or nonfreedom to determine one's own behavior has been much debated in both ideological contexts. In practice, however, it is difficult to justify punishment unless one assumes that the deviant chooses his activities, which is an assumption most legal system personnel make. On the other side, psychiatric rhetoric often states that man's behavior is determined by his environments and his heredity, but in practice the position is more ambiguous and reveals the Protestant and medical background of the ideology. For Calvin, the only thing that is determined outside of the individual is election or nonelection (read *deviant identity* or *nondeviant identity*). In psychiatry, the only thing that is out of the patient's control is his disease (deviance). The deviant is expected to cooperate with treatment. He is expected to try to get well (Parsons, 1951, chap. 10). But this view is nonetheless quite different from the view of the punishment ideology, which explicitly holds the deviant responsible for his deviant act.

Law views the individual as free to choose between good and evil. Order in the society is therefore maintained by societal efforts to structure the options available to individuals so that they will choose to behave in an orderly manner and by mobilizing the individual's conscience to do the right things. The law provides sanctions that encourage the rational actor to make the "right" choice.

Psychiatry, in its extreme forms, sees such efforts as a waste of time. A healthy personality will behave in socially desirable ways because his socialization experiences or constitution have determined that he will do so. His personality structure is such that he will obey the law as well as the informal norms by which society regulates behavior. If the deviant fails to obey the rules, punishment is essentially a waste of time—as well as unjust—because he is unable to behave otherwise. The society must work toward changing the deviant individual and doing away with the pathological aspects of his personality. This process, whatever the specific method, is called *treatment.*

In the law, sanctions are evoked by the deviant act. There

is no specific need to be concerned with what the individual believes or with the structure of his personality. What the individual is will, sooner or later, be reflected in what he does. What he does shows you what he is. While the law limits social control to responding to a temporally specific act by the offender, treatment concerns itself with the history and current functioning of the individual. If the personality structure is in need of treatment, waiting until the individual commits a crime in order to treat him is irresponsible.

This brings up the issue of limits on the process of social control. The criminal law provides the individual with procedural "rights" designed to guarantee that his understanding of, and his evidence about, the alleged crime will be heard and that only fair punishments will be given out. This reflects the punishment ideology's focus on the act. The major problematic issue is the nature of the act that the individual committed.

Psychiatric theory guarantees fairness through the professional ethics of its practitioners. It finds legal rights inappropriate, since they may prevent the patient from receiving help when he needs it. That the patient may not want the help that is in his own interest may only be another symptom of his disorder. The limits on psychiatric social control are the individual's needs. The professional dedication of the treatment agent is to help the individual to a healthier personality structure. His professionalism prevents abuses that might arise if the power were given to someone who did not have the individual's best interests at heart. In this sense, psychiatry clearly has a much more optimistic image of what people typically do with power than the law does.

Law and psychiatry also have different views of the relationship between the deviant and the control agent. For the legal theorist, the individual chooses what he does and thus is expected to resent suggestions that what he did was wrong. The deviant is expected to resist social control. He may come to see the error of his ways and repent, but the most likely means of reform is through his learning that crime does not pay. The legal procedure thus provides for an adversarial process that allows the individual to express his view of his act. Psychiatry, following a medical model of sickness, assumes that anyone who is ill will usually seek a cure for his illness since illness usually involves some sort of suffering. The deviant is assumed to suffer from his deviance and to want help.[6]

The Rise of Psychiatric Control

We have suggested that psychiatry, in some ways at least, replaced the church as a system of social control. However, it developed a life of its own. The differentiation of church and state and the consequent end to the use of law to enforce religious principles was one of the great achievements of the eighteenth and nineteenth centuries. This differentiation of religion and law climaxed in the French and American revolutions at the end of the eighteenth century.

However, the separation doctrine did not apply to the new science of psychiatry and its allied discipline of social work. Despite the formal similarities between psychiatric depictions of deviance and that of Christianity, psychiatry proclaimed itself a secular doctrine. Indeed, psychiatry and social work vehemently claimed that they were sciences and thus independent from, or even in conflict with, traditional religions. Thus, although the doctrine of the separation of church and state prevented state enforcement of ecclesiastical morals, there was no immediately apparent reason why psychiatry and the criminal law should not cooperate fully.

In the late nineteenth and early twentieth century, psychiatry and social work penetrated many aspects of the criminal law. Having both the prestige of positivist science and the argument that psychiatry (since it sought to "help" the individual by helping him overcome his problem) was more Christian and humane than the criminal laws, the psychiatric approach to deviance began to penetrate various sectors of the law. Juvenile courts were developed in which the concern focused on the child's problems and his well-being rather than his crime. The institutions of probation and parole developed as part of a changed penal philosophy in which the reform of the criminal rather than retribution or deterrence was the focus.

During this period as well, the insanity defense was increasingly broadened and movements to decriminalize other types of deviance, including drunkenness, prostitution, gambling, and homosexuality began.[7]

However, in the second half of the twentieth century a pattern developed in Supreme Court rulings that can only be described by its evolutionary significance. In case after case, the Court began to sharply distinguish between psychiatric and legal controls. The seminal case was *Robinson* v. *California* (1962). In that opinion, the Supreme Court ruled unconstitutional, on the grounds of "cruel and unusual punishment," a California law that made it illegal to be a narcotic addict. Justice Stewart, writing for the majority, pointed out that the statute did not forbid using or possessing a narcotic. It punished the status of being an addict. If this were permitted, he reasoned, the state could punish someone for being a leper or being mentally ill.

Two of the dissents are even more interesting than the majority opinion. Justice White noted that the argument of "cruel and unusual punishment" was so unusual that the majority was clearly "hard put to find a way to ascribe to the framers of the Constitution the result reached ... rather than to (the majority's) own notions of ordered liberty" (*Robinson* v. *California*).[8] Clearly, this is precisely what the Court was doing. They were creating a differentiation of function between law and one branch of medicine (psychiatry). The nature of that intention was spelled out well in Justice Clark's dissenting opinion. He objected that the law was an "enlightened" one and that the majority was "instructing the California legislature that hospitalization is the *only treatment* for narcotic addiction—that anything less is a punishment denying due process" (*Robinson* v. *California*). Justice Clark's interpretation was only partially right. In succeeding years, the courts have held that any treatment outside of prison under the jurisdiction of the medical profession is acceptable, but unless the medical profession controlled the sanction, sanctioning status was cruel and unusual punishment.

The decision in *Robinson* was largely praised or damned on the basis of the assumption that it was the first step toward abolishing victimless crimes. This has proven incorrect. Both the Warren and Burger Courts and other appellate courts have consistently held that the *act* of committing these crimes is still criminal but that the state may not punish the status of being that type of criminal. The judiciary has similarly distinguished between the act of being drunk in public and being a chronic alcoholic (*Powell* v. *Texas*), committing a homosexual act and being a homosexual (*Perkins* v. *State*), and found unconstitutional statutes against being a vagrant (*Goldman* v. *Knecht*).[9] The courts have also attacked other penetrations of psychiatry into the legal system. The most notable is its ruling requiring stricter legal procedures in the juvenile court and thus abolishing the treatment basis of the juvenile courts (In re Gault 387 U.S. 1, 1967). There is growing evidence that in both legal and academic circles this differentiation is spreading to include other aspects of the relationship between law and psychiatry (Gould and Namenwirth, 1972; Matza, 1964; Kittrie, 1971).

What has happened is that the courts have institutionalized in the legal system a differentiation of function between two institutions. That it was not arbitrary and corresponded with basic concepts about the normative functions of criminal law and psychiatry is indicated by the quick acceptance of these rulings and the absence of any serious legislative challenges.

The Development of Therapeutic Control

The immediate impact of the *Robinson* decision was small. Psychiatry was not very heavily involved in drug abuse control, and where it was it had generally operated separately from the criminal law. Police found that most addicts could be arrested for acts anyway. Possession of narcotics and possession of narcotics paraphernalia were the most common illegal acts. Evidence of possession was, at least occasionally and perhaps often, "planted" on known addicts.

In the late 1960s, however, a national crisis around heroin use developed. We have argued elsewhere that this crisis was primarily symbolic and was probably not a result of a major increase in heroin use, although there clearly was a major in-

crease in the use of some other drugs (Lidz and Walker, forthcoming, chap. 5). Both psychiatry and the law enforcement
system responded with massive increases in antiheroin programs.

The relationship between these two systems of social control developed a number of changes that we wish to describe
here. The *Robinson* decision seemed to call for a relationship of
substantial independence between the criminal justice system
and psychiatric treatment. Empirically, though, such peaceful
coexistence never prevailed.

In the city we studied—which we called Riverdale—the
newly developed clinic began with a definite adversarial relationship to the police and the courts (Gould and others, 1974).
There was tremendous uncertainty and anxiety among clinicians
concerning the treatment they could expect from the local
police and courts. The clinicians feared that the clinic would be
closed or at least kept under constant surveillance and that they
themselves might conceivably be arrested.

The law enforcement community did not fear that the
clinic would be able to close the court down, but there was a
common conviction that the clinic would make the police and
the court's work ineffective by allowing addict criminals under
the clinic's protection to escape punishment. The law enforcement community's first response to the clinic was to assimilate
it into their own competitive-adversarial relationship with the
addicts (see Lidz and Walker, forthcoming, chap. 7).

Whatever their rivalries, though, the legal and psychiatric
systems shared a common element: They both processed the
same people. This made some sort of interaction between the
systems virtually inevitable.

At first the clinic took a controlled adversarial position
vis-à-vis the courts. Clinicians would go to court *for* their patients, trying to forestall the possibility of the court taking
punitive action. The clinicians were trying to argue in court for
the *primacy* of the doctor-patient relationship. They followed
their professional morality, tried to demonstrate to their patients a communality of interest, and at the same time tried not
to lose patients to the penal system. But, in the process of argu-

ing to the court that they would "take care of this guy," they were forced to acknowledge that the court had some interest in successful treatment.

Once it became clear that such an argument might serve as a defense, defense lawyers began to request that the clinic send a spokesman whenever one of its patients appeared in court. This was the first sustained pattern of cooperation between any court personnel and the clinic. From this point on, it was only a short step for defense attorneys to begin sending their clients to the clinic to receive treatment. Defense lawyers argued for treatment primarily because they saw it as a more favorable disposition than prison. They were still seeing this primarily as advantageous to their clients vis-à-vis the punitive system of the court. It was simply a good bargain. One manual on defense strategy shows how the treatment ideology began to be raised in court: "A lawyer should acknowledge that his client is addicted, should show that the crime in question is related to the addiction and should demonstrate that the client is being treated for his addiction and is being rehabilitated. If a favorable disposition of the case cannot be obtained in that way, the attorney can then proceed according to normal defense strategies" (Rafalsky, 1972, p. 409).

It is extremely important to recognize that *the use of treatment as defense was raised in the course of plea bargaining sessions, not in the course of formal courtroom proceedings.* The judge was simply asked to accept what the prosecution and defense had already agreed on, namely, that probation that would allow treatment to continue was more useful than a prison sentence. The institution of plea bargaining has been described at length elsewhere (Newman, 1956; Sudnow, 1965; Blumberg, 1967), but for our purposes here it is sufficient to note that plea bargaining is a negotiating situation between defense and prosecution in which *the formal procedure of the courtroom is considerably weakened.* The distinctions between the presentation of evidence, determination of guilt, and sentencing are forgone, and all three elements are interwoven in an undifferentiated process of negotiating a disposition *acceptable* to both the defense and prosecution. Plea bargaining also weakens the normative review for proper procedure by the appellate court. By raising support for treatment goals in the course of plea bargaining, then, the defense was able to disregard the points of normative contradiction, both substantive and procedural, between the criminal law and psychiatry. Since both defense and prosecution sought expedient dispositions and plea bargaining was a less restricting method for selecting dispositions, plea bargaining became the procedure through which to conduct discussions that would have been inappropriate in the course of formal proceedings. Since the judge merely ratified the agreed-on disposition and the mutually agreed-on disposition was very rarely appealed, the entire process was largely beyond the scope of judicial review.

When we look at these earliest legal-medical interactions, then, we see that each side was simply trying to use the other to reach its own professionally mandated goals. There was uneasy cooperation, but each system was responding to the other as an *external* threat or resource.

The cooperation did not end here, however. Slowly there evolved the elaborate system of cooperation that we call *therapeutic control*.[10] This involved both a pattern of cooperative interaction between the two systems and a cultural pattern of existential beliefs and moral principles that mandated the interaction pattern.

The patterns of cooperative interaction between the two systems involved turning the police into an outreach system for the clinic, and the clinic into the corrections system for the law enforcement system. The courts and the clinic operated as a two-stage decision-making system tied together by referrals.

The police operated as an outreach system for the system of therapeutic control. Early in the clinic's history numerous outreach procedures were tried. Clinical staff gave lectures at schools, PTAs, and community centers, and held long conferences with other mental health professionals and paraprofessionals in an effort to generate referrals. Successful patients were encouraged to recruit their friends, and the clinic even assigned several staff members to work on outreach. As the system of therapeutic control developed, however, these efforts slowed almost to a halt. While patients not referred by the courts continued to present themselves for treatment, they were not encouraged. In spite of statistical evidence to the contrary, Riverdale Clinic staff generally believed that patients without "legal pressures" on them could rarely be successfully treated. This led one applicant to ask, "You mean we've got to go out and get busted before we can get cured?"

Decision making about who would actually be treated was a threefold process. First the defense attorney and the prosecutor would meet to discuss whether there was a case against the defendant, and whether treatment was a plausible disposition. Since the evidence usually involved a disagreement between the addict and several police officers, the chances of an outright dismissal were small. On the other hand, only "hard core" addicts might be refused the chance to get treatment of some sort. While there were several criteria of "hard coreness," the most critical was previous treatment failures. It is theoretically important to note that the sanction here (reversion to penal incarceration) is based on a status that is not constructed on the basis of criminal acts but rather on treatment failures.

In the second step, if the defense attorney and the prosecutor agreed that treatment was appropriate, the defendant was encouraged by his attorney to apply to the clinic. If he had not previously failed in treatment, he was allowed to choose his type of treatment. If he had failed and his reputation was bad, he was told that he had better get in-patient treatment or the court would jail him anyway. At the clinic, the defendant-potential patient applied for treatment. There he had to convince a group of ex-addicts and a professional who ran the "intake" unit that he was sufficiently motivated to succeed in treatment. Once again, the status-act dimension of this decision was confused. Motivation in this context was not a psychological state but a series of external forces, such as marital, legal, and financial difficulties.

Finally, the clinic provided a letter to the court stating that the addict was in treatment. On the basis of the prosecutor's recommendation, the court then sentenced the addict to a suspended sentence and probation, with the stipulation that probation would be revoked and the suspended sentence executed if the addict did not fulfill his treatment obligations.

This pattern of cooperative interaction would have seemed a gross compromise of professional principles were it not for the belief, held by both court and clinic personnel, that addiction in American society presented a special problem that could not be managed by either system separately. The core of these beliefs can be summarized as follows:

1. Heroin presents a major threat to American society and to the health and well-being of the addict. Both the clinic and law enforcement agencies have a duty to respond to it.
2. Therefore searching out and controlling drug users is in the best interests of both society and the individual.
3. Preventing further drug use is more important than administering punitive sanctions for drug use, and rehabilitation treatment is thus the preferred response to drug use.
4. Addicts cannot always be expected to see their interests in treatment and typically have to be coerced into it.
5. The importance of the drug problem is so great that anyone who has a drug problem should receive some form of treatment, even if he is charged with a crime not directly related to drug use.
6. Since treatment is not a punishment, legal technicalities of evidence, guilt determination, and sentencing are less important for the court's decision than the existence of a personal drug problem.
7. The clinic has primary responsibility for determining the appropriate treatment program for the individual and keeping the court, in the person of the probation officer, apprised of patient participation.
8. Punitive sanctions are appropriate in enforcing compliance with universalistic "clinical" performance standards and only those standards. A person with a drug problem who has demonstrated his inability to benefit from treatment deserves incarceration.

These beliefs were not the private property of the drug specialists. The first two beliefs were repeated daily in both printed and electronic media in the early 1970s. The third and fourth points also received wide circulation. It is important to remember that the dedifferentiation we are discussing, although not generally discussed in its specifics, was based on widely held perceptions of national crisis and was congruent with aspects of public policy as enunciated by both the President and Congress.

Pressures for Therapeutic Control

Therapeutic control poses an interesting theoretical paradox. What we have described is a dedifferentiation, in one substantive area, of two generally differentiated systems of social control. *However, this takes place in spite of a maintenance of this differentiation at the societal institutional level.* Thus, the Supreme Court did not overturn *Robinson,* different departments of both federal and state bureaucracies continued to manage and support the two control systems, and law enforcement and psychiatric national meetings on drug abuse continued to be held separately. Thus the dedifferentiation we call *therapeutic control* evolved only on the local level. But the evidence is strong that such a dedifferentiation evolved not only in Riverdale but in most localities across the country.

The question is what sorts of pressures produced these local dedifferentiations. A major component of these pressures was the perception that there was a national crisis of heroin use that must be met in order to preserve civil order. We have expressed some skepticism that this crisis was "real," but it was perceived as real, and thus it was real in its consequences.

By 1970, there were already serious questions about the adequacy of either institutional framework to cope with the developing drug crisis. Classic penal punishment was apparently not effectively deterring individual drug users ("Addict Diversion," 1972, pp. 667-668; Kleeman and Posner, 1971; Kassis, 1972). The courts were "seeing" the same drug defendants over and over again, in what was sometimes called the "revolving door" of drug use and penal sanction. The courts' perception of a crisis may not have reflected any real increase in recidivism. The demand for increased police pressure and more arrests meant, of course, the stepped-up surveillance of those addicts the police knew, which resulted in those addicts reappearing in court more often. But to law enforcement personnel the situation appeared to be deteriorating.

In the process of applying increasingly severe penal sanctions, the penal facilities available to the courts were apparently becoming seriously overloaded with "drug crime" convicts. Here again, the perception of crisis emphasized the problem. At no point during the crisis had more than one third of the prisoners in the Riverdale State Jail been arrested for drug crimes or even been known to use heroin; in the context of the drug crisis they stood out as a special cause of crowded prisons. Without a single exception, every policeman, probation officer, and lawyer we observed expressed the belief that heroin cases were overcrowding the jails.

The penal response of the legal system was apparently ineffective in combating the perceived spread of drug abuse. Punishment is often justified as a deterrent not only to the offender who is punished but also to the "potential" offender. In the face of the widespread perception that the incidence of drug abuse was increasing dramatically, legal system personnel were almost forced to conclude that the penal sanctions were an ineffective deterrent for the population at large.

The final problem the courts had was more subtle. Like the clinic, court personnel learned about drugs from the addicts. Using the tried and tested excuse-making techniques described by Matza (1964), the addicts tended to describe their drug use to the law enforcement personnel in terms of uncontrollable needs. While the police greeted such claims with unmitigated skepticism, the court personnel were uneasy. Seven of the eight assistant prosecutors we observed expressed serious reservations about the efficacy of punishing addicts. Given their perception of their own lack of expertise when dealing with heroin, the prosecutors found it hard to reject the expertise of the clinicians and the addicts who claimed that the addict "needed" treatment.

An example from our field notes should clarify this pattern:

[DeJean (the prosecutor) and I were talking and waiting for Nelson (a defense attorney) to finish talking with his client when a defendant came up.]

Defendant: "Excuse me, you're the prosecutor, aren't you?"

Prosecutor: "Yeah."

Defendant: "Can't you and me settle this thing without him?" (pointing to the public defender on the other side of the court).

Prosecutor: "What's on your mind?"

Defendant: "Well, I mean, you're not going to send me away, are you?"

Prosecutor: "Why shouldn't I, you were dealing, weren't you?"

Defendant: "Yeah man, but I had a big habit to support. Where else was I going to get $75 a day? Besides, what good is it gonna do to send me away? I need treatment."

Admittedly it was unusual for an addict to do his own bargaining, but defense lawyers made similar arguments; hence the following interaction:

Prosecutor: "What about Jones?"

Defense Attorney: "He's an addict. I'm gonna send him to the mental health center."

Prosecutor: "He's been arrested eight times before."

Defense Attorney: "Yeah, but he's a *junkie.*"

At the same time, some major problems were becoming evident at the clinic. While applications to drug treatment programs had not yet begun to decline, senior clinicians believed that a large segment of the drug-abusing population "needed help" but were not seeking treatment on their own. Patients who applied for admission to treatment programs were all too likely to terminate treatment against the advice of the clinicians. This largely resulted from conflicting ideas about what the clinic should be on the part of the addicts and the clinicians. Many addicts wanted to use the clinic as a way of reducing their drug habit and getting out of family and school troubles, and as a short-term way around the courts. The clinicians could not accept such a use of the clinic (Gould and others, 1974, pp. 157-158).

Clinicians found that patients were not sufficiently cooperative with treatment regimens. Clinicians were worried that patients were selling their methadone on the black market, were involved in various criminal activities that were supposed to be forgone by patients, and were not participating whole-heartedly in therapy programs. Like the court personnel, the clinicians were faced with addicts who could plausibly claim to know a great deal more about addiction than the clinicians did. The message that they got from the addicts led them to believe that it was naive to believe that most addicts would accept treatment without court pressure.

By 1970, the import of these inadequacies in both control systems was apparent to both legal and psychiatric system personnel. The "crisis" of drug abuse provided a key context for the evaluation of these inadequacies in several ways. First, both clinic and court personnel felt themselves to be under considerable pressure from the public (and for the clinicians, from "Washington") to do something about the crisis. These pressures were more concrete than they might seem. The clinic felt that a favorable public image, both locally and nationally, was essential to continued funding from the National Institute of Mental Health. The law enforcement community, particularly the prosecutor's office, was thoroughly enmeshed in local politics. Their political sense told them that conflict with the Riverdale Clinic, and thus the University Hospital, would not look good in the newspapers.

Second, the crisis provided a rhetorical basis for arguing that "something must be done." Recalcitrant colleagues could be appealed to in the name of the welfare of the community. The professional principles that prevented cooperation seemed in the context to be "mere technicalities," and the American pragmatic spirit predominated. Whatever these "technicalities," they saw themselves as "doing a good thing."

Let us now consider the practical advantages that each role incumbent saw in such an accommodation. Defense attorneys, as we have already noted, tended to favor some cooperation because "treatment" was generally perceived by both them and their clients as a more acceptable disposition than incarceration. Of course, to the clients, it was a less acceptable disposition than simple probation, but judges were extremely reluctant to grant simple probation to "drug offenders," especially "repeaters." Some defense attorneys told our observers that they preferred "treatment" to simple probation because they felt that clients with a "drug problem" required some sort of intervention before they ended up with a case that would require incarceration.[11]

From the prosecution's point of view, the main advantage of a symbiotic relationship with the clinic was that it facilitated plea bargaining. Especially in the lower courts in Riverdale, the docket was always jammed. The prosecutor's biggest problem was to keep cases moving without "giving away the court." In the context of the crisis, drug cases were seen as a major cause of the overloading of the docket, and a simple disposition that required little of the court's time was a major help in managing the docket. Not all of these drug cases involved violations of narcotics control laws. Many involved "the kinds of crimes that addicts typically commit to support their habit" (Sudnow, 1965). In these cases, the defense usually claimed that the defendant's "drug problem" was at the core of the case and that the prosecutor could easily dispose of the case by sending the defendant to the clinic. Even if the prosecutor was not convinced of the ultimate efficacy and preferability of treatment as opposed to punishment, he generally found treatment to be a useful disposition because it significantly increased his ability to manage a large docket.

The probation officer's role in the therapeutic control system was particularly important, because he was given the responsibility for invoking the punitive sanctions to support treatment. His reasons for taking on this role, therefore, are particularly important. Probation is one of the major inroads of psychiatry into the court system that took place early in the twentieth century. As the enforcer of the sentence (which the

judiciary hands out on the basis of the seriousness or nonseri-
ousness of the crime), the probation officer is an arm of the
criminal law. However, probation officers frequently come from
social welfare backgrounds and often espouse psychiatric principles. As an organized profession, probation officers are heavily
committed to treatment (Diana, 1960).[12] Thus most of the probation officers in Riverdale were strongly disposed to cooperate
with the clinic. Furthermore, being a probation officer in Riverdale was a frustrating job, as it is in many other jurisdictions
(Diana, 1960). While they are supposed to "supervise" the probationers and see that they stay out of trouble, the most idealistic of Riverdale's probation officers saw supervision as a form
of therapy, a chance to "do some good." But with caseloads of
120 probationers per officer, there was little prospect of success. Thus the chance to be a part of a treatment system that
seemed likely "to make a difference" was irresistible. One
might argue whether or not therapeutic control helped any
addicts, but there is no question that it helped the morale of the
probation officers who were assigned to handle the drug cases.

Finally, the clinicians saw advantages in cooperation arising from the coercive sanctions available to the courts. The
clinic's interest in coercive sanctions was first generated by
problems of recruitment. Senior clinicians became convinced
that they could help only those addicts who wanted to stop
using drugs *prior* to their application to the clinic and that any
addict would want to give up heroin mainly because of "real-
world" pressure—primarily from the police and the rest of the
legal system, but also from family, school, or other systems.

It follows from these two beliefs that the clinic could
best fulfill its mission if the police were exerting the maximum
feasible pressure on "prepatients." To be sure, clinicians never,
to the best of our knowledge, actively aided the police in pursuing any particular street addict,[13] but clinicians were able to
communicate a "You catch them, we'll treat them" posture to
the police. The implication of this philosophy was that the
clinic was complementary to the constellation of the criminal
justice system, rather than antagonistic or even orthogonal to it.

The second advantage clinicians saw in cooperative relations with the legal system dealt with the ongoing problem the clinic had with patients leaving against the advice of clinicians. This was a source of continual frustration to clinicians, who typically saw treatment as a lengthy process (generally several years), while patients often wanted to terminate treatment after a few days or weeks. Since most of the treatment regimes relied on in-program peer pressure, a constant turnover of the patient population drastically reduced the effectiveness of group dynamics. Yet, when program participation was wholly voluntary, the clinicians had few effective resources to sanction patient withdrawal.

The clinicians found this problem could be greatly mitigated if continued participation in a particular program was a condition of probation. Then, if and when a patient thought about withdrawing from the program, he would know that he would have to serve the prison sentence that was suspended when probation was granted. From the clinician's perspective, this scheme had the benefit of building coercive sanctions into the treatment system, with the added advantage of having those sanctions administered by someone who was not technically part of the system. This added advantage was important, since it permitted clinicians to impress on their patients their "helping" role without tying that to a "punishing" role.

Conclusion: The Origins and Structure of Dedifferentiation

We began this paper by noting that, although there has been some discussion in the literature of the persistence of undifferentiated structures in modern societies and of the processes of dedifferentiation in decaying empires, there have been no reports of dedifferentiation in modern societies. We have discussed in some detail the origins and nature of the differentiation between psychiatry and criminal law and between their respective sanctions, treatment and punishment. In 1962, the U.S. Supreme Court extended that differentiation to include the social control of heroin. In the late 1960s and early 1970s, a number of significant changes took place in the relationship between psychiatry and the criminal law in controlling heroin. We believe that the description we have presented justifies treating these changes as a partial dedifferentiation of two functionally differentiated systems in one substantive area. The alternative interpretation, that the level of differentiation of the two professions in this area was not substantially less than in other areas where medicine and the law interact, seems to be ruled out on the basis of the data presented. Likewise, it seems hard to argue that therapeutic control was a temporary disorganization, since it persisted more than five years after taking final form.

The major question is "How does such a process occur?" and, equally important, "What controls prevent it from happening more often?" Perhaps the first thing to be said is that the differentiation between treatment and punishment, while firmly institutionalized in most other areas, was not so in heroin control. The clinicians who ran the Narcotics Addiction Unit and other similar clinics did not have a tradition of treating heroin addiction as a psychiatric disorder and were thus susceptible to the rather undifferentiated formulations of addicts' motives that the addicts themselves provided. The addicts' own accounts of their motives, which we described earlier, also reflect the relatively superficial level at which the differentiation was institutionalized.

Another critical dimension was the pressures placed on both psychiatric and law enforcement personnel by the "drug crisis." In combination with the pervasive American pragmatic world view, this generated the belief that "something must be done." For reasons that we have detailed, both law enforcement and psychiatric administrators came to believe that two differentiated control systems would not "work." In the context of what seemed like a national crisis, ethical and procedural "technicalities" seemed to be an unaffordable luxury.

However, this is not a sufficient explanation. Therapeutic control involved behavior that routinely violated the professional ethics of both lawyers and psychiatrists as well as legal notions of due process. These control mechanisms had to be circumvented. The principal violations of legal ethics involved the breakdown of adversarial proceedings and lack of procedures for guilt determination prior to sentencing. The prosecutor was also required to ignore his mandate to see that criminal acts are punished. The procedural difficulties were not an organizational problem because the control mechanisms came into play largely at the appellate level. Since the court-related aspects of therapeutic control were accomplished in plea bargaining, no records of the process were kept on which to base an appeal. Furthermore, since both parties agreed to the disposition, there was rarely anyone who found it in his or her interest to appeal. The prosecutor could freely ignore his mandate to punish the guilty by using ambiguity in the societal legitimation of punishment and emphasizing the rehabilitative functions of both treatment and punishment.[14]

Therapeutic control also involved normative violations on the part of psychiatry. Central to the doctor-patient relationship is the idea that the patient freely cooperates with the doctor's treatment plans. Although psychiatry has always treated some patients against their will by committing them to psychiatric hospitals, this was always justified on the basis that the patient had lost his or her reason and could not see his or her interest in treatment. The controls on violations of these norms tend to be vague and are based largely on the professional association and collegial relationships. As far as we have been able to ascertain, the existence of the coercive relationships involved in therapeutic control was not generally known in psychiatry apart from the clinicians who were involved in it. The leading psychiatric journals do not discuss the matter. Between 1970 and 1975, the *American Journal of Psychiatry*, the official organ of the American Psychiatric Association, contains not a single mention of anything vaguely like what we have described here.

It seems probable that the localized character of the dedifferentiation functioned to prevent its destruction by societal-level professional and legal controls. This led to the paradox that the formal law prescribed two highly differentiated systems of social control of heroin, while the practical operations of heroin control involved a relatively undifferentiated system organized on a local level with almost no institutionalized accountability for its structures and procedures. It seems pos-

sible, although by no means proven, that such a dedifferentiation could not otherwise have been maintained.

Notes

1. Compare this with Durkheim's view of the develop-
mental changes in social control (Durkheim, 1933).
2. The whole discussion of the Protestant origins of
psychiatry might seem peculiar in light of Bekan's (1958) discussion of the Jewish mystical influences on psychoanalytic
thought. However, it is important to remember that psychiatry
as a system of control was already almost a hundred years old
when Freud began to study psychiatric disorders. Furthermore,
a close reading of Bekan's work makes it clear that Freud used
the Kabala as a source for treatment techniques and beliefs
about the structure of the mind. The basic concept of a bad act
reflecting a corrupt agent was taken for granted by Freud.
Finally, it should be noted that the conflict between Freudian
and more Protestant concepts of mental illness persists in the
arguments over genetic or constitutional factors in mental illness.
3. Rothman (1971) records that the early American
asylum superintendents had an obsessive concern with the
causes of mental disorder rather than treatment or study of the
disease process. We believe that this is best understood by seeing
that the new secular account of deviance could accept the
whole Calvinist account of deviance except for the idea that
God willed the deviance. The cause of the deviance had to be
naturalized.
4. We have perhaps oversimplified this distinction. A
criminal intent of the action that—following Kenneth Burke
(1945)—we treat analytically as part of purpose not actor, is
clearly a precondition for a legal crime. Likewise, neo-Kraeplin-
ian psychiatry, which defends the Calvinist version of psychiatry against Jewish and other heretical versions, emphasizes fitting this patient into a scene in which his disorder is minimized,
much the way the reprobate's relation to secular community
was supervised by the church.
5. Alcoholism, juvenile crime, homosexuality, child
molesting, and abuse are some other prominent boundary areas.
6. Christian theology would, of course, have the deviant

suffering after death rather than in this life, but fear of hellfire should yield the same result. Of course, in Calvinist theology man can do nothing about his own salvation—a position that corresponds to biological schools of deviance. American thought has always been more comfortable with the Arminian position that man participates in his own salvation and has generally expected that therapy can be successful.

7. Several of these had origins not only in psychiatric thinking but also in libertarian thinking, which held that they should not be sanctioned at all. This later element should not be overemphasized, however. It is worth noting that the major effort to decriminalize prostitution through the courts was made on the basis that prostitution is a "disease" (State v. Anderson, 280 Minn. 461, 159 N.W. 2nd 892 [1968]).

8. (1962) 370 U.S. 689. Likewise, Lon Fuller (1964), although approving of the outcome as in tune with constitutionally based natural law, objected to the Eighth Amendment basis of the decision as inappropriate. *Robinson* v. *California* 370 U.S. 687 (1972).

9. *Powell* v. *Texas,* 392 U.S. 514 (1968); *Perkins* v. *State,* 234 F Supp. 333 (1964); *Goldman* v. *Knecht,* 295 F Supp. 897 (1969). In this discussion, we have relied heavily on Larry C. Berkson, *The Concept of Cruel and Unusual Punishment* (1975). This is a matter of some embarrassment to Lidz, who in *Contemporary Sociology* reviewed the book negatively, as too narrow to be useful to sociologists. He wishes to apologize.

10. The term "therapeutic control" and some of its conceptualization came from Crane (1972).

11. Given that we were employees of the local drug program, these statements are somewhat suspect. We believe that we persuaded these attorneys that we were not partisan to treatment, but that would not be easy to demonstrate. See also the position that Rafalsky (1972) took on this subject.

12. As any reading of *Federal Probation* or any other journal in the field will show.

13. In 1972, however, there was a serious debate within the upper echelons of the clinic staff as to whether to turn over to the police some information they had about dealer organizations in Riverdale.

14. We do not mean to imply that this was always or even usually done cynically, but it certainly was on occasion.

References

"Addict Diversion: An Alternative Approach for the Criminal Justice System." *Georgetown Law Journal,* 1972, *60,* 667-671.

Bekan, D. *Sigmund Freud and the Jewish Mystical Tradition.* Boston: Beacon Press, 1958.

Blumberg, A. *Criminal Justice.* New York: Quadrangle, 1967.

Burke, K. *A Grammar of Motives.* Berkeley: University of California Press, 1945.

Cohen, A. *Custom and Politics in Urban Africa.* Berkeley: University of California Press, 1969.

Crane, L. E. "Legal Control of Heroin Users: A Therapeutic Model of the Criminal Process." A paper presented to the Society for the Study of Social Problems, 1972.

Diana, L. "What Is Probation?" *Journal of Criminal Law, Criminology and Police Science,* 1960, *51,* 189-204.

Durkheim, E. *The Division of Labor in Society.* New York: Free Press, 1933.

Eisenstadt, S. N. *The Political System of Empires.* New York: Free Press, 1969.

Erikson, K. *Wayward Puritans.* New York: Wiley, 1966.

Fuller, L. *The Morality of the Law.* New Haven, Conn.: Yale University Press, 1964.

Gellner, E. "Post-Traditional Forms in Islam: The Turf and Trade, and Votes and Peanuts." *Daedalus,* 1973, *102* (1), 191-206.

Gould, L., and Namenwirth, Z. "Contrary Objectives: Crime Control and the Rehabilitation of Criminals." In J. Douglas (Ed.), *Crime and Justice in American Society.* Indianapolis: Bobbs-Merrill, 1972.

Gould, L., Walker, A., Crane, L., and Lidz, C. *Connections: Notes from the Heroin World.* New Haven, Conn.: Yale University Press, 1974.

Haskins, G. *Law and Authority in Early Massachusetts.* New York: Macmillan, 1960.

Kassis, R. L. "Drug Rehabilitation: Is a Separate Drug Court the Answer?" *Pacific Law Journal,* 1972, *3,* 595.

Kittrie, N. *The Right to Be Different.* Baltimore, Md.: Penguin, 1971.

Kleeman, N. J., and Posner, A. K. "The Comprehensive Drug Rehabilitation and Treatment Act: Treatment in Lieu of Prosecution." *Massachusetts Law Quarterly,* 1971, *56,* 171.

Lidz, C., and Walker, A. *Crisis and Accommodation: The Moral Structure of Heroin Use and Control.* Forthcoming.

Lipset, S. M. *The First New Nation.* Garden City, N.J.: Anchor, 1967.

Lubove, R. *The Professional Altruist.* Cambridge, Mass.: Harvard University Press, 1965.

Maine, H. S. *Ancient Law: Its Connection with the Early History of Society, and Its Relations to Modern Ideas.* New York: Dutton, 1861.

Matza, D. *Delinquency and Drift.* New York: Wiley, 1964.

Mayhew, L. "Ascription in Modern Societies." *Sociological Inquiry,* 1968, *38* (2), 105-120.

Miller, P. *Orthodoxy in Massachusetts.* Cambridge, Mass.: Harvard University Press, 1933.

Newman, D. "Pleading Guilty for Considerations." *Journal of Criminal Law, Criminology and Police Science,* 1956, *46,* 780-790.

Parsons, T. *The Social System.* New York: Free Press, 1951.

Parsons, T. "Evolutionary Universals in Society." *American Sociological Review,* 1964, *29* (3), 339-357.

Pollock, F. and Maitland, F. W. *The History of English Law Before the Time of Edward I.* (2nd ed., 2 vols.) Boston: Little, Brown, 1952. (Originally published 1895.)

Rafalsky, T. "The Addicted Client: Rehabilitation as a Defense Strategy and the Role of the Attorney in the Rehabilitation Process." *Contemporary Drug Issues,* 1972, *1,* 399.

Rothman, D. J. *The Discovery of the Asylum.* Boston: Little, Brown, 1971.

Sudnow, D. "Normal Crimes: Sociological Features of the Penal Code." *Social Problems,* 1965, *12,* 255-270.

Weber, M. *The Protestant Ethic and the Spirit of Capitalism.* New York: Scribners, 1958. (Originally published 1905.)

11   *Travis Hirschi*

Causes and Prevention
of Juvenile Delinquency

Explanations of juvenile delinquency require consideration of two sets of elements. These are, on the one hand, the driving forces, the reasons or *motives* behind the act and, on the other, the obstacles that stand in its way, the *restraints* that inhibit its occurrence. In principle, it is possible to construct an explanation of delinquency that gives each set of elements, if not equal weight, at least some role in the outcome. In practice, equal treatment of motives and restraints turns out to be difficult. Once the theorist tends in one direction or the other, logic quickly takes him to an extreme position. As a result, theories of delinquency usually focus on one set and ignore or exclude the other. Theorists favoring motives of course find support for their position in human nature, the logic of science, and in the brute facts of experience. Those favoring restraints find, in the same places, equal support for their views. The choice between these extremes then takes on the character of an all-or-none political or ideological decision, with the student asked to choose between causation and deterrence, between social science and law, between the liberal and conservative approaches to public policy.

This chapter argues that this choice is a product of misunderstanding of the nature of delinquency causation, that there is no necessary conflict between the idea that delinquency is caused and the idea that it may be deterred, between social science and law, or between the liberal and conservative approaches to public policy. In the process, it presents a theory of delinquency consistent with—well, human nature, the logic of science, and the brute facts of experience.

Historically, under such headings as "social disorganization" and "social control," restraint theories have dominated social science. In modern theorizing, under such headings as "strain" and "subculture," the tendency is to favor motivational theories, a tendency that is increasingly coming under attack. Motivational theories draw strength from their association with the idea that delinquency is caused. At the same time, resistance to motivational theories draws strength from alleged difficulties in the concept of causation as applied to human behavior. Given that causation is at the heart of the controversy, it is necessary to examine this concept with care.

The word *cause* has several meanings in social science and in ordinary usage. All of these meanings, at first glance, favor attempts to construct motivational theories of delinquency.

First, there is a tendency in both ordinary usage and in social science to equate "causes" with *forces* or *motives*. According to this equation, to find the causes of delinquency is to find the forces or motives behind it. Causal explanations thus account for delinquency in a positive sense and may be contrasted with restraint explanations, which tell us only how delinquency is prevented. The power of this tendency may be understood by attempting to equate "causes" with restraints or obstacles, an equation that is in principle equally justified but that is contrary to common usage.

In the legitimate scientific use of the term, a *cause* is simply a "nonspurious correlate" of delinquency. In the world of research, factors predictive of delinquency do not come labeled as "motives" or as "restraints." They come merely as measures of such things as social class, size of family, or intelligence. If one of these measures turns out to be correlated with

delinquency, the researcher interested in theory must decide
whether it belongs to one class or the other. However, since
most research on delinquency is atheoretical, the question of
the meaning of the correlation is rarely addressed. The researcher remains neutral on theoretical issues and simply follows the
long tradition in social science that allows calling correlates of
delinquency *causes* or *determinants* of delinquency.

Calling correlates causes is perfectly legitimate if certain
conditions beyond correlation are met. But the tendency to
confuse cause in this neutral scientific or statistical sense with
cause in the sense of force or motive contributes to the illusion
that research agrees with theory that "causes" are more important than restraints. It also supports the view that "causes" far
removed from the delinquent act, such things as social class, size
of family, and intelligence, are forces actually producing such
acts.

A final source of support for motivational theory is the
connection between "cause" and the *postulate of determinism*.
Social science is based on the assumption that all behavior,
"down to the last sneer," is determined by prior events. This
seems to mean that any item of behavior is *required* by its
causes. Positive explanations square better than negative explanations with this assumption because they suggest that delinquency is the product of forces over which the individual has
little or no control.

For several reasons, then, it seems better or more scientific to focus on motives rather than restraints. Once this decision is made, it quickly becomes self-confirming. The forces
introduced to explain delinquency become sufficiently strong
that it is hard to imagine restraints having much effect anyway.

This usually happens whether the explanation is restricted to a single "cause" of delinquency or involves a complicated set of causes. For a recent example, consider the connection between "learning disabilities" and delinquency. Such
disabilities could be a cause (in the statistical sense) of delinquency, although the connection has not been firmly established. Suppose such a connection were established. How would
it be explained? Congressman Claude Pepper (D-Fla.), sponsor-

ing the bill to provide funds for the treatment of learning disabilities, offers the theory that learning-disabled delinquents are "venting their rage at the cruelties and injustices of which they have been the brunt" (*Youth Alternatives,* 1977, p. 3). If he is correct, increasing the penalties for their crimes or more careful supervision or surveillance of them is not likely to have much effect on their behavior. In his theory, the cause creates a good reason or a strong motive for delinquency, and this event having taken place, not much can be done to prevent the behavior that follows.

The same conclusion may be reached from major sociological theories. In one, sometimes called "strain theory," delinquency is the result of frustration of the desire to succeed in American society. The resulting discontent is said to be "intense" or "acute." In other words, delinquency is an attempt to relieve considerable psychological pressure. For such purposes, many kinds of delinquent acts will do, and the threat of punishment is not likely to be taken very seriously. In another popular explanation, sometimes called "subculture theory," delinquency results from exposure to people whose values or beliefs require delinquency. In this theory, the source of pressure or motivation to delinquency is social rather than psychological. The delinquent is "living up" to what others expect or to his own beliefs. Delinquency, then, is in one sense a moral obligation or duty. And, as is well known, people will often follow duty in the face of risk and pain. In both theories, then, the motivation to delinquency appears sufficiently strong that the behavior is going to occur virtually regardless of what is done to reduce its benefits or increase its costs. The forces producing delinquency are strong enough to neutralize almost any set of restraints short of locks and bars. The *ordinary* restraints on behavior may therefore be ignored by the theorist, and, if any of these theories is true, they should be ignored by the framers of public policy as well.

The obvious explanatory power of motivational theories leads, in the end, to the conclusion that something is wrong with them. They explain "too much" delinquency (Matza, 1964). They deny the effectiveness of restraints and even the legitimacy of punishment. Those convinced that these are errors then try to locate the general source of what appears to be an inherent difficulty in this kind of theory. Not surprisingly, they typically find it in the concept of causation.

We might expect those who consider causation the root of error in social scientific theories of delinquency to devote at least some attention to the meaning of the concept. Unfortunately, they are even more careless of its meanings than those who accept and use it. As a consequence, the student encountering such grand pronouncements as "the search for *the causes* of crime is illusory" (Morris and Hawkins, 1970, p. 46) and "I have yet to see a 'root cause' [of crime] " (Wilson, 1975, p. xv) may not know whether he has encountered an attack on particular theories of crime, a denial of plain and obvious fact, or some peculiar meaning of the word *cause*. In most cases of this sort, he has encountered all of these things and more. James Q. Wilson, for example, concludes that the idea that crime is caused is both contrary to fact and the requirements of public policy. He says, "If causal theories explain why a criminal acts as he does, they also explain why he *must* act as he does, and therefore they make any reliance on deterrence seem futile and irrelevant" (1975, p. 58, emphasis in original). Wilson first confuses the idea that delinquency is caused with particular motivational theories of delinquency. He then concludes there is something defective in the idea of causation and advocates a return to the assumption that criminal acts are "the product of a free choice among competing opportunities and constraints" (Wilson, 1975, p. 62).

Advocates of motivational theories draw confidence in the wisdom of their approach from the notion that "cause" in all its meanings is on their side. Advocates of constraint theories reject "cause" in all its meanings because they, too, believe it favors their intellectual opponents.

The fact is, however, that the concept of causation is perfectly neutral in all this. Causes may be forces producing delinquency. They may also be obstacles preventing its occurrence. For most social scientists (at least outside criminology), a cause of delinquency is merely some factor associated with delinquency independent of prior causes. (Since the number of possible causes is by definition limited, this statement only appears to be circular.) For example, poverty is a cause of delinquency if poor people are *more likely* to be delinquent regardless of what caused them to be poor in the first place (and if poverty comes before delinquency). The procedures for establishing such causal connections are essentially statistical. These procedures treat as arbitrary the distinction between causes that positively produce an effect (as in "smoking causes lung cancer") and causes that prevent an effect (as in "vaccination prevents smallpox"). Further, they allow us to know that one condition causes another without knowing how or why the causal connection exists (smoking and lung cancer is again an example). Once causal connections have been established, the factors linking cause and effect are the subject of conjecture and, hopefully, of research to determine whether the conjecture is consistent with the evidence, but the fact of causation itself is not evidence in favor of one conjecture or another.

This statistical definition of causes is contrary to the common idea that there is a necessary connection between causes and their effects, that if some condition is a cause of delinquency, all persons in that condition will be delinquent. If this idea were true, to say that poverty is a cause of delinquency would be to assert that all poor people will be delinquent. It would follow that locks, guards, and the threat of punishment could have no ultimate effect on their behavior. It would also follow that poverty is *not* a cause of delinquency, because, obviously, not all poor people are delinquent! It may seem strange that social scientists who believe in causation would subscribe to such silliness. Yet many do (for examples, see Hirschi and Selvin, 1966), and many more are accused of doing so when they do not (for examples, see Morris and Hawkins, 1970, pp. 52-53; Wilson, 1975, p. 58).

Some believe that accepting a probabilistic definition of cause implies a retreat from the postulate of determinism. Actually, it does not. To assume that delinquent acts are caused by prior states or events is not to assume that they are determined by any single state or event, but only by some combina-

tion of *all* states and events present at the time they are committed. The postulate of determinism is essential to social science.
It asserts that delinquency can be completely explained. It
directs us to continue the search. It does not tell us where to
look or when we have found what we were looking for.

In short, the concept of causation does not commit the
student to any particular theory of delinquency, or to any prevention strategy or combination of strategies. Poverty may be
found to be a cause of delinquency without implying anything
about the effectiveness of deterrence; deterrence may be found
to be a cause of (non)delinquency without implying anything
about the importance of poverty. If there are causes of delinquency, which there are, and if delinquency can be prevented,
which it can, we have made a mistake somewhere if our explanation of delinquency requires that we state the contrary.

Historically, a major method for avoiding all this trouble
was to restrict "explanation" to the statistical definition of
causation mentioned earlier. Using some variant of this definition, the researcher would attempt to locate causes of delinquency by comparing samples of delinquents and nondelinquents. If his data led him to believe he had found a cause,
he would simply report this fact without worrying about how
the cause worked. This procedure often resulted in discovery of
a large number of causes. For example, the broken home,
mother's employment, and the size of delinquent's family (the
larger the number of children in the family, the more likely
each of them is to be delinquent) were often among the causes
enumerated. All could be seen as providing motives to delinquency or as reflecting the adequacy of restraints. As long as
the researcher did not take the "how" of these relations too
seriously, these causes could not be seen as "incompatible" with
each other. It is only after some of them have been "explained"
by theory that such problems arise.

The task, then, is to construct a theory that allows the
various causes of delinquency to operate without competing
with each other. Let us take the major causes[1] of delinquency
as our starting point. In the United States, these are sex, age,
race, educational performance, IQ, social class, place of resi-

dence, and family disruption. The child most likely to be charged with delinquency is a nonwhite male, about sixteen, with a considerable history of difficulty in school, who grew up in a fatherless family in an urban slum. How might these causes be explained?

A Restraint or Control Theory of Delinquency

Delinquent acts are acts contrary to law. Since the law embodies the moral values of the community (and insofar as it does not, the task of explaining delinquency is even easier), it follows that (1) delinquent acts are contrary to the wishes and expectations of other people; (2) they involve the risk of punishment, both formal and informal; (3) they take (and save) time and energy; and (4) they are contrary to conventional moral belief.

If these assumptions are true, it follows further that those most likely to engage in delinquent acts are (1) least likely to be concerned about the wishes and expectations of others; (2) least likely to be concerned about the risk of punishment; (3) most likely to have the time and energy the act requires; and (4) least likely to accept moral beliefs contrary to delinquency.

This, in brief form, is an example of control theory. It asserts that the delinquent is "relatively free of the intimate attachments, the aspirations, and the moral beliefs that bind most people to a life within the law" (Hirschi, 1969, preface). Such theories assume that the potential for asocial conduct is present in everyone, that we would all commit delinquent acts were we not somehow prevented from doing so. Put another way, they assume that we are born amoral, that our morality has been added by training and is maintained by ties to other people and institutions.

In control theories, the important differences between delinquents and nondelinquents are not differences in motivation; they are, rather, differences in the extent to which natural motives are controlled. Control theories thus focus on the restraints on delinquent behavior, on the circumstances and desires that prevent it. Factors traditionally viewed as causes of delinquency, such things as poverty or "learning disabilities," remain potential causes and retain whatever significance their statistical relation with delinquency allows. They are not seen, however, as producing delinquency in the same way that friction produces heat. Instead, they are interpreted as factors that weaken the conscience or reduce the effectiveness of controlling institutions. Such causes do not require that the individual become delinquent; instead, they affect the likelihood that he will be exposed and that he will give in to temptation.

While these theories do not imply that the delinquent act is produced by any single cause, they retain the assumption that it is determined by all causes present at the moment it is committed. Some of these causes are the calculations and desires of the actor himself. It is he who wants sex, money, or peace; it is he who decides they may be had by robbing a liquor store; it is he who concludes that no policeman is near the scene. If he miscalculates the risk-benefit ratio, so does everyone, once in a while. If he is "compelled" to commit the act, it is not by forces peculiar to him, but by forces common to all of us. These theories thus locate the immediate causes of delinquent acts in the desires of the actor and his evaluation of the situation. While such causes provide reasons and motives, they cannot be interpreted as forcing the actor to act against his will or as freeing him from responsibility, since they originate with him.

Control theories come in a variety of forms and borrow from several social science disciplines. Since all of them agree that people require training, guidance, and at least a little supervision if they are to become and remain law abiding, no useful purpose is served by suggesting that one is superior to the others.

One important variant considers the effectiveness of child rearing or the adequacy of socialization as the key to delinquency. Learning theories of the control variety assume that the purpose of socialization is to teach law-abiding conduct, that the delinquent has been *improperly* trained or *inadequately* socialized. They assume that we must learn to be law abiding, that some lessons are more to the point than others, and that some of us are better teachers and better pupils than others

(Nettler, 1974, pp. 215-249). Theories that focus on learning are *not* control theories insofar as they assume that crime is a product of socialization, that the delinquent has been properly trained or adequately socialized from the point of view of those training him. Such a view makes crime social rather than asocial behavior, the product of positive rather than negative causes. On the whole, psychologists have favored learning theories of the control variety, while sociologists have preferred theories based on quite different assumptions about the nature of crime and the value structure of American society. It goes without saying that the choice between these views should be a matter of evidence rather than disciplinary allegiance or policy advantage.

A second way to account for delinquency from a control perspective is to consider the effectiveness of institutions, such as the family and the school, and the extent to which they work together or at cross purposes in the control of delinquent conduct. Such an analysis may follow groups through the life cycle, noting variation *over time* in the likelihood that they will commit delinquent acts, or it can compare groups *at one point in time* with respect to their institutional affiliations and loyalties. Such explanations assume that all individuals are equally well socialized. They therefore concentrate on external rather than internal controls. Although they cannot explain all variation in delinquency among individuals, they are often effective in accounting for differences in delinquency rates across groups and over time. These were once known as *theories of social disorganization*. They assume that delinquency is evidence of institutional breakdown and failure. Their competitors are theories that deny that some institutions are more effective than others in meeting human needs and in controlling the behavior of their members.

Let us explore some of the traditional causes of delinquency from this perspective.

The Family and Attachment to Others. Sociologists use terms such as "significant others" or "reference groups" to refer to those people we consider important, to those whose good opinion we value, to those capable of influencing our behavior.

These ideas correctly imply that there are still other people not very important to us. The danger with such concepts as applied to delinquency is that they suggest that each of us *has* significant others or important reference groups, which may or may not be the case. Thus sociologists sometimes say that "behavior is an attempt to maintain and enhance favorable judgments from our reference groups," which implies that delinquency, as behavior, has similar sources. Control theory reminds us that while we are all closer to some people than others, it does not follow that we are all equally close to someone. It reminds us that some of our behavior must be interpreted as reflecting lack of interest in the opinion of others.

One set of people we are expected to be close to, at least in childhood, is parents. *Parents do not want their children to be delinquent* (although they may in some cases want the product of the child's delinquency, such as the color television set "found" on the way home). We may therefore assume that delinquency often says something about the quality of the relation between parent and child.

And, indeed, those least attached to their parents are most likely to commit delinquent acts. Evidence for this assertion comes from a variety of sources and cultures. However this dimension is measured, whether by asking the parent or child or by observing their behavior with each other, and whatever it is called, whether "cohesiveness," "respect," or "love," the results are the same. Academic opinion differs about whether the father or the mother is more important as a controlling agent. As of now, the best guess is that they are equally important, partly because the child tends to view them as a "team," a view that is often correct (McCord and McCord, 1959, p. 105; Hirschi, 1969, pp. 100-107).

Those who do not care or think about the reactions of their parents are more likely to commit delinquent acts because they have less to lose. Risking the good opinion of some other person is easy when that person's opinion is not valued anyway. There are, to be sure, many sources of lack of concern for parental opinion. Some parents are simply less "worthy" of respect: They have fewer resources with which to coerce or buy conformity; they do not live up to the adolescent's standards of appearance and demeanor; they are easily fooled and manipulated. (Put more objectively, they have less money and education.) Still others do not care to earn the love or respect of their children, being consistently cruel to or neglectful of them (McCord and McCord, 1959).

Lack of attachment to parents easily spills over into lack of "respect" for teachers and the police, for adults in general. This spillover is both psychological and structural. A good deal of the controlling power of adults outside the family lies in the threat of reporting the child's misbehavior to his parents. When this threat is removed by parental impotence, the sanctioning power of all institutions is reduced. By the same token, when relatives, friends, neighbors, and teachers do not or cannot report the misbehavior of the child, whatever control his parents might exercise is no longer possible.

Given the centrality of the family in the system of internal and external (psychological and structural) control, its absence from most sociological theories of delinquency is something of a mystery. The mystery is deepened by recent efforts to justify the absence: "We do not accept . . . that delinquency may result from differential attachment to parents, and learning processes which result in children being differentially attached to moral authority in general—especially at a time when the hold of the nuclear family is, by all accounts, being weakened" (Taylor, Walton, and Young, 1973, p. 184). One way of reading such statements is that the family is no longer important in the control of delinquency because the family is no longer important in anything. However, when we look at adolescents whose allegiance to their families is profound (the vast majority), we see the error in assuming that because the hold of the family has weakened for some it has weakened for all. In fact, once we admit variation in the effectiveness of family control, it becomes apparent that the family may become more important as a cause of delinquency as the number of "weak" families grows.

Variations in the effectiveness of family control help account for many of the major correlates of delinquency. Girls are more closely supervised by their parents than boys and are more likely to be emotionally dependent on them, as well as on other adults. (As a consequence, there is evidence that girls are more likely than boys to "suffer" from family disruption—Toby, 1957.) Low-income and ethnic minority families are less able to control their children, for the variety of reasons mentioned earlier. In addition, such families are more likely to be disrupted and to live in neighborhoods where control is made difficult by the lack of support from the community at large.

In a much-quoted statement on the policy implications of these facts, Wilson (1975, p. 54) says, "If a child is delinquent because *his family made him so* ... it is hard to conceive what society might do about *his attitudes.*" Such enlightened pessimism being the order of the day, it may be worth repeating that control theory does not suggest that the family *makes* the child delinquent in a way contrary to the implications of deterrence "theory." (Nor does it suggest that all the families that will ever be exist now—a suggestion admired by those wishing to conclude it is too late to do anything about the family anyway.) In fact, there is no reason to believe that those wishing to increase the costs and decrease the benefits of crime may not do so as well (and as cheaply) by strengthening the family as by increasing the number of policemen.

The School: Commitment to or Stake in Conformity. Perhaps the best predictor of delinquency in American society is difficulty in school. For three quarters of a century, there has been a large grain of truth in the statement that "truancy is the kindergarten of delinquency." The school is expected to engage the attention and maintain the interest of the child for some ten to fifteen years. Yet, for many, it is quickly clear that education is not their game, that proficiency in reading, writing, and arithmetic is not going to come. Given the hours and years such "students" are expected to remain in school, we should perhaps wonder at how so many manage to avoid serious involvement in delinquency. In any event, those who do poorly in school are considerably more likely than those who do well to end up in trouble with the law. There are several ways to explain these differences from a control perspective.

One line of thought suggests that, in the school as in the

family, the bond of affection or respect is crucial. The poor student simply learns to dislike school and therefore to deny the legitimacy of the school's authority. While true, such analysis is incomplete, since the school has other resources at its disposal. Institutions that prepare adolescents for the future may rely on their interest or investment in that future as a means of controlling them. The student who aspires to be a doctor or lawyer and who has worked long and hard to attain the grades required for access to these professions will presumably not want to risk his investment by engaging in delinquent acts. He is committed to, or has a stake in, conformity (Toby, 1957).

The student with low grades in the "prevocational track" does not have such an investment. His prospects for future status are not bright; there appears to be little connection between his present behavior (inside or outside the classroom) and his adult life. He will end up in a low-paying (or a high-paying) manual job, virtually regardless of what he does during the school years. He therefore has no stake in conforming to the rules; the risks from engaging in delinquent acts are slight; he is therefore more likely to engage in them (Stinchcombe, 1964).

Another consequence of the school's lack of relevance to the student is that it frees him from the shackles of childhood. Completing one's education, whether by graduation or by simply giving up, is to become in one sense an adult. Consistent with this premise, those who complete their education while still in school are much more likely to adopt attitudes and behavior patterns normally reserved for adults. They are more likely to smoke, drink, date, and be interested in automobiles. It is wrong to conclude that such freedom to behave in adult ways, coupled as it is with the normal freedom of childhood magnified by lack of concern for school, is particularly painful. It is not. In fact, it is a species of happiness. It is also highly conducive to delinquency.

In sum, the poor student is less likely to be concerned about the good opinion of the adults who run the system; he is unlikely to accept the argument that education is the royal road to success; and he is more likely to behave like an adult. Adult behavior on the part of children comes close to being delinquent in its own right and is, in any event, conducive to actual delinquency.

As might be expected, school performance is also an important key to many of the other correlates of delinquency. As of now, it appears to account for the marked differences in intelligence between delinquents and nondelinquents (Hirschi and Hindelang, 1977). It accounts for much of the differences by class and race, and it helps us understand part of the effects of family disruption. If "learning disability" turns out to be important in delinquency, it stands ready to account for that relation, too. (Actual school performance explains only a little of the considerably lower delinquency rate of girls. Girls are, however, much more likely than boys to be sensitive to the opinion of teachers, so that "school" in general explains still more of this difference.)

In general, it appears that the school has become the major institution of social control in American society. Or perhaps it has become the major generator of delinquency in American society. Which of these views is more nearly correct? Or are they identical? Again, control theory suggests that the former view is appropriate, that school failure represents not a motive for auto theft, but instead a reduction in the potential cost of apprehension for this crime. The school may "fail" to win the interest and loyalty of many of its pupils, but it does not *make* them delinquent. And there is no good evidence that efforts to pretend that all students are equal in academic ability (by eliminating IQ tests, tracking, and by inflating grades) fool anyone but the pretenders.

The Peer Group or Gang. The adolescent free of such adult institutions as the school and the family is free to take up with others in a similar situation, and he clearly tends to do so. The peer group, or gang, has thus for a long time been correctly seen as a concomitant of delinquency. At one period in American theorizing, the gang came to be seen as the key link in the chain, the most important cause of delinquency. The attitudes and values that produce delinquent behavior, it was said, are a product of gang membership. This image of delinquent behavior as a product of group membership was especially appealing to sociologists, partly because it suggests that delinquency too is social rather than asocial behavior. If true, control theory would be in trouble: Delinquency would be a product of training rather than a consequence of lack of training; it would result directly from strong rather than weak bonds to others; it would be moral rather than amoral behavior (at least from the perspective of the group in question).

Fortunately for the theory, the image of the gang as an "intimate group" bears little resemblance to the facts. Delinquents do tend to associate with delinquents, just as kids interested in chess tend to associate with each other, but the ties among delinquents are not equal in quality to those among other peer groups. On the contrary, there is now considerable evidence that gang members tend to see each other as unpredictable and untrustworthy, that their ties to each other reflect their weakened ties to other social groups (Suttles, 1969; Klein, 1971; Yablonsky, 1966; Hirschi, 1969).

Consistent with this revised image, it is now clear that gangs organized around or for delinquent activity—if they exist at all, are extremely rare. The bases of gang membership are age, sex, ethnicity, and territory (Suttles, 1969); the sources of cohesion in the gang are external rather than internal—all members are caught in a common situation, they are to some extent forced together rather than attracted to each other (Klein, 1971). And, indeed, gang members are only slightly more likely than nongang members to commit delinquent acts (Thrasher, [1927] 1963; Suttles, 1969).

Belief. Belief has played a major role in sociological theories of delinquency. In perhaps the most famous of these theories, the person becomes delinquent because of "an excess of definitions favorable to violation of law over definitions unfavorable to violation of law" (Sutherland and Cressey, 1968, p. 75). The basic assumption in some theories is that we cannot act contrary to our beliefs unless forced to do so. This means that criminals and delinquents either have beliefs or values that require delinquency or that they are under considerable pressure to act contrary to beliefs that forbid delinquency. Control theory offers an alternative to these views: The belief system of the delinquent neither requires nor forbids delinquency. Rather, it makes the choice between law-abiding and delinquent behavior a matter of expediency. This amoral or instrumental belief system asserts that "It is okay to get around the law if you can get away with it," that "Everybody does it, so you have to do it first," and that "Suckers deserve what they get."

These beliefs are consistent with (or effects of) the delinquent's alienation from conventional persons and institutions. That is, they reflect and rationalize the position of the unattached. Such beliefs are reasonably seen as "causes" of delinquency in the sense that those holding them are as a consequence more likely to commit delinquent acts. Now consider the following: "If causal theories explain why a criminal acts as he does, they also explain why he *must* act as he does, and therefore they make any reliance on deterrence seem futile and irrelevant" (Wilson, 1975, p. 58, emphasis in original). We have at least partially explained why a criminal acts as he does, but we have not implied that he *must* act as he does, nor have we suggested that deterrence is futile and irrelevant. On the contrary, the theory suggests that deterrence should be effective, that in the extreme case it is *all* that stands between the crime and the potential criminal. Wilson and others who would use deterrence *against* causal explanation have both the logic of causation and its implications for deterrence simply wrong.

Age. One of the most troublesome correlates of delinquency, both in terms of accurate measurement and of explanation, is age. The tendency of delinquency as measured by official records to increase rapidly in early adolescence is clearly established. This increase is not readily explained by changes in the adolescent's beliefs, his attitudes toward or performance in school, or by changes in family structure. Rather, it appears to be a function of the increasing responsibility granted and required of the child at this time.

That greater responsibility is required is evident: The law allows a child of seven to get away with things it hesitates to ignore in a youth of fourteen. By the same token, it is even less tolerant of the same behavior in an adult of twenty-one. These varying attributions of criminal responsibility on the basis of age go back a long time. That they remain with us is clear in statistics on criminality and in the provision of separate legal institutions for juveniles and adults. And, whatever the trends in the juvenile court, it seems safe to assume that in one form or another they will remain with us always.

In this case, the law again presumably reflects the sentiments of the community as a whole. Thus it seems reasonable to assume that at the same time the requirement of legal responsibility is increasing, the granting of social responsibility is increasing at the same rate. In other words, as the child becomes more accountable to the law, he becomes less accountable to adults in general, especially to his parents. Delinquent behavior is thus most likely to *occur* and is most likely to be defined as *delinquent* at the point where the line of decreasing tolerance (by the law) crosses the line of increasing freedom from adult supervision. This point of maximum likelihood of "delinquency" is probably the point at which the child first appears to be physically mature.

Such a conception helps explain how delinquency in adolescence can be predicted from school performance and from family and school "misbehavior" at an early age. It is not so much that the child suddenly "becomes delinquent" in middle adolescence as that he has in many cases been "delinquent" all along.

Summary

Causes of delinquency are often interpreted as motives propelling the individual to crime. Such interpretations suggest that, once a cause has operated, not much can be done to prevent delinquent acts; that restriction, supervision, and the threat of punishment are unlikely to be effective. They also suggest a statistical relation between cause and effect sufficiently close that at least "most people" exposed to the cause should become delinquent.

Many social scientists, convinced that deterrence can be effective and certain that most people exposed to the causes of crime do not become criminals, have concluded that the con-

cept of causation is inappropriate to the study of delinquency
and that the search for causes should be abandoned.

Still, it remains true that causes of delinquency can be
(and have been) discovered. It also remains true that adolescents
exposed to the causes are amenable to restriction, supervision,
and the threat of punishment. Since this is so, it must be that
the *interpretation* of causes as supplying the motive force behind delinquency is the root of the problem.

An alternative interpretation is that the traditional causes
of delinquency do not produce delinquency directly but rather
by affecting the system of internal and external controls. In
other words, causes free the potential delinquent from concern
for the ordinary costs of crime. In this interpretation, the benefits of crime—such things as money, revenge, sex, and excitement—are available at the moment the crime is committed to
anyone committing it. Crime is not a response to unusual
psychological needs or the product of a profound sense of duty.
It is, rather, the product of ordinary desires operating on people
ill equipped to resist them.

It follows that delinquent behavior may be prevented by
restoring its ordinary costs (removing its causes), by providing
its benefits in other ways, and by adding extraordinary or more
certain penalties. The genius of most social groups is that they
are able to control the behavior of their members without frequent resort to severe penalties. Those who say this cannot now
be done ignore the fact that it is being done, cheaply and efficiently, in countless collections of basically amoral creatures.

Note

1. Causes, it will be recalled, are nonspurious correlates of
delinquency. To call some factor a *cause* is to say nothing about
how or why the correlation exists. Those who see something
sinister in ascribing causal status to membership in a particular
group are interpreting causes as forces or they are assuming that
causes have a necessary relation with their effects. As will be
clear, in the present instance this interpretation is specifically
denied. (The assumption has already been addressed.)

References

Hirschi, T. *Causes of Delinquency.* Berkeley: University of California Press, 1969.

Hirschi, T., and Hindelang, M. "Intelligence and Delinquency: A Revisionist Review." *American Sociological Review,* 1977, *42,* 571-587.

Hirschi, T., and Selvin, H. C. "False Criteria of Causality in Delinquency Research." *Social Problems,* 1966, *13,* 254-268.

Klein, M. *Street Gangs and Street Workers.* Englewood Cliffs, N.J.: Prentice-Hall, 1971.

Matza, D. *Delinquency and Drift.* New York: Wiley, 1964.

McCord, W., and McCord, J. *Origins of Crime.* New York: Columbia University Press, 1959.

Morris, N., and Hawkins, G. *The Honest Politician's Guide to Crime Control.* Chicago: University of Chicago Press, 1970.

Nettler, G. *Explaining Crime.* New York: McGraw-Hill, 1974.

Stinchcombe, A. *Rebellion in a High School.* Chicago: Quadrangle, 1964.

Sutherland, E. H., and Cressey, D. R. *Principles of Criminology.* Philadelphia: Lippincott, 1968.

Suttles, G. *The Social Order of the Slum.* Chicago: University of Chicago Press, 1969.

Taylor, J., Walton, P., and Young, J. *The New Criminology.* New York: Harper & Row, 1973.

Thrasher, F. M. *The Gang.* Chicago: University of Chicago Press, 1963. (Originally published 1927.)

Toby, J. "Social Disorganization and Stake in Conformity: Complementary Factors in the Predatory Behavior of Young Hoodlums." *Journal of Criminal Law, Criminology and Police Science,* 1957, *48* (May-June), 12-17.

Wilson, J. Q. *Thinking About Crime.* New York: Vintage, 1975.

Yablonsky, L. *The Violent Gang.* Baltimore, Md.: Penguin, 1966.

Youth Alternatives: A Publication of the National Youth Alternative Project, 1977, *4* (4), 3, 14.

Index

Date Due

BRODART, INC.   Cat. No. 23 233   Printed in U.S.A.